Praise for *When We Move to Heaven*

"We have seen our share of serious incidents, but this one was unlike any other. I have been a member of the Troutville Fire Department for over 20 years and this is the most tragic fire our department has experienced during that time. Meeting someone who has been through so much pain and heartache yet can still be so positive in her outlook is very comforting. Her messages are always so powerful and uplifting, it is hard to believe the terrible pain she has been through and yet she can still touch so many hearts with her message. Linda's words are an inspiration."
—Greg Sleboda, Fire Chief, Troutville Volunteer Fire Department, Troutville, VA

"From brokenness to healing, from healing to healer Linda Street has made her journey. To read her story in *When We Move to Heaven* is to be given a passport to travel the hard road of pain only to discover the "peace that passes all understanding."
—Dr. Charles G. Fuller, Retired Senior Pastor, First Baptist Church, Roanoke, VA

"Linda Street, whom I first knew quite literally when she was a toddler, is an amazing and fascinating woman whose life was hammered in January 2003 by a most unthinkable, crushing tragedy, and yet she was able to bring herself out of it in a manner that should be an inspiration to everyone."
—Donald Davidson, Director of Museum, Indianapolis Motor Speedway, Indianapolis, IN

"There is no education or training that could have ever prepared me to hear Linda tell the account of her painful tragedy... Linda courageously took every overwhelming painful step in her journey of grief and felt every emotion to its' greatest depth. It was in that darkest place that God intimately and personally comforted her with His presence... Every therapist and pastor should read her story. Everyone who is going through a painful time in life will be so encouraged by Linda's story. It will make you fall on your knees in awe of God's power and faithfulness. This is not just a traumatic story, but an account of someone's faith in God as she walked the most painful path. Linda models for all of us how to walk through the darkest path and see God."

—*Martha M. Furman, LPC, LMFT, Total Life Counseling, Inc. and Gentle Shepherd Hospice, Salem, VA*

"As a professional aerobatic pilot, I've had the opportunity to meet many private and professional pilots. They all have a passion and a purpose that has propelled them into the world of flying. Linda's unique story riveted my attention. Two years after losing her husband and children during a tragic fire, Linda turned to flying to help her keep her sanity. Even for the most experienced pilots, flying requires extreme mental and physical stamina as well as 100 percent focus. Flying is many things to many people. For Linda, I believe her faith and flying are her saving grace. I commend Linda for writing *When We Move to Heaven* and for sharing her message with others."

—*Patty Wagstaff, Patty Wagstaff Airshows, Inc., St. Augustine, FL*

"Linda's story is living proof that the God of all comfort, who comforted her during her deepest sorrow, will use her pain to comfort others. I believe those who read her book and hear her story can find hope and healing and strength."

—*Sheriff Ronnie Sprinkle, Botetourt County, VA*

"From the ashes of the life she once knew, Linda shares with us her dark and lonely journey through the valley of the shadow of death that took the lives of her husband and two small children. Her steadfast faith and perseverance in the midst of this devastating tragedy will not only inspire you but give you confidence that no matter what, God is true to His word and He will never leave you or forsake you. Linda is truly a remarkable woman of faith and courage and her story will strengthen and encourage your heart."

—*Don Eckenroth, Gentle Shepherd Hospice, Roanoke, VA*

"It isn't often that a story comes along and so completely grabs your heart as *When We Move to Heaven* by Linda Street. This gut-wrenching, straight-from-the-heart true story is real and human, painful and hopeful—and challenging. If God was faithful in Linda's life, with all she went through—and there's no doubt He was—then we can expect no less in our own. Thank you, Linda, for writing this moving, faith-filled account."

—*Kathi Macias*, Speaker, Bible Teacher, and Author of 21 books, including *BEYOND ME: Living a You-First Life in a Me-First World* (New Hope Publishers, Summer 2008), *How Can I Run a Tight Ship when I'm Surrounded by Loose Cannons?* (New Hope Publishers, Fall 2008), *My Son, John* (Sheaf House, Fall 2008), *Mothers of the Bible Speak to Mothers Today* (New Hope Publishers, Spring 2009)
www.kathimacias.com

When We Move to Heaven:

A family love story

Isaiah 52:7
How beautiful upon the mountains
Are the feet of him who brings good news…

Linda Street

Second Edition

Copyright © 2018 by Linda Street-Ely
When We Move to Heaven: A family love story
2nd Edition
By Linda Street

Published 2018 by Paper Airplane Publishing, LLC

Paper Airplane Publishing, LLC.

http://paperairplanepublishingllc.com

All rights reserved. Except for brief quotations in critical articles or reviews, no part of this book may be reproduced in any manner without prior written permission from the publisher: Paper Airplane Publishing LLC, P.O. Box 9067, Liberty, Texas 77575. (936) 334-1642.

Library of Congress Cataloging-in-Publication Data
Linda Street-Ely
When We Move to Heaven: A family love story
2nd Edition
Pages: 282

Summary: "True story of God's love shown in one woman's journey after tragedy." — provided by publisher

ISBN-13: 978-1-947677-00-5 (Paperback)
1. Christian 2. Grief 3. Testimony 4. Faith 5. Inspiration 6. Linda Street-Ely

Printed in the United States of America

All scripture quotations, unless otherwise indicated, are taken from the New King James Version®. Copyright © 1982 by Thomas Nelson, Inc. Used by permission. All rights reserved.

Scripture quotations marked (NIV) are taken from the HOLY BIBLE, NEW INTERNATIONAL VERSION®. NIV®. Copyright© 1973, 1978, 1984 by International Bible Society. Used by permission of Zondervan. All rights reserved.

Quote by Charles Swindoll from *Growing Wise in Family Life* taken from *Strong Family* by Charles R. Swindoll. Copyright © 1991 by Charles R. Swindoll. Used by permission of Zondervan.

Unless otherwise noted, all poems/verses are written and copyrighted by Linda Street.

www.WhenWeMovetoHeaven.com

Table of Contents

Dedication i
Acknowledgments ii
Letter to the Reader viii
Foreword by Dr. Jimmie L. Clemmons ix
Foreword by Reverend Dan Drake x
Letter to Mycol xi
Prologue 1

PART I—The Before

Chapter 1: Changed Forever 4
Chapter 2: The House 11
Chapter 3: Winds of Change 20
Chapter 4: Nana's Funeral 27
Chapter 5: Alaska and Sealy 34
Chapter 6: The Offer 42
Chapter 7: Going Forward in Faith 49
Chapter 8: What's Spiritual Warfare Got to Do with Me? ... 57
Chapter 9: Becoming Grandparents 62
Chapter 10: The Move 67
Chapter 11: Back in Texas 77

PART II—…and The After

Chapter 12: The News.. 92
Chapter 13: First Memorial Service 103
Chapter 14: Second Memorial Service 119
Chapter 15: "Why…?" 131
Chapter 16: Searching…and Waiting 149

Chapter 17: Tasting the Vomit 175
Chapter 18: Recognizing the Sifting 191
Chapter 19: The Courier 200
Chapter 20: A Firefighter's Gift 213

Part III—The Eternal

Chapter 21: A Second Trip to Sudan 232
Chapter 22: Where Does It All Lead? 252
Epilogue: Walking with a Limp 258
A P.S. from Rusty 260

Dedication

To My Lord and Savior, Jesus Christ, without whom this entire story is impossible; and to Mycol, Austin, and Jessie, who have given me tremendous gifts of strength and courage, until we are together again.

Acknowledgments

I would like to acknowledge every person who has shared their love and compassion. How can I express to so many people the depth of my gratitude? Undoubtedly I will fail to include some people in this space, yet not for lack of gratitude. Some people I am unable to name because there have been so many acts of kindness done anonymously. But God knows who you are, and I am grateful.

Brother Jim, who moved to Heaven before this book was published, I love you and look forward to seeing you there.

To my daughters, Angie and Missy, thank you, with hugs into eternity. You girls are remarkable, amazing, and incredibly forgiving of the times I couldn't be much of a mom to you. You are two of the strongest people I know.

Every firefighter, police officer, and emergency response personnel who responded to the fire in the early morning hours of January 27, 2003, thank you for your selfless giving to so many.

Rusty, my Bro, I don't think I could have finished the book, or life itself, without you. I love you and thank you for being the brother I didn't get at birth, but now have into eternity.

Lynna, thank you for your trademark patience. I have long looked up to you, and you continue to be an inspiration to me. For all you've given up for me, thank you.

Mike Ely, thank you for your compassion and encouragement, for loving Mycol, Austin, and Jessica, without even having met them yet.

My sister, Barbara, thank you for your constant prayers and support, even when you were tearing apart at the seams with me. And to you and your family, thank you for loving my family and me so deeply and for helping to strengthen my faith.

My sister, Diane, thank you for your loving kindness, your deeply compassionate heart, and your example of tenderness toward all living things.

Mamacita, my precious Mamacita, I love you with all my heart. Thank you for loving me as your own daughter, and most of all, thank you for giving birth to Mycol, for raising him to be the man he was and is. I know the reunion in heaven was sweet when you arrived.

Mom, you know me well. Thank you for encouraging me to finish the race.

Reba, thank you for being such a great sister to Mycol, a fantastic aunt to Austin and Jess, and an understanding sister-in-law to me.

Kurt, how could I ever thank you for the gift of love you created in that video? And so many other gestures of love–you are always willing to do whatever it takes to help, out of selfless compassion.

Wes, thank you for honoring God and Mycol by becoming a model husband, father, and leader.

Aunt Marge, thank you for being with me, in the toughest times and in times of laughter. You were my partner in adventure.

Kathi Macias, my wonderful editor. You pulled it all together for me and patiently helped me endure the writing of this book.

Aunt Teen, my precious aunt, who also moved to heaven before this book was printed. What an anchor you have been for me, and for so many; you have been called a saint.

Bill Potter, my cousin who is more like a brother, always willing to be and do more than I could ask.

Jean Pollard, Berniece Kinnison, and John Dantonio, thank you for gently handling the pieces of me in those first moments, and so many times since.

Ronnie Sprinkle, what a gem you are. Thank you for all the good you do for so many.

Don and Kim Eckenroth, thank you for being so true to the promptings of the Holy Spirit. Your crown in heaven has got to be humongous!

Mike Ross, Scott Butler, and John Weber, attorneys of the good kind who went far beyond professional obligations to pray with me and stand as disciples of Christ with encouragement and help.

Mary Jo Lagoski, my knock-out gorgeous (I promised you I'd say that!) counselor. You took me on as a client but call me your friend. Thanks for working from your heart.

Martha Furman, my first counselor; thank you for helping me through those first traumatic moments.

David and Barbara Lino, Terry Cherry, Betty Dudley, Jeff Stephens, Mike Grooms, Lane Hasson, Mark Vaughan, Art Hearne, Linda Shelton, April Bates, and all pastors, Sunday school teachers, children's choir teachers, thank you for investing in the lives of my family.

Mary Lynn Barrett, you are such an angel. Your prayers for me are always uplifting and you never stop giving me hope, and thanks for finding Tom Parrish.

Tom Parrish, thank you for writing *Stepping Into Eternity*, and for caring so much about all of God's creation.

Rob Krause, my "little brother", what an awesome young man you are. God uses you in so many ways. You have already touched many people and I know you will continue to go where God has put it in your heart to go.

Dane Parish, my "Hammerman", thank you for pressing on toward the goal, and helping see to it I did too. I can only imagine the embrace when you entered heaven.

Howard and Annette Sumpter, we couldn't have asked for more loving, compassionate neighbors. Your constant willingness to serve others is a shining example of Christ's desires for us.

A.J. Arney, thank you. Thank you for trying. I know the fire has been heart breaking for you. Thank you for showing me the loving memorial you have made.

Lisa Arney, for being there from the beginning. For walking the property and finding the U-Haul. Even though you didn't know what it meant, you went looking for something, out of compassion. And because of your willingness, and your caring, I know God has been happy to use you in His plan.

Cheryl Wellington, thank you for so many years of cherished friendship. I thank God for you, my friend.

Richard and Nancy Ediger, thank you for your strength in prayer and in deed, helping with so many necessary tasks that were beyond my ability.

Tom Meritt, thank you for not being the status quo funeral director. Our family would not have been as well served without you.

Tom, Terri, Jeremy, and Adrienne Camp, thank you for spending time with me, listening and praying with me.

Beth and Greg Reed, and Graham and Trina Stephens, thank you for the gift of time–the time you gave me, and the time with my family that you shared with me. I imagine Mycol and Greg now together, in awe of seeing all the people of the Old Testament.

Tim and Tamara Burke, thank you for your graciousness, for taking the time to tell me how my family has inspired your faith, and for saving the seedlings you grew from the seeds Austin and Jessie gathered for you.

Savannah Mallette, you are one very special young lady and I love you very, very much. Thank you for your precious, sweet personality, and for being my son's special friend.

Mike and Julie Mallette and all the other Mallettes, what a blessing you will always be.

Mary Morris, a good friend to Mycol and to me, and to all of Mycol's family, thank you for being there so many times.

Jeff and Jennifer Schauss, thank you for your compassion, and for being willing to give up the shelf Mycol built for me so I could have it in my new house.

Brian Dannenfelser and Scott Chiropractic, thank you for taking care of my physical ailments during so much stress and trauma.

Richard Farmer, thank you for offering your expertise on historic homes, and all the time you put in on my behalf to fight the insurance company.

Jim and Christin Pivero, thank you for so much time and effort put in to helping during the crisis, and for continued prayers and support at all times.

ACKNOWLEDGEMENTS

Anthony Schreiber, thank you for taking me out of my shell and teaching me to fly. Your dedication is unmatched.

Cliff Hyde, thank you for making flying available to me, and your wisdom along the way.

Nicole Malachowski and Patty Wagstaff, two of the most accomplished women pilots, thank you for your strong encouragement, woman-to-woman, to keep going for it.

Donald Davidson, thank you for your friendship, for telling me I could write this book, for believing in it all.

Dan Drake, you understand spiritual warfare, thank you for understanding on a deeper level what all this means, and for helping so many people battle and win.

Lina Lawson, thank you for creating a cover design that fits perfectly with Jessie's drawing.

Jan Coates, thank you for encouraging me and opening up so many doors.

To the reading group: Annette Abbott, Dorothy Brooks, Cindi Dunn, Joanne Lowe, Sarita Poage, Suzanne Teleki, Lucy Turoff, Ruth Winn, Susan Senechal, and Bob Joyce, your willingness to read through the manuscript and your honesty helped tremendously.

To our many, many other family and friends who have prayed for me and who have offered encouragement, compassion, hope and help in such a variety of ways, not just in finishing this book, but in staying in the race at all: Pete and Nancy Adamson, Zeke Barlow, Byron and Alane Barnfield, Scott and Carol Briggs, Kevin and Sally Carani, Elizabeth Carey, Chris Collins, Dick and Jan Copenhaver, Lisa Costigan, Fred and Laura Dallas, Gayla Davis, Jay and Sandie Davis, Dave and Cindy Fassett, Ron and Sandra Fielder, Tim Geiger, Don Glover, Kelly and Karen Hartman, Jerry and Donna Henderson, Bill and Marsha Holschuh, Walter and Mary Sue Jamison, Corey and Carey Jones, David and Sharon King, Terry and Cindy Kizer, Mike and Kathy Lay, Mike and Dena Lee, Linda Long, Steve Lovelace, Cody Lowe, Adam and Donna Marcum, Gary and Radha Merrick, Connie Miller, Cris Morris, Dan and Julie Murray, Steve Musselwhite, Andrea Parish,

Marshall and Mary Ann Perry, Mike Paulsen, Dave Petersen, Mark and Tracy Potter, Will, Rebecca, Jon, and Jan Potter, Jan Powell, Mike and Susan Rash, Dane Ray, Jim Reilly, Dean and Brenda Rimbach, Don and Julie Seagraves, Mary Kay Sisemore, Brent and Aphia Stephens, Tom and Vicki Stovall, Mike Strothers, Marie Strom, Terry and Ann Tanner, Tony Tsounakas, Ashley Tucker, Fred and Ruth Ungerer, Amy Vaughan, Burt and Shelly Williams, John and Jamie Wilson, Russ Wright, and for every person who has touched my life with help and hope, grace, forgiveness and wisdom, thank you.

Letter to the Reader

It is my goal to take you on a journey, one that is partly mine, partly yours. By bringing you as close as I can through many steps of my own, it is my prayer that you will find something in my journey that helps you along yours.

There will be times when things don't seem to make sense–and that is the reality I hope to convey.

It is difficult to take a journal created over time and written from raw pain and turn it into a book with purpose. If our story reaches one person, if one life is turned around by the power of the Holy Spirit, if one person accepts the gift of salvation because of this book then it has been successful.

May you be blessed,
Linda Street

Foreword by Dr. Jimmie L. Clemmons

Once in a lifetime an event, tragedy, or circumstance totally and completely shifts your attention from yourself to someone else. In that brief moment of time nothing in your world can be compared with the devastation of the other person's pain.

This story tells of such an occurrence. It tells the death of a love story, the loss of an identity, the search for meaning, the reluctant desire to find new life, and the grace of God in restoration. This book will break your heart, cause you to forget your small concerns, and enable you to rejoice in the life-giving grace of God.

Most people struggle with trivial concerns that keep them from appreciating the fresh joys of the Lord each day. It is my prayer that by reading *When We Move to Heaven: A family love story* new appreciation for life and new faith will germinate in your heart from the ashes of Linda Street's story. It was with heartfelt love that I initially entered Linda's life, and through that opportunity my own life has been encouraged. At the moment of Linda's loss, I began to gain a friend for life. Literally "through the valley of the shadow of death," death was overcome.

Reading this book will cause you to face the realities of life: Sometimes the best of God's children die young; life seems to have no answers for the grieving, but answers can be found in the most unlikely places, when you least expect it.

Dr. Jimmie L. Clemmons, Pastor
North Main Baptist Church
Liberty, Texas

Foreword by Reverend Dan Drake

All of us during the course of our lifetimes as members of Adam's race will face our share of trial and disaster, tragedy and triumph. But the greatest struggle any of us ever faces is the one within ourselves.

We struggle to come to terms with who we are, why we are here, and what should we live for! Most of these questions are decided for us either by our fears or by our faith.

Linda Street has journeyed through not only the "valley of the Shadow of Death," but through that most horrific and terrifying of all events—the untimely, unforeseeable, and apparently senseless loss, not only of a loved one but of all that she loved: the home of her childhood dreams, her husband, her children.

Yet though she has been deeply impacted by these terrible events, her life in the final analysis has not been defined by them, but through the grace of God, by the depth of her faith in her Lord Jesus Christ!

I count Linda as a personal friend and often find strength to do "the next right thing" through recounting to myself her story.

It is my prayer, that as you read this book, you will find the strength to allow faith not fear to guide you; that hope in the goodness of God will draw you forward to discover that it is God who will give to you the oil of gladness instead of the spirit of mourning. (Isaiah 61:3)

To Linda and to Rusty and my friends at North Main Baptist Church: May God bless you all as you sow seeds of hope and courage in a world to whom hope has been all but lost.

Reverend Dan Drake
Director of Projects, Jacob's Well
Sugarland, Texas

Letter to Mycol

Dear Mycol,

Your great strength and commitment toward God, your love for me and for your family, have inspired me and given me the courage to write this book. For I have thought many times, how would I ever live without you?

A friend told me once his vision of us together in heaven. He said he envisioned my arrival a great celebration, family greeting me, thanking me for writing this book.

I'm not sure what heaven is like, but when I get there I believe it will be even better than anything I can imagine…

It is my hope this book will honor you; not only you, though—God too. For it is His will we seek.

Until then, may I be faithful to continue your work as the courier who wanted only to bring good news.

Love,
Linda

Prologue

On the night my life changed forever, I spent considerable time on my knees, praying for my family and for our church. Division and infighting had infiltrated the ranks of our beloved congregation, and I was determined to do battle at the source.

"Satan, get out of our church," I demanded, wondering even as I did so why I had spoken aloud. The words had no sooner left my lips than I felt a heavy, oppressive presence press in against me on all sides.

"How will you feel if you lose your family?" hissed a voice, not audibly but distinctly, and from somewhere outside of me. The sense of evil was so powerful that I felt as if I were being smothered.

"Oh, God," I cried out, pleading specifically for the protection of my husband and two small children, "please protect Mycol! God, please protect Austin! Oh, God, please protect Jessie!"

Then, despite the evil and terror that surrounded me, I prayed, "But not my will be done, but Yours."

And I slept…

PART I

The Before...

1 Corinthians 15:51
We will not all sleep, but we will all be changed—
in a flash, in the twinkling of an eye...
(NIV)

Chapter 1

Changed Forever

January 26, 2003, was, in many ways, a night like any other…and yet it was the night that drew an indelible line between the before and after of my life.

It was the fourth Sunday I had been away from my husband, Mycol, and our two younger children, Austin, five, and Jessica, four, who were busy settling into our new home in Virginia. Angela and Melissa, my two older children from a previous marriage, were already grown and had started families of their own, making us proud grandparents. Mycol, Austin, Jessie, and I had just relocated over the Christmas holidays to Troutville, Virginia, in beautiful Botetourt County, just outside Roanoke, from the Houston suburb of Kingwood, and we were thrilled to finally be living in the 212-year-old log house that had once belonged to my beloved grandparents, Nana and Pop-Pop. I had returned to Houston to continue working until Mycol's business loan came through and he could start his own trucking business. Then I would return to Virginia and become a fulltime, home-schooling mom. I could hardly wait! The separation was hard on all of us, but there seemed to be no other choice at the time. If all went as planned, we would be together again in just a few weeks.

Of course, we talked on the phone and communicated via email every day, and this day was no different. Mycol had called earlier to tell me about the church they had attended that morning: First Baptist in downtown Roanoke. They were trying a different church each Sunday until they found the one that was "just right." First Baptist was a bit larger than the other churches they had visited, closer in size to the one we had attended in Texas. Mycol said he could be comfortable there, though he had felt that way about the other churches too, and this one was more of a drive.

When I asked Austin what he thought of First Baptist, he said, "It's okay, but *Rain-bow For-est Bap-tist Church* is still the best!"

I laughed, remembering how Austin had raved about *Rain-bow For-est Bap-tist Church* ever since attending it on the first Sunday of their church visits. Mycol had said the people there were extremely friendly, but I couldn't help but wonder if Austin had simply fallen in love with the way he declared each syllable when he proclaimed the church's name in a singsong way.

After that we talked about Virginia's cold, snowy weather, and then finished our conversation with repeated declarations of how much we loved and missed each other. Finally, reluctantly, we hung up, with the promise that we would talk again later.

The phone rang about ten o'clock that night. It was Mycol, checking in for our routine good-night call, but it was obvious he wasn't his normal cheery self.

"What's wrong?" I asked, once again wishing we weren't separated by so many miles.

His tone was unusually serious as he answered, "I'm tired. I need to get these kids into bed." He went on to tell me how much he missed me, and then said he and the kids were planning to leave Virginia on Wednesday to drive to Texas so we could all be together for a few days. That meant I would see them by Thursday night! My heart leaped at the thought. Now I had something to look forward to all week.

We discussed the possibility of going to the rodeo while they were in the Houston area, which was an outing all four of us would enjoy. And then Mycol mentioned again how cold it was there in Virginia. I asked if he was keeping the doors to the kitchen and the home school room closed, and he assured me he was, but the winter wind was blowing and it was still very, very cold in the old log house.

I then reminded him of what the home's former owner had told us about the fireplace keeping the house really warm. Mycol said he remembered that, but didn't indicate whether or not he intended to use it.

We talked about our prayer requests, and then Mycol brought up some divisive church issues regarding our former place of worship in Kingwood. I had told him there was going to be a meeting to discuss the situation, and he encouraged me to attend, stressing the fact that Satan would continue to attack that church because of some of its outreach and missions ministries. We had both come to understand that spiritual warfare is a reality.

As we talked I could hear the kids in the background. Austin was running through the house, his usual happy self and clearly not ready for sleep. Jessie had a tummy ache, so Mycol needed to go tend to her and then get them both into bed. He told me he missed me, that he looked forward to when we'd all be together, and then repeated that he was very tired and needed to get to bed as well. But I just didn't want to let him go.

"I'm not ready to hang up yet," I said, "but I know you have to go and get the kids settled down. Call me as soon as you get up, okay?"

"We're an hour ahead of you," he said. "You won't be at your office by then."

"That's okay. Just leave me a message as soon as you get up, and I'll call you when I get there."

"Okay. I just want you to know something. I know that I really, really love you," he said, as he had for years.

And with that, we ended the call. As I got ready for bed, I pondered all that had happened in the past few months, replaying in my mind all those great childhood memories at the old log house and thinking of all that lay ahead for us in our dream home. I thought of the pasture and hayfields where our children and grandchildren would play, making treasured childhood memories of their own; the pond, the creek, the seven springs from Tinker Mountain; the Allegheny, Blue Ridge, and Appalachian Mountain ranges watching over us; and the adventures that awaited us on the Appalachian Trail just outside our back door. True, we would now be farther away from Mycol's family in Texas, but we would be closer to several members of mine.

I thought back eighteen years to when my grandmother had sold the home to A.J. and Lisa Arney, and how I'd wanted to buy it at the time but couldn't afford it. Now, nearly two decades later, A.J. and Lisa had called to offer us the chance to buy the house back. We had jumped at it and made the move. Now all we had to do was wait for Mycol's business loan to come through, and then I could quit my job in Houston and go home to my family. How greatly I missed Mycol and our children! How I longed for Austin to mingle his little fingers with mine and click our fingernails together again, something he started doing as a baby when I'd rock him to sleep, and to feel Jessie's precious tiny fingers pinching the skin around my elbows as she cuddled up in my lap when I'd rock her to sleep. I was already missing our regular mealtime together, hearing our children say grace, which always ended with an enthusiastic "God, please bless this food so we can grow big and strong and jump real high!" In the meantime I would just have to be satisfied with the few days we would have together this coming weekend.

I reminded myself to let Cheryl, my dear friend and former neighbor–and currently my hostess–know that I wouldn't be staying with her that weekend, as Mycol and the kids and I would probably stay with one of Mycol's sisters, either Reba or Lynna. But I so appreciated Cheryl's hospitality and generosity in opening her home to me while I finished up my last weeks of work in Houston. Cheryl and I might be living miles apart in the future, but I knew we would always remain close.

And then I prayed. Kneeling at the side of the guest bed in Cheryl's house, I offered my prayers to the Lord, first for the things Mycol had requested, which included getting the trucking business going and his adjustment to all the changes that would entail. I then thanked God for the many blessings He was pouring out upon us and asked Him to use me for His glory.

After that I prayed for the church in Kingwood, the one we had been a part of for so long and that was now being attacked by demonic forces.

Then I did something that was very out of character for me, particularly when staying in someone else's home. I spoke out loud and said, "Satan, get out of our church!"

The eerie, evil presence that quickly descended upon me struck terror into my heart. It was as real as anything I have ever experienced with my physical senses–maybe more so.

"How will you feel if you lose your family?"

The question came from outside me, but it sent a chill right through me, as I began to call out for my family's protection.

"Oh, God," I cried, "please protect Mycol! God, please protect Austin! Oh, God, please protect Jessie!"

Then, despite the darkness and terror that surrounded me, I prayed, "But not my will be done, but Yours."

And Then It Was Morning...

Amazingly I was soon able to fall asleep. When I awoke the next morning–Monday, January 27, 2003–I got up, left Cheryl's house, and headed for work, already looking forward to Mycol's message, which I knew would be waiting for me when I got there.

I arrived at 7:15 a.m., which was 8:15 in Virginia, so I knew Mycol was already awake, but when I walked into my office and looked at my phone, the message light wasn't blinking.

That's strange, I thought. *He must be sleeping in.*

Minutes later Cheryl called from her cell phone. "Linda, have the police called you?"

I frowned. *The police? Why would they be calling me?* "No," I said. "Why?"

"They were just here looking for you, but you had already left."

"Who was there?" I asked, a feeling of unease beginning to creep into my stomach. "What did they want?"

Silence. Cheryl's phone was dead. She had been having trouble with her cell phone and intended to get a new one, but just hadn't gotten around to it yet. I tried to call her back but couldn't get through, so I called the police station.

"This is Linda Street," I said, as soon as I heard the dispatcher's voice. "I understand someone is trying to find me."

"Yes," she said. "Let me get a sergeant."

It seemed a very long time as I waited for the sergeant to come to the phone. All I could think was, *Please, God, don't let it be bad! Why isn't Mycol calling me? Why didn't I call him back last night, when I was praying for their protection?*

The sergeant finally came to the phone and told me there was a number in Virginia I needed to call. For a moment I thought it was a number where I would reach Mycol. I thought that whatever was going on, he was getting the message to me about where he was. Then the sergeant gave me the number to the Botetourt County sheriff's office.

I asked the sergeant what this was about, and at first he contended that he didn't know, but I didn't believe him. There was no way he would receive an emergency communication from another state and not get any of the details.

"Yes, you do," I insisted. "Tell me. What's going on?"

After a brief hesitation, he replied, "It's something about a fire. You need to call the sheriff's office there."

I was shocked, stunned, terrified, and numb all at once, my heart racing as I forced my trembling fingers to dial the number in Virginia. *Oh, God, please, please let them be okay! Let them just be in the hospital and not able to get to a phone. Please, God! Please... I should have called Mycol back last night! Oh, why didn't I call him back?*

A dispatcher answered and said they would have the sheriff call me back because he wasn't there in the office. Since I had no other choice, I hung up and waited.

Finally, after what seemed like forever but was actually only a matter of minutes, the phone rang, and even as I picked up the receiver, I knew my life would never be the same.

Psalm 37:3-7

Trust in the LORD, and do good;
Dwell in the land, and feed on His faithfulness.
Delight yourself also in the LORD,
And He shall give you the desires of your heart.
Commit your way to the LORD,
Trust also in Him,
And He shall bring *it* to pass.
He shall bring forth your righteousness as the light,
And your justice as the noonday.
Rest in the LORD,
And wait patiently for Him

Chapter 2

The House

The news of my grandmother's passing had come as no surprise. In many ways, our family–her children and grandchildren–were relieved, at least for Nana's sake, to see her reach the end of a long, slow decline. Nana had no regrets about choosing the assisted living facility that had served as her home the last thirteen years of her life; in fact, before she stopped speaking, she often reassured us that she was happy there.

Nana's ninety-seventh year marked a personal victory for the strong-willed woman who had been determined to surpass her father's ninety-six-year sojourn on this earth. Had she been able to speak near the end, I am certain she would have proclaimed her victory loud and clear. And yet we knew how happy she was to finally have moved on, released from this life to join Pop-Pop, her one and only love, in Paradise.

And so, in spite of our loss, we were able to rejoice in her passing, though the timing didn't seem quite right to Mycol and me. My husband and I had long dreamed of leaving our suburban Houston residence and moving to the beautiful Blue Ridge Mountains of Virginia. Now, just as that dream seemed about to become a reality, we would not be able to share our joy with the one person in our family who would have appreciated and understood it more than anyone else.

Pop-Pop's parents had owned the old place, eight acres of scenic Virginia land at the base of the Appalachian Trail, graced with a charming two-story, 212-year-old log home that now appeared might soon become ours–Mycol's and mine. Built on a slope, with a walk-out basement and an old stone fireplace, our dream home held many fond memories of my childhood. Seven natural springs bubbled up from Tinker Mountain into a creek that flowed across this lovely property, nestled among the Appalachian, Allegheny, and Blue Ridge mountain ranges, and though some might call the old log home a cabin, Nana would never have stood for it. "A cabin doesn't have bathrooms and a kitchen and separate bedrooms and living room. A cabin is just one or two rooms," she would object. This was a house, not a cabin, and now, if all went as planned, it would soon be our home.

By today's standards, the home wasn't much–at least not its size. But I never thought of it as being small; rather, I preferred to think of it as cozy. It was built of thick, hand-hewn logs, etched by the powerful axe strokes of muscular men centuries earlier, men who worked together like musicians in an orchestra to create a majestic house that commanded the attention of every passerby who drifted along the winding Catawba Road, now a two-lane paved road that paralleled the Appalachian Trail. Time seemed defeated by this particular structure– my beloved log house–an ambassador of Botetourt County, its very essence a messenger of significance, of history, and of deep and abiding love.

The stately limestone chimney stood atop the house like a sentinel, silently pronouncing its presence, broad-shouldered from the two fireplaces that stood one on top of the other, at basement level and main floor, supporting a long, proud neck that overlooked the roof. The imposing mountains behind the house and its rising chimney were somehow reminiscent of the young shepherd boy David going out to meet Goliath with nothing but his slingshot and his faith in God. That chimney had its heritage to boast, having been the original chimney for the house. It had, at one time, been carefully dismantled, carried across Catawba Road, and used as the foundation for a home built for my great grandmother. When that house was torn down years later, the mighty chimney finally returned to its original home and was reconstructed by my Pop-Pop's loving hands, as he renovated the old house, complete with plumbing and electricity.

I had daydreamed of that home many times over the years, as far back as my early twenties when I was raising Angie and Missy, the two daughters from my previous marriage, throughout my marriage to Mycol, and most recently during the final days I sat beside Nana's bed in the nursing home. Sometimes I read to her, even when she couldn't respond; other times I prayed; still other times I let my mind wander, back to those joyous, fun-filled days of my youth when so many of my kinfolk gathered together at the Virginia homestead during holidays and family vacations. My mouth still waters at the memory of Nana's persimmon pudding bubbling on the stove, with its tantalizing aroma wafting through my childhood and into adulthood.

And then there were the cows, which Nana had named Harriet and Gertrude. As I sat beside her bed and watched Nana sleep, I smiled at the memory of those gentle bovines meandering among the walnut, oak, and hickory trees, on their way to take a long, slow drink from the pond my Pop-Pop had made. Four of Nana's eight acres were pastureland, while on the other four, which sat on the opposite side of the log house, hay grew and seemed to cry out for children to come and roll down their gentle slope—"log rolls," we called them.

For years our extended family had journeyed from four different states to meet up at Nana and Pop-Pop's log house, I with my parents and two sisters, and my eleven cousins and our aunts and uncles. We were quite a crowd when we got together.

As children we took turns paddling around the pond in the old canoe, gazing up at the mountains and pretending to be explorers. My sister Diane, two years older than I, often wished the rest of us would tire of playing explorer in the canoe. She would have preferred we run over to the hayfield on the other side of the house, granting her some valued solitude from rambunctious siblings.

My little sister, Barbara, two years younger than I and the baby of all the grandchildren, preferred to stay close to the house, often clinging to one of the older generation while discovering the goodies in Nana's garden or playing on the balcony porch that stretched the entire length of the house and overlooked the pasture.

I, of course, was the middle child, and quite curious. I remember getting in trouble once when I chased Harriet and Gertrude through the pasture. I thought it was fun, but Nana admonished me, "You'll make their meat tough!" I stopped chasing them, at least when Nana was watching, but with this much room to run and play I could easily find other things to do. The old red barn, which stood watch between the house and the fresh spring-fed creek below Tinker Mountain, had a knack for drawing me to adventure. There were good places to hide, trees to climb and lots of nature to discover, beautiful scenery all around. Whether playing with cousins in the house, chasing Harriet and Gertrude through the pasture, climbing the mountain, or paddling the canoe in the shady pond, I loved this piece of earth more than any other.

My memories of visiting Nana at the old log house inspired a poem about her, which I wrote just a couple of years before she left us. By that time I was in my thirties and writing quite a bit of poetry. During one of the last times I had a chance to sit at her bedside, I wrote another poem, this one a tribute to Nana's love for Pop-Pop.

The words for that second poem first began to float around in my mind and take shape one day when I noticed her staring at Pop-Pop's picture, which hung directly above the head of her bed. Nana was sitting in a wheelchair, gazing up at his picture, the last portrait of him before he died. It was obvious in Nana's expression how deeply she missed the only man she had ever loved. And there was much to miss about that great man, for he was an athlete, a chemist, an inventor, and a businessman, but most of all, a Christian, a true diplomat of all that is important. After a year as a professional football player with the Philadelphia Eagles, Pop-Pop used his degree in chemistry to obtain over 100 patents, including U.S. patent number 2,748,584, a way to reclaim and recycle grease used in journal boxes on trains. He had the exclusive market for his invention, and his company did well, but he always remained faithful to tithing, even while supporting a family of six throughout the Great Depression. Though I was only seven years old when he suffered a fatal stroke, I knew the stories of Pop-Pop's kindness and generosity, which helped me know my grandfather better.

"He looks so young," Nana remarked, over and over again, as she sat in that wheelchair and gazed longingly at Pop-Pop's portrait. "I don't know why the Lord has kept me here all these years."

"I don't know either, Nana," I told her. "But I do know you miss him."

Pop-Pop was the love of Nana's life, and I understood how blessed she felt to have shared those precious years with him, but I could only imagine how much she missed him once he was gone. The longing in her eyes and in her voice as she looked at her husband's face had a profound effect on me, as I considered how very blessed I was to have Mycol. I so cherished our relationship and the life we had together. I knew how completely Nana looked forward to her reunion with Pop-Pop in heaven, and I couldn't imagine ever missing Mycol for so many years.

But now, in September of 2002, Nana was gone, reunited at last with her beloved husband. Though I knew I would miss her terribly and I so regretted not having her around to share our joy at finally being able to bring the log house back into the family again, I also wanted to celebrate as I thought of how completely happy my precious grandparents were at that very moment.

Of course, Pop-Pop would have been just as happy as Nana at the thought of Mycol and me and the kids moving into the log house. Pop-Pop had inherited the place before I was born and began restoring it in the mid 1960s. After he passed on, Nana held on to the house for several years, continuing to use it as the family gathering place, but the upkeep of so much acreage, as well as the house, eventually became too much for her to handle alone. When I was in my early twenties, Nana decided she couldn't keep up with the maintenance anymore, and so she sold the house to A.J. and Lisa Arney, both of whom had grown up in Botetourt County. In fact, when A.J. was young, he used to pass by the log house every day as he rode the bus to school, and each time he would say to himself, *One day I will buy that house.* When he discovered Nana was putting it up for sale, he snatched it right up, fulfilling his childhood dream.

I was crushed by the transaction, for I had always considered it "my" beloved log house and assumed it would stay in the family. In fact, when I first learned of Nana's desire to sell the house, I tried to convince other family members to pitch in so we could all buy the house together. I wanted to keep it in the family to use as a vacation home and a place for reunions, a place to recapture and even relive those glorious times of summers gone by and to pass along to our children the chance to make memories of their own. Some of my relatives thought it was a great idea but, like me, they simply didn't have the resources to make it happen. Others just weren't interested. And so the homestead passed to A.J. Arney, a homegrown Botetourt boy, and his bride, Lisa, a committed Christian woman.

Once I finally came to terms with the fact that someone other than our family would live in the house, I made a point to stop by and visit it when I went to Virginia to see Nana. A.J. and Lisa were always warm and welcoming, especially since they knew how I felt about the place, so they weren't surprised when my last words to them before leaving were always the same: "If you ever want to sell it, call me."

Eighteen years later, with an entirely different generation of children having run through the pasture, picked berries on the mountain, and sailed their toy boats in the spring-fed creek, the Arneys decided to take me up on my offer. I was at work when I got the call.

"Linda, this is Lisa Arney."

Her name didn't ring a bell at first because I only saw her every couple of years, and I certainly wasn't expecting to hear from her at that time. She must have picked up on my hesitation because she explained, "I live in the log house that was your grandparents'."

I smiled. "Oh, yes, of course! How are you, Lisa?"

"I'm fine," she answered, and then jumped right in to the purpose of her call. "Do you still want this house?"

She might as well have asked me if I'd like to win the multi-state power-ball lottery. "Of course, I still want it," I answered eagerly, before I even knew how much they wanted for the house or if it would work out for us to move halfway across the country.

In a matter of minutes I was on the phone with Mycol. "Honey, you're not going to believe this," I chattered, my heart thumping nearly as fast as the words spilled out of my mouth. "I just got a phone call from the couple who bought the log house from Nana. They've offered to let us buy it!"

Mycol didn't miss a beat. "Tell them we'll take it."

"Are you sure?" I asked, surprised that he hadn't wanted to think about it for a while or learn more details before answering. After all, he had never been with me when I made the trips to visit Nana and the house that by then belonged to the Arneys. "You haven't even seen the place, and you've never been in Virginia."

"I know," he said, "but I also know how much it means to you. You've longed for that house, and it's everything we both want, right?"

He was certainly right about that. Though he had never physically been to the log house, he had heard me talk about it so many times that I was sure he could envision it in his mind. And we had discussed our mutual desire to get away from the city, to take our two preschoolers and move to the country where they could be raised in fresh air and old-family ways.

And so, though we knew absolutely none of the details of how this move could take place, we agreed that it would happen, even as the shock of such a major decision seemed to ripple through the phone wires. It was obvious, even then, that our lives were about to change dramatically.

He Looks So Young

Time stopped;
Standing still he keeps watch over her
As the nurses come and go,
Giving medicine,
Feeding time.

She thinks he looks so young because
She is nearing centurion age.
Closing her eyes carries her lovingly back to him,
Where she longs to be.

Long forgotten,
She once loved to watch their many grandbabies
Come to visit and play.
Now long waits between feeding,
Changing,
Bathing,
Fill the days.

Unforgiving time
Moving slower than its hour hand
To keep her from himc
Hanging on the wall above her bed.
She repeats, "He looks so young."

Oh, night, come quickly
That our beloved matriarch
May cease this amalgamation
She once could separate
Between night and day.

No kind nor gentle soul

Desire farewell
As she seeks the lilies,
Remembering
When they first met.

A college girl's first love
Forever;
A real man's hero, smart and strong.
Whom many called a giant
Whom she called Bill
Who waits for her with his patent
quiet
patience
And never leaves her side.

The aides don't think he's young at all—
He reminds them of their grandfather.
Little do they know.

Much do they miss
Of the roaring youth they leased,
She
And Bill.
Long apart
But not really.

He waits with her
And loves her,
Ready to help her cross
And return to him.
She, meanwhile, gazing at his last portrait,
He looks so young.

Chapter 3

Winds of Change

Mycol and I had decided to withhold the announcement of our exciting news until the sale closed, hoping Nana would live long enough to know we were moving into the historic log home that she and Pop-Pop had loved so much. But now she was gone, and we were preparing to leave our Texas home and drive to Virginia for Nana's funeral. While there, Mycol, a native Texan, would be seeing the beloved and much-talked-about house for the very first time.

I smiled at the realization that my daily routine would soon be changing, not only because of our impending move but also because I would no longer be working outside the home as I had been doing for several years now. For the five and a half years that Mycol and I had been parents together, the importance of raising our own children at home far outweighed any desire for material things. It had been just a matter of logic that I would be the one to continue to work after the birth of our son, Austin. Mycol's job meant long hours and more physically demanding work for about the same pay as mine but with no other benefits. It was an easy decision at that time for him to be the one to stay home to raise the children. Most people were surprised when they learned of our non-traditional family life, but once they saw Mycol's devotion and Christian leadership as a husband and father, they realized what a uniquely gifted man he was.

Many times I came home from work to find the usual line-up of Hot Wheels and Matchbox cars, which streamed from one end of the house to the other, and I would gently step over the thick traffic so as not to disturb the flow our son had so carefully arranged. Watching our children play with the little cars always brought back sweet memories for me, as they had been my favorite toys, too.

Austin Chad Street was born eight minutes after noon on Wednesday, February 26, 1997, in the front seat of his granny's car in the middle of traffic on a very busy road in Houston. My mother-in-law was driving, I sat next to her, and my fourteen-year-old Melissa was in the backseat. Missy was excited about the birth of her new brother, and since she lived with Mycol and me, she would get to witness his birth and the first few years of life, until she moved out on her own. My other daughter, Angie, was living with the girls' dad in Indiana, but we kept in close contact and she too was eager to see her new little brother. The girls loved Mycol and had developed a close and trusting father-daughter relationship with him, beginning when they were ten and seven years old.

As my mother-in-law concentrated on getting me to the hospital on the day of Austin's birth, Mycol followed behind us, but the traffic was heavy and he couldn't quite catch up in time. Actually, that front-seat delivery turned out to be the easiest birth I experienced, with nobody telling me what to do or how to do it. I remained sitting up, and very soon I was holding Austin in my lap. Twenty-one months later Mycol and I welcomed our baby girl, Jessica, although this time we made it to the hospital in time for the birth.

To differentiate between the two sets of children, we often referred to Austin and Jess as "the babies," or "The Buddy" and "The Jester," although, in her typical dry wit Missy insisted her position remained "baby of the first litter." Austin and Jess bonded immediately and became close friends and constant playmates. As they became aware of their close relationship and compared their love for one another with the love they saw between Mycol and me, Austin and Jess wondered whether they too would one day be married. In their innocence, they discussed it between themselves one day and then decided to ask me about it.

Austin, who had recently turned five, came to me with the confident leadership of a little man. "Mommy," he said, looking up at me with his big brown eyes shining, "am I going to marry Jessie like you and Daddy are married?"

I smiled inside and out, thinking how his question felt like a high compliment to our parenting. Since becoming a father Mycol had often said to me, "The best thing a man can do for his children is to show them how much he loves their mother." Clearly, Mycol's message of love was reaching our children.

"No, Buddy," I answered. "You will marry someone else when you grow up."

He seemed okay with that, as he turned to his little sister and said, "Jessie, we aren't going to get married. You have to marry someone else, and I do too."

Austin was kindergarten age and Jessica a preschooler when Mycol and I began home-schooling. I drew up the lesson plans, and Mycol carried them out. But because he felt less than competent as a teacher, we had discussed switching roles. The timing seemed right, now that it looked like we would be moving to Virginia. We had already discovered that I would not make as much working as a paralegal in Roanoke as I did in Houston, and so we had begun formulating plans for Mycol to re-enter the workforce. I was looking forward to staying home and being a fulltime parent again, as I had been years ago with Angie and Missy, and with the news that my older daughters were each expecting their first child, our excitement grew as we looked forward to being young grandparents.

One evening, as I stood in my living room amidst the traffic jam of Hot Wheels, I remembered driving to work one morning and having to squeeze through a particularly thick traffic snarl. I passed slowly next to one of two lanes where a severe accident had occurred. What I witnessed in the accident's aftermath shook me deeply. At least two cars had been involved. One of them–the closest to my lane–was facing traffic. The entire top of that car had been sheared off. Sitting atop the rear seat was a firefighter, holding what was obviously a person covered by a blanket. That scene burned itself into my mind and chilled me to my very core. I thought of all the people who would be affected by the loss of that one person–the victim's family, the others in the accident, the emergency response personnel, and even their families. At that moment I prayed for the victim's family, and I prayed for strength for the firefighter. It had to be a traumatic experience, regardless of how much training he had.

I called Mycol the minute I arrived at my office. As I tried to get the words out to describe what I had seen, I became more and more emotional. "I just wanted to tell you I love you," I cried.

"I know," he said, his voice so gentle and reassuring that it spoke volumes about his understanding. "You sometimes make fun of me because I always say 'I love you' every time you or I leave, but we never know if it might be the last time. We aren't promised tomorrow, and I would want the last thing you hear me say to be 'I love you.' That's why I do that."

A God Thing

I shook my head to dislodge the memory. Mycol was right, of course. Every moment is precious. But right now I had to focus on getting us all ready to go to Nana's funeral. It would be a long drive from Kingwood, Texas, to Troutville, Virginia.

"Honey," I said to Mycol later that evening, "Aunt Marge asked me if I'd read my 'Nana' poem at the service on Saturday."

Mycol's face brightened. "Really? That'll be cool."

"Yes, but you know how nervous I get in front of people."

"It's a good poem, and it's your family. You can do it."

Aunt Marge was one of my mother's sisters, and I adored her. My parents, sisters, and I usually spent Thanksgiving with Aunt Marge, Uncle John, and their four children, and often spent some summer days as well in their suburban Chicago home. Besides that, Aunt Marge and Nana were very close, so when she asked me to read my poem at the funeral, I don't think I could have told her no.

As Mycol and I continued to plan our trip to Nana's funeral, he said, "Looks like I'll get to see the log house before we buy it after all. I was kind of hoping I wouldn't, just for the adventure. But that's okay. I don't mind seeing it first; I just hope I like it."

"Oh, I think you will," I assured him. "It's everything we've always wanted: a log home on acreage out in the country. It'll be perfect for us and the kids."

Mycol's big brown eyes lit up. "I can't wait to climb up to the Appalachian Trail. This is going to be so awesome! One day I want to hike that whole trail, from Maine to Georgia. But most of all, Bebe," he said, using his pet name for me as he slipped his arms around me and leaned in for a kiss, "I'm happy because it's the house you've always wanted."

"You're so good to me," I said, my voice barely above a whisper as I realized I had done nothing to deserve such a loving husband, and yet there he was, gazing at me with adoration. "I really hope you fall in love with it too. I do have such beautiful memories there. And it's so neat that you agreed to buy it without ever seeing it."

"It's a God thing," Mycol said. And he was absolutely right. Though we seemed to be in a season of change, I was secure in God's love for us, and in the love Mycol and I shared for one another. Everything seemed so perfect…

Nana

I still call you Nana.

Although that name abandons
The sophistication that you are
And my childhood was long ago sung to sleep
Lively memories rise rich and sweet
As your persimmon pudding
In a fine china bowl
On a velvet tablecloth
Next to a wavy glass partition
In the dining room
Of an Evanston apartment,
Only a short walk–even for short legs–
From elephant ears and rock candy
And chocolate phosphates
(at the dime store where we exchanged your dimes for books of paper dolls).

I still call you Nana.

Even though I am now capable of saying "Grandmother" —
Next year I will be three
Again
For the thirteenth time.
Innocence preserved in recollections of summers
Riding down a long, winding road,
A full day's trip and into the night,
As we searched for the familiar glow
That beckoned from the front porch of the log house.
And you on the porch
Awaiting arrival of three granddaughters
Tucked into the backseat of a station wagon,
Eagerly competing to be the first to spy

You waiting on a wooden porch chair,
Welcoming us to adventures that sprang memories.
Fourteen grandchildren snapping beans from your garden,
Chasing cows in the pasture,
Climbing a mountain out your back door.
And you were Nana all the time.

I still call you Nana.

An exclusive moniker no one else deserves.
Who would have known the Princess Pocahontas
Would bring together Indian native and Englishman
To give us this adoring grandmother,
Emerged through skyscrapers of Philadelphia
And school days with Princess Grace
To be crowned Nana?

Chapter 4

Nana's Funeral

I was nervous as I walked to the podium to share my private thoughts and read the poem I had written as a tribute to Nana. My grandmother's father had been a prominent architect in Philadelphia, and he had raised his daughter among "society" folks. Nana had also been a schoolmate of Princess Grace and was a direct descendant of Princess Pocahontas. But to us, the grandkids, she was just Nana.

There wasn't a dry eye in the sanctuary by the time I read the closing line and then made my way back to my seat. As the service continued my mind drifted back to one of my more recent visits with Nana. I'd had the "Nana" poem framed in an ornate white metal frame, which she proudly displayed in her room at the assisted living facility, eagerly pointing it out to all who entered. On my way to visit her one day, I stopped at a bookstore to look for something with Robert Frost's poem "The Tuft of Flowers." Nana's health was declining and it was becoming difficult for her to carry on much of a conversation, so I thought she might enjoy hearing some poetry during our time together. I found a little paperback of Frost's poems and bought it, then took it with me for our visit.

When I arrived I discovered that Nana's roommate's son had already purchased the exact same book as a gift to his mother. I smiled when I saw it and learned that when the son came to town to visit, he often read to his mother and Nana from this book. *At least now I know she likes Frost*, I thought. And so I settled in and began to read, first "The Tuft of

Flowers" and then "The Road Not Taken." But after a few lines Nana mustered the energy to whisper, "Too poetical."

I wasn't sure if she said *poetical* or *political*, so I asked, "Too poetical?"

Her response was weak but emphatic. "Yes."

I still wasn't sure what she meant by that, but I did understand that she didn't want to hear any more poems by Robert Frost. I put the book down and looked around the room for something else to read to her. I spotted a newspaper and asked if she wanted me to read that, but she took another shaky breath and whispered, "Too boring."

I was fresh out of ideas until I saw the framed poem I had written for her the year before. "How about this one?" I asked, holding it up for her to see.

Her smile spread across her face and lit up her eyes. It was obvious she loved my poem, and I was deeply touched by her approval. And so I read my very special "Nana" poem to her, and when I finished she declared, "Now that's a real poem!"

My poem, compared to Robert Frost's, was a *real* poem–at least as far as Nana was concerned. In that very special, even sacred moment, I felt closer to my precious grandmother than ever before. Of course, I didn't know then that it was the last time I would see her alive.

Some time after the funeral I received an email from my cousin Mark, who had been unable to attend the service but had heard about the poem. He asked to read it, and I decided to send him "He Looks So Young" as well. I had never shared that particular poem with the family because I was concerned that it might sound as if I had been hoping Nana would soon pass away. But by then I was more comfortable sharing it.

I soon received another email from Mark in which he thanked me for allowing him to read the poems, terming them "exquisite." He said my poem about Nana had transported him into the past and brought back a flood of wonderful memories. He also said that "He Looks So Young" reflected wise and gentle handling of a very delicate situation, and he applauded my writing talent and encouraged me to "keep up the good work." He then ended with the words "I look forward to a rendezvous some day at your new digs in the old log house."

The old log house. As I sat there listening to the remainder of Nana's funeral service, my thoughts drifted from one place to another, finally coming to rest once again on the old log house in the Virginia mountains. That beloved house seemed to pop into my mind nearly anywhere or anytime. Perhaps it was because it was always there in my heart, just waiting to be called up.

And then it was time for the pall bearers to carry Nana's casket. Mycol had been asked to join my male cousins in this final honor and tribute to my grandmother, and I watched him with mixed emotions. As I meditated on the end of life, I recalled a story from Nana's past that helped lift some of the heaviness of the day.

A black lady named Christine had helped to raise Nana's father from the time he was born. Christine and her family lived with and were employed as domestic workers by my great-grandparents. Christine was only twelve when my great-grandfather was born, and he quickly became her "baby Erskine," as the two of them developed a bond that lasted their entire lives.

Many years after "baby Erskine" grew old and passed away, Nana visited Christine, who was then living with her daughter. Christine was quite elderly by then and had become blind, so her daughter explained to her that "baby Erskine's baby" had come to visit.

Christine was so excited. "Now don't you worry none 'bout Christine," she said to Nana. "I'm goin' up there to heaven to be with the Lord, and when it's time for you to come up there, you don't need to be afraid. No, don't you be afraid. I'm just gonna reach a hand on down from the clouds and pull you on in."

I smiled, as the warmth and reassurance of Christine's faith seemed to settle upon me, nearly a century after she had spoken those precious words. It was a wonderful reminder that the work and the message of love are timeless.

The Announcement

Though sadness and relief marked the ending of Nana's life on earth, an underlying joy bubbled inside me at the realization that Mycol and I were bringing the log house back into the family. This would be a rebirth of sorts, and as we made the drive from the funeral home to the cemetery, passing right by the log house, Mycol and I shared the exciting news in the car with my mother.

"Mom," I said, "we're going to be making an announcement later, but we want you to be among the first to hear it."

She raised her eyebrows, obviously curious as to what could be so special that we would bring it up during our farewell to Nana.

Nearly giddy with excitement, I burst out, "We're buying the log house!"

Mom gasped, as our news brought forth so many vivid, wonderful memories of her own. She knew how much that place meant to me, and we could feel our excitement growing as the three of us discussed it during the remainder of the ride.

And then we were there. We got out of the car and joined the others, as we said our last goodbye to Nana and laid her body to rest, next to Pop-Pop's. From there we made our way to Aunt Teen's house, an old farmhouse I had often visited as a child. The farmhouse was just around the corner from the cemetery, not far from Nana's beloved log house.

Aunt Teen was actually my great aunt, a spunky, tenderhearted, five-foot tall eighty-seven year old who had definitely contributed her share of memory-making to my childhood. She and Uncle Lum had raised chickens and cows, and I remember going to the chicken house and squeamishly grabbing warm eggs from under the hens. Uncle Lum was the one who first introduced me to fishing, and he also served as our tour guide for my first trek up the mountain when I was eight years old. We all had missed Uncle Lum since he passed away six years earlier, but now the resurgence of my Aunt Teen and Uncle Lum memories only added to my eagerness to move into the log house less than a mile down Catawba Road.

Aunt Teen's house was already full of people by the time we arrived: cousins, aunts, and more distant relatives, friends, and neighbors. Neither Angie nor Missy was able to come to Nana's funeral, but Mycol, Austin, Jess, and I were happy to be there with so many family members. We took comfort in being together, knowing that it was Nana's time to leave this life and be with the Lord–and with Pop-Pop–and knowing she was ready and wanted to go.

As we visited and reminisced with loved ones, Jan, one of my bubbliest cousins, asked me for our current address, and then told us she had a long drive home and wanted to get going. Mycol and I tried to stall her until we could make the announcement to the entire family about buying the log house, but when Jan asked why we wanted her to stay longer, I whispered our news to her. She was so excited that she agreed to put off her departure so she could be there when we told everyone else. Jan was the only one besides Mom and my two sisters and daughters who knew about our pending move.

Meanwhile, we filled our tummies with Aunt Teen's good country cooking and talked with family members we hadn't seen in years, exchanging memories, hugs, and laughter. Time slipped away too quickly, and I soon noticed that the afternoon was nearly gone. At Jan's urging, I looked around for Mycol, hoping he would take the speaker's role, but I couldn't find him. With increasing anxiety, I searched inside and out, but couldn't locate him or the kids. It turned out he had taken them, along with some of the other dads and kids, up the mountain for a new adventure.

When Jan repeated that she really had to get going but didn't want to miss out on hearing me make the announcement, Mom took me by the hand and led me into the dining room, where she declared, "Attention, everyone! Linda has an announcement to make!" The chatter died down quickly, and all eyes fixed on me. Though I was reluctant to say anything without Mycol and the kids present, I decided to go ahead.

"You all know how special that log house has always been to me," I said. "You heard me read about my memories in the poem, and about what that place means to me. I've loved it all my life. Well..." I paused, exchanged an excited glance with Mom, and then said, "Mycol and I have bought it and will be moving in around November."

Scattered gasps were followed by cheers, applause, and laughter. The house was soon abuzz with the news, and it really seemed like a good way to honor Nana following her funeral. Several of my cousins and their spouses said they would be coming to visit frequently, and I felt on top of the world…though I still regretted that Angie and Missy weren't able to come, and that Mycol and Austin and Jessie weren't there with me at that moment. I always felt so incomplete without them.

"There are times when I think it might be better
to have my future predictable,
but looking back, I'm always grateful
God didn't tell me ahead of time."
—Charles Swindoll, *Growing Wise in Family Life*

Chapter 5

Alaska and Sealy

Our announcement brought immediate reaction from all present, as memories of the log house were cherished by everyone in our family. Aunt Marge, though sharing in our excitement, expressed her amazement at what she considered our unpredictable but exciting lifestyle.

"You're always doing unusual and exciting things, Linda," she commented. "I just never know what you're going to do next. I thought you were planning to move to Alaska."

"We were," I agreed, "but that's changed."

She raised her eyebrows. "What happened?" she asked, in her typical Aunt Marge tone, full of intrigue and adventure.

I knew my aunt's questions had nothing to do with the fact that she thought we should go to Alaska rather than move into the log house, for she loved that old log house as much as any of us. She too had spent many childhood summers romping through the pastures and hayfields, climbing the mountain, and playing in the creek. Back then, however, they had used the log house as a storage place for apples, and the spring water was cold enough that they didn't need refrigeration. They could even put fresh milk in a carton and set it in the stream of icy water springing from the mountain. That was before too many people knew the secret beauty of Botetourt County, before houses were built along the opposite side of the winding road. It was before my grandfather, Aunt Marge's dad, refurbished the old house and returned it to a cozy home, a perfect place for making memories.

No, Aunt Marge had no problem with our moving into that wonderful old home; she wanted to know how it had all come about. I smiled at her curiosity and interest, glad to share the story with her. "A few years ago, Mycol felt the Lord was urging him to go to Alaska."

Aunt Marge looked at me in her curious but patient way, which made me chuckle. "I didn't want to be disrespectful or anything," I continued, "but I didn't get that same message. Wouldn't God speak to me too? But Mycol said, 'When you hear God speak to you, it's like nothing else you can describe. It's something totally different, and you just know.' So I said, 'Okay.'"

I paused long enough for Aunt Marge to utter a "wow," and then continued.

"So we put our house up for sale, and between the two of us we sent hundreds of resumes to businesses in Alaska. But nothing ever came of it. I got a couple of phone interviews, but nothing beyond that. No one in Alaska wanted to hire someone from Texas. They don't like to hire outside the state because they're afraid you'll bail after your first taste of their long, dark winters."

"I remember that," Aunt Marge declared. She had lived in Anchorage for a few years when Uncle John was in the service, and she nodded her head in sympathy as I continued.

"Then Mycol suggested we fast and pray and ask God to lead us and clarify His message. So we did a three-day fast, read scripture, and prayed together every morning before I left for work and every evening when I got home, plus separately during the day. Meanwhile, we continued sending resumes, but still nothing happened. We looked at hundreds of homes on the Internet, thinking we'd be moving to Alaska soon.

"I finally said, 'Mycol, why don't you go to Alaska? I mean, if God spoke to you to go and I'm not hearing it, and we didn't get any clear confirmation from the fast, the house isn't selling, we're not finding work there, why don't you just go for a weekend? You could look at houses while you're there.' So we planned a trip for him to visit Alaska the weekend of his thirty-fifth birthday, which is March eighth."

"What a wonderful birthday present!"

"It was," I agreed. "He didn't find any houses that captured his interest, but the beauty of Alaska sure captured his heart. So we planned a family vacation there for about ten days in August. The four of us and our niece Hannah went. And Alaska is beautiful! But the best part for me was seeing Mycol so excited about being there. He was in love with the place."

Aunt Marge smiled. "I can certainly understand why."

"But what we couldn't understand was if God wanted us to go to Alaska, why weren't we moving? Why hadn't the house sold? Why had neither of us secured employment? We just didn't get it. Finally I said, 'Mycol, maybe God just meant *go*, not *move*. And we did go, so maybe that was all there was to it."

"We don't always understand God's ways," Aunt Marge observed.

I nodded. Mycol felt we were supposed to move there, but we also shared Aunt Marge's sentiment that we can't always understand God's ways. I had even jokingly said to Mycol, "Watch God move us east instead of west," but I didn't really think it would happen.

A Change of Direction

So many times during those days of uncertainty I had told Mycol that I wondered why he would feel God urging us to go to Alaska. At one point he said, "I don't know, but I hope it's not because my life is going to be cut short."

I remember thinking that was an odd comment for a man of thirty-six to make. "Don't say that," I had told him. "I couldn't live without you."

But Mycol just responded with his usual words of caution. "We're not promised tomorrow. When the Lord calls me home, I'm ready."

It seemed he had been saying that often lately, but dismissing the uneasy feelings dredged up by that thought, I went on to explain to Aunt Marge that even though things hadn't worked out for us to move to Alaska, Mycol had still been determined to get our kids out of subdivision life. We finally came to the conclusion that if God wanted us to live in Alaska, we'd be there. Since that hadn't happened, and since my office was on the far west side of Houston and we were living on the far north side, we decided to look into buying some property toward the west. I would be closer to the office, and we could get the lifestyle we wanted for our family. We hadn't totally given up on the idea of Alaska, but we reasoned that it wouldn't hurt to go ahead and move somewhere else until something changed. We were just eager to leave the "master planned community" and get the kids away from there before the materialism that was so characteristic of that area took hold of them.

And so we had explored the small Texas town of Sealy, a rural area close to my office. There was one piece of property there that Mycol really liked. It was twelve acres with a pond, fully fenced, and off the main road, a peaceful country setting in a nice country town. Unfortunately, the listing agent didn't seem eager to sell it. All the other lots in that area were sold except this one, and Mycol had to be persistent just to get the agency to show it to us. They kept saying we shouldn't want it because there were no trees on it, but we told them we knew how to plant trees.

So we finally took a look at the property, and though our house was still on the market, we bought the twelve acres in Sealy and began to get excited at the prospect of moving.

We were supposed to close on the property the week of September 11, 2001, but because of the terrorist attacks, the banks were closed. Finally, on Friday, September 14, the day President Bush declared a National Day of Prayer, we were set to complete the transaction. The title company had scheduled us for 1:00 p.m., but prayer services were being conducted nationwide at the noon hour, and we weren't about to miss that. We attended a prayer service, arrived a bit late to closing, and then finally signed the papers that made us the proud owners of a treeless twelve acres in Sealy, Texas.

We left the title office and headed straight for our new property to have a picnic. Opening the back doors of our "all-the-way van," so dubbed by our son because it was much bigger than the minivan and you have to say it with your arms spread wide because it was all-the-way big, we made enough room to spread out a blanket and open the cooler that held all kinds of goodies just right for celebrating: cheese sticks, juice pouches, and peanut butter and jelly sandwiches. After we ate, the kids and I walked over to the pond so they could look for frogs and turtles and practice skimming stones. Meanwhile, Mycol walked along the property's perimeter with his Bible and prayed. He still wrestled with the move to Alaska not working out, but more than anything, he did not want to be disobedient or outside the will of God. And so he prayed as he walked around our property with his Bible, asking God if this was right. When he completed his prayer walk, he told me he had peace about buying this land, even though he didn't understand and still thought we would move to Alaska one day.

As we continued to visit the Sealy property over the next few months, still waiting for our house to sell before building or moving an older home onto it, I began to get a very strong sense that we would never live there, even though that was our plan. I shared this with Mycol, but I also agreed to continue pursuing the house-hunting as though we were going to live in Sealy, until God showed us otherwise.

Our prayer for the Sealy property was the same as with the move to Alaska: If it was not God's will, we asked Him to close the doors. While we may have wanted these things, if they were outside God's will, we didn't want them that badly.

Our preference was to move an old house onto the property and then restore it. We found a few possibilities, but every time we wanted to put a contract on one, it either sold before we could secure the contract or the contract fell through because we still hadn't sold our house in Kingwood.

We also both liked log homes, so we looked into building one, but every time we started talking about it I'd say, "There's really only one log home I like!" And, of course, Mycol knew exactly which log home I was talking about.

During that time, we received five contracts on our house. The first four fell through for various reasons, and we ended up spending almost two years with our house on the market. But even as we waited for the house to sell, we took many trips out to Sealy and began to make memories there–picnics at the property, skipping stones on the pond, playing at the city park and stopping to eat at Tony's, our favorite restaurant. After moving here from Greece, Tony had become a successful businessman in America, and he always seemed overjoyed to see us. He'd kiss the kids, give me a hug, then pick up little Jessie and take Austin by the hand and take them to pick out a piece of candy from the jar on the register. Tony became a good friend on our trips to visit our treeless land.

Our Little Evangelist

Retelling the story to Aunt Marge brought back so many fond memories of the things we had encountered leading up to that moment, including one very special day when we were riding in the "all-the-way-van." Mycol and I were up front, and both kids were in the rear-most seats, when we heard Austin whisper, "Jesus, come in my heart. Jesus, come in my heart. Jesus, come in my heart."

We turned around and saw Austin lying on his back, eyes closed, feet up against the window, praying with all the pure desire of a four-year-old. When he finished his prayer, he sat up, turned to his little sister, and said, "Jessie, you know what you have to do? You have to ask Jesus to come into your heart." Austin Chad, our little evangelist!

Mycol and I looked at each other, amazed, grateful, and deeply touched by the gift of being able to witness this event. We didn't know what led to Austin's asking Jesus into his heart at that precise moment, but it is what we lived and taught at home, and of course, we took him to church and church school. The timing and the decision were his.

By nature, Mycol and I are relatively quiet people. We enjoyed sitting quietly together, observing our children. We often commented on what they were doing as we watched and analyzed their stages of development, but mostly we just sat and cherished the moments. So, as was typical for us, Mycol and I listened without comment to our son as he prayed to Jesus and witnessed to his little sister. This was one of those important and tender moments of life, and we just let Austin be Austin.

As we heard him invite Christ into his heart, we were both very moved but did not dare speak for fear of interrupting this sacred event. Besides, we didn't know what might happen next, and we didn't want to crowd the airwaves with our needless words when our children might come up with something memorable. We talked about it later, of course, but not at that point.

Austin is a thinker; he's analytical. He would contemplate and then act. I imagine he had been thinking of all he had learned, and then, at that very moment, he acted. The brief evangelistic message he spoke to his sister was all he said. Jessie, of course, was only three, so she looked at him but didn't really respond. She was busy playing with one of her toys, and her mind was on other things. I know she heard Austin because her eyes registered acknowledgment of his comments, but all she said was "Okay."

The sound of Aunt Marge clearing her throat brought me back to the present, and the look on her face told me she knew I had been lost in pleasant memories. But it was time to continue my story and explain to my aunt how we had gone from having picnics on our treeless lot in Sealy while we waited for our house to sell, to purchasing the log house of my dreams.

For Our Daughters

Sisters, look not for sand to grow your garden.
Seek the blessed ground that lends
Rich nutrients where flows a living river.
Plant your seed and strengthen
Roots and grow your harvest
Where provision overflows.
Be like Deborah; for direction
Turn to Him. He will protect you
From the lions and will make
You strong and wise
When you rely on Him.
If your faith is in your limited
Understanding your harvest will
Likewise be incomplete.
Study the wisdom of Deborah.
Learn the faith and reach
For His goodness. For you, my sisters,
Have so much potential: success
Yet to be achieved,
Only invisible when you draw
On the wrong gauge.

Chapter 6

The Offer

It was in April, more than a year after Mycol's first trip to Alaska, when I received that surprise call at my office from Lisa Arney, who had to remind me, "We're the people who bought the log house from your grandmother."

Aunt Marge's face lit up as I related that part of my story. I'll never forget Lisa's next question: "Do you still want the house?" That question has echoed in my mind for a very long time since.

This was the one house I had dreamed of owning for as long as I can remember, the one house I've always loved. And yet it felt out of reach somehow, not to mention impractical. But that day, as I sat in my office with the phone pressed to my ear and that wonderful house being offered to me, all I could do was blurt out, "Yes! Of course!"

I couldn't believe Lisa and A.J. had kept my number all these years and they were ready to sell. That's when I had finally been able to see the reason we hadn't moved to Alaska, and why I had sensed we would never live in Sealy. It was as if I could hear God saying, "Wait till you see what I have for you!"

Mycol and I had no idea how we would accomplish this move. We knew we would have to sell the house, even though it had already been on the market quite a while, and now we had twelve acres in Sealy to sell as well. In addition, one of us would have to find work in the Roanoke area.

But none of those details mattered at that moment. All I knew was that I was finally going to see my dream come true. I would finally get to live in the log home with Mycol and our two younger children. And someday, I thought, we would entertain our grandchildren there, just as my grandparents did.

Aunt Marge was fascinated as she listened to our intricate tale unfold, but that was just the beginning. I told her how Mycol and I had continued to be faithful in fasting and prayer, listening for direction from God. As we did, we felt the Holy Spirit speak to us, and things began to unfold, one step at a time. Something unseen but clearly present was affirming these exciting changes in our lives, and we could hardly wait to see what lay ahead...

A Natural-Born Leader

One of the details I shared with Aunt Marge was about our family's nighttime routine. Mycol and I and the kids would sit on the floor between Austin and Jessie's beds, sing a song from their children's Bible story book, read a Bible story, ask some questions about the story, sing another song, and then have a family prayer. Teaching Austin and Jess to pray brought Mycol and me so much joy in our Christian parenting: walking in our faith, acting on our belief in our responsibility to God for the gifts He had given us, these children He had loaned to us.

One evening, about six months before moving to the log house, during our regular Bible story time, Jessie asked, "Mommy, when we move to heaven, will we get to see Jesus?" As she bounced around the room with her usual endless energy, she wanted to know when she could see this Jesus she already knew about.

"Yes, baby girl," I responded, "we will."

Jess was happy with my answer and continued her busyness as she hopped from her bed to Austin's and back again.

She asked about seeing Jesus several times after this, but this first time Mycol and I were really taken aback by what we heard from our little Jester. We would talk about it privately later, but as with Austin's asking Jesus into his life, we didn't dare interrupt the moment, so we didn't discuss it between us right then. How could a three-and-a-half-year-old possibly understand something it takes some of us a lifetime to grasp? And yet, she did.

That night, after we finished our bedtime routine and tucked the kids in, Mycol and I went to our room, eager to talk about Jessie's question. Neither of us had used the phrase "move to heaven" before. Where did she get those words? And where did she get the idea? We knew her understanding had not come from either of us. But from that time on, when we talked about Jesus, Jess would ask about moving to heaven and getting to see Him, our wonderful Savior.

Shortly after that, while reading the Old Testament book of Judges, I suggested to Mycol that we should have named our daughter Deborah instead of Jessie. Judges is a collection of stories about the time when Israel had no king. It tells of the strengths and weaknesses, trials and triumphs of those who filled in as leaders for the nation, and their personal relationships with God. Deborah was one of those strong and faithful leaders for Israel. Because of Deborah's faith in God and her strong personal relationship with the Lord, and because she listened to God and trusted Him, He used her to outsmart and conquer Israel's enemies. Jessie's strong faith, her confidence in the Lord, and her natural leadership reminded me of Deborah.

In fact, one of the children's choir teachers once told me that the teachers all knew that if they could make Jessie happy, the whole class would follow her. If they wanted the children to stand, all they had to do was get Jess to stand. Likewise, if they wanted them to sit, they had to focus on Jess. Whatever she did, the other kids would follow.

I thought about how many parents of teen girls struggle as their children mistakenly focus their move to independence on the opinions and approval of this world, this society. I thought about the way some young girls dress to attract attention, how they are manipulated by advertising and how it affects their behavior. If only our little Jess could teach older girls this confidence in the Lord through her spiritual maturity. Even at such a young age, Jess had no fear. She loved completely. In fact, she inspired me to write the poem "For Our Daughters" as advice to older girls.

Confirmation and Direction

There were still a lot of details that I hadn't fully explained to Aunt Marge, but she was thrilled to hear the story up to that point. The rest, however, was yet to unfold.

As Mycol and I had continued to fast and pray and listen for direction from God, I began to record our journey, chronicling our prayers in a journal. I'd pray and ask God to lead me to a section of scripture and to speak to me through His Word. Then I listened to what the Holy Spirit spoke to my heart. At the same time Mycol was fasting every Monday, and his relationship with the Lord strengthened in a way that amazed me.

I could feel things happening, as our lives seemed to be moving in a new direction. There was an energy level I could sense; life was getting interesting, and I wanted to be able to look back and read my prayers again as this exciting time unfolded. It was so obvious that God's Holy Spirit was affirming these changes in our lives.

On May 6, 2002, I prayerfully opened to the book of Job in the Old Testament and, wondering if we were right in our desire for this log house, I thought about how some people appear to "have it all together." Sometimes we wonder why nonbelievers are so successful by our worldly terms; sometimes we wonder why we aren't living in circumstances we desire. But all people will have to deal with consequences of their spiritual decisions after this life. I asked God to speak to me through His Word; I asked Him to speak to me about the house situation, how we were going to afford this deal, about anything He wanted to speak to me about. I just wanted to hear Him.

As I continued to read the Scriptures, seeking God's will for our family, I realized I wanted my life to count for something, and neither Mycol nor I wanted that log home so badly that we would be willing to turn from what we understood to be God's will. We prayed specifically that what we really wanted was God's will, and if that meant "no log house," that was fine with us. We knew there was no material thing–no house, no job, no car, no anything–that could ever be as important as the will of God.

Meanwhile, A.J. and Lisa had asked us for a commitment so they could begin to make plans for building their new home across the street from the log house. We knew we could trust God with the direction our lives would take, but we just didn't know how things would work out.

I read Matthew 9:10-13. *God desires mercy, not sacrifice.* He repeated it in Matthew 12:1-8, where He says that even though His disciples may have violated a Sabbath law, they were hungry and He was merciful in wanting them to be fed. Mycol and I were adamant that we did not want our desire for this house to interfere with our relationship growing in God. These verses in Matthew meant to me that God's priority is that we be fed by Him. I think we were seeking that.

Not long after reading those words, my sister Barbara called, very excited. She told me something that was very out of character for her. She said she had been praying and she asked God to lead her to where He would have her read in His Word. She then opened to Psalm 107:1-9, where the Lord gave her a vision to share with us: being in deserts, hungry and thirsty, searching for a city in which to settle. In this psalm the Lord heard the cry of the Israelites and brought them to a city to settle, and then filled them to quench their hunger and thirst and blessed them with His unfailing love.

Psalm 107:1-9 OH, give thanks to the LORD, for *He is* good! For His mercy *endures* forever. ²Let the redeemed of the LORD say *so*, Whom He has redeemed from the hand of the enemy, ³And gathered out of the lands, From the east and from the west, From the north and from the south. ⁴They wandered in the wilderness in a desolate way; They found no city to dwell in. ⁵Hungry and thirsty, their soul fainted in them. ⁶Then they cried out to the LORD in their trouble, *And* He delivered them out of their distresses. ⁷And He led them forth by the right way, That they might go to a city for habitation. ⁸Oh, that *men* would give thanks to the LORD for His goodness, And *for* His wonderful

works to the children of men! ⁹For He satisfies the longing soul,
And fills the hungry soul with goodness.

Barbara could hardly contain her excitement at receiving this guidance, this particular part of scripture at this particular time. We all agreed that these verses felt like a confirmation that God was opening doors and making the way for us to move. We knew we must remain attentive and cooperative. If this was indeed God's plan, then He would make the way.

About that same time I was in a Christian bookstore and saw a coffee tumbler with the scripture Jeremiah 29:11: "'For I know the plans I have for you,' declares the LORD, 'plans to prosper you and not to harm you, plans to give you hope and a future.'"(NIV) I bought two of those tumblers, sent one to Barbara, and kept one for us.

This is getting really exciting, I wrote in my journal. *Mycol says he can feel it that God is going to do something big with this.*

We kept our focus on listening to God. Within days of our fast and prayer concerning selling our house and moving, a young couple named Jeff and Jennifer called and asked to see the house. We soon learned that this couple had been house-hunting for quite a while and were nearly ready to give up when they found ours listed online and decided to look at "just one more house."

They offered us our full asking price, and soon we celebrated the sale of our Kingwood home and moved into a town home nearby. Selling the house brought us one step closer to buying the log house; selling the Sealy property would be our next focus. Moving into the town house for six months would give A.J. and Lisa time to build their new home on their property on the other side of Catawba Road, just across from the pasture that would soon be ours.

"Its just like that old TV show, 'Get Smart.' Maxwell Smart would take a step forward and a door would open, but never until he took that step."
—*Mycol Street*

Chapter 7

Going Forward in Faith

Before Nana passed on we were keeping the news of the log house secret from most of our friends, at least until we could see things a little clearer. But Barbara was in on the secret almost from the beginning, and we prayed and fasted together for direction. Even though Mycol and I desperately wanted to raise our children out in the country, we wanted more than just the log house–we wanted God's will. The fact that Psalm 107 came to Barbara during prayer and fasting and that it spoke to us of our own experience, of our desire to settle in what we considered a better place and raise our children in a more desirable setting, brought an incredible significance to this particular psalm. It soon became a stronghold of promise to us, of God answering prayer, confirming as we listened.

As I prayed and meditated on this passage of scripture, the parallel really began to sink in: Israel, freshly delivered from Babylonian captivity, praised God for His unfailing love for those who cried out to Him in their crisis. We felt like this in that we had wanted to leave the subdivision lifestyle for years, wanting to raise our children in a different environment, and we could finally feel God hearing our cries and answering our prayer. *This may not be Alaska, but it's an answer to our prayer,* we thought.

As we continued to pray and seek God about the details of this move, Mycol would say, "It's just like that old TV show, 'Get Smart.' Maxwell Smart would take a step forward and a door would open, but never until he took that step." And Mycol was right. That was exactly the way things unfolded for us–one step of faith at a time. As the path illumined with each consecutive step, we began sharing our news with more of Mycol's family, as well as our friends who lived nearby.

Securing the Finances

Selling our house to Jeff and Jennifer meant a significant transition for me. This was the house I had purchased sixteen years earlier, at the end of my first marriage. Angela and Melissa spent most of their childhood in that house in Kingwood, going to Kingwood schools, attending church and day camp in Kingwood, making friends and establishing a life in that Houston suburb. Then Austin and Jessie came along, and the two of them knew the Kingwood house as their only home. Closing the door for the last time was difficult for all of us, and Mycol and I had to comfort Austin as we pulled out of the driveway that final day.

We stayed in Kingwood for another six months, moving into a townhouse near the San Jacinto River. Packing up sixteen years' worth of household belongings took a while, and since the townhouse would be a temporary residence, we decided to live out of boxes as much as possible. Meanwhile, in Troutville, A.J. and Lisa were nearly finished building their new home on the other side of Catawba Road.

Again in August we fasted and prayed concerning the sale of the twelve acres in Sealy. Within three days of our fast, we received a contract on the Sealy property. While waiting for the Arneys to finish building their home and move out of the log house, the twelve acres in Sealy sold at a huge profit. We had owned that property just less than a year, having purchased it the week of 9/11. With the timing of that investment in mind, we had to wonder where else we could possibly have put our money at that particular time and earned better than a fifty percent profit in less than a year. When we finally settled with the Arneys on a sale price, it turned out to be exactly what we could afford, with the additional profit from the Sealy land to add to our down payment.

In September, after Nana's funeral, we stopped by the log house so Mycol could see it for the first time. Lisa Arney told us that over the years there had been a couple of other people who had expressed interest in buying the house. She had kept all the phone numbers, including the number of a well-to-do Texan who had at one time offered cash for the place. Lisa confessed that they had called him first, but when he was unable to make the purchase at that time, she called us. When the fellow Texan came by later, cash in hand, Lisa informed him they had already entered into an agreement with us.

After Nana's funeral and before leaving Virginia, Mycol and I wanted to visit the three banks we had corresponded with in an effort to find the best mortgage. Prior to visiting those banks, we prayed with my sister Barbara and her husband, Mike.

When we went to the first one, which was a local bank, we were told they couldn't offer us a loan because I was planning to qualify on my current job in Houston. That being the situation, they had to consider this a second home, even though we owned no other real estate at the time. The risk, they said, was too great that I might not find work in Roanoke and would have to continue working in Texas, eventually growing weary of the situation and missing my family, who would already be living in the log house. Not knowing us, they were concerned that I might quit my job, even without a viable financial alternative, and therefore put the mortgage in jeopardy.

Mycol and I walked out of the bank and found Mike and Barbara waiting for us. We told them it was a no-go, and then we all agreed that we would keep searching for the open door, and this bank wasn't it. As Mike and Barbara began their long drive home to Indianapolis, Mycol, the kids, and I went on to the second bank, also a local one.

This banker seemed flustered. He couldn't really tell me whether or not they could offer a second home loan. But as we talked, something else struck me. When I had walked into his office, Austin was with me. Quiet and well behaved, Austin had spotted the banker's desk toy–a box filled with sand, a few small rocks, and a small wooden rake, which the man referred to as his "Zen relaxation thing." Austin was fascinated. Though the banker didn't say anything, I could tell he was very nervous as Austin carefully raked the sand.

During this time, Mycol had been waiting in the car for Jessie to wake up. When she did, Mycol brought her into the office to join us. As soon as the banker saw her, he grabbed the desk toy and said abruptly, "Okay, guys, this is going up."

Now I don't have a problem with his not wanting sand everywhere; that would be perfectly understandable. But the man's abruptness clued me in that he clearly had no children. More important, he scared Austin. Our son thought he had done something wrong, and he quickly climbed up on Mycol's lap and began to cry softly. We had to reassure him several times that he had done nothing wrong.

The meeting continued in that same atmosphere, and neither Mycol nor I felt comfortable with the man. He kept making phone calls to ask questions regarding our loan application, and after more than an hour, we still didn't have a clear answer from him, so we left and called the last bank on our list.

I told this third banker that we were in town and would like to stop by. As Mycol pulled the car into the parking lot, there was the banker, waiting at the door. He opened it and said, "You look like a Linda!"

This friendly gentleman invited us in, and like the previous banker, he had a desk toy. It was a box with little pins that you would place over something, like your hand, and make an impression, then set it up on the desk. But unlike the previous banker, this man was not at all nervous around children. In fact, he took the toy, crouched down to the kids' level, and showed them how it worked. He even asked if he could make impressions of their hands so he could save them on his desk. By that point, he had won all of us over.

In addition to his congenial personality and the respect he showed our family, when I said, "I just need to know if you can do a second home finance or not," he opened a folder on his desk and pulled out a piece of paper. "I was just waiting for you," he said. "Here's your approval letter." And so our loan was assured.

Lost Rings and Found Candleholders

In October, while still living in the townhouse in Kingwood, the autumn storms hit, bringing a deluge of rain. The San Jacinto River rose out of its banks, flooding nearby homes, including our town house. I was at work when it happened, and Mycol had to grab as many things as he could from the bottom floor and put them upstairs. Then he took the kids and left. I met them at the home of a friend who offered us a comfortable, dry place to sleep. When we returned to the townhouse the next day, we found a few inches of water on the floor.

After the flood waters began to recede, the four of us went out for a walk and happened by the local fire station where one of our friends from church, Kelly Hartman, worked. Kelly was a Houston firefighter and welcomed us into the fire station for a visit. Having four children of his own, "Mr. Kelly" was excited to show Austin and Jessie the big fire truck. He picked them up and carried them around the truck, explaining all the gadgets. We thanked him for the tour but soon had to head back to the house for dinner. From that time on, every day when Austin and Jess got out their little cars, one of them would inevitably find a fire truck and say, "I'm Mr. Kelly!"

Not much was damaged in the flood, but lots of things had to be cleaned, sanitized, and re-packed. It was an inconvenience, but we had lots of help from friends in our Bible study group. Together, we went back through every single box, keeping a special lookout for Mycol's wedding ring, which he had lost two years earlier.

Mycol had always fiddled with that ring. When we were dating, he wanted a gold nugget ring like our brother-in-law Rusty's, so I bought one for him on Valentine's Day before we were married. That ring became his wedding ring. He liked it, but it was bulkier on his finger than he had expected it to be. Twisting the ring around his finger and moving it off and on became a habit when his mind was occupied elsewhere. Two years had passed since he first noticed it missing and asked his mom to watch for it in case he had dropped it during a visit to their nearby home.

His mom never found the ring and probably forgot about it over time. Mycol soon told me he was afraid the ring was lost and asked if we should get him another one. Knowing the ring had been uncomfortable for him, I was not eager to replace it. "It's not the ring that makes us married," I assured him.

That ring hadn't appeared when we boxed up everything for the temporary move to the townhouse, and it didn't appear when we re-boxed after the flood. But true to his personality, Mycol had a positive attitude about the flood, the damage it caused, and the entire situation. His comments encouraged me as we cleaned out the debris, and he kept saying, in his usual happy-go-lucky way, "At least we're all okay."

While cleaning up from the October flood, we came across some items from my office that I had packed up two years before when I changed jobs. One of those items was a candleholder, a gift to me from Austin. When our young son saw that the candleholder he had given me had been packed away all that time, he was not happy with what he considered my disobedience. He had bought the gift for my desk at work, and I knew my forgetfulness hurt his feelings. I felt so badly that I wrote a poem about the incident and called it "The Candle Holder." My son's precious gift, the candleholder, once again graces my office desk, and will be on every office desk I have in the future.

A Wrinkle in the Plan

We finally closed on the log house and property in November. We were getting close to a moving date and had confirmed what we had suspected all along–that I would not be able to make as much money in Roanoke as I was making in Houston. I had spent months looking for a job in Roanoke, but when it became obvious that the paralegal profession seemed to be drawing only about half of Houston's pay, we decided to hang up my paralegal certification and trade it in for a set of keys and a semi-truck for Mycol.

This was not as flighty as it may at first sound because Mycol enjoyed driving and had worked in freight transportation for years before we started our family. What at first seemed like a wrinkle in our plan was now beginning to look like a good thing. By switching roles and Mycol re-entering the work force, I could stay home and home-school the kids, which is something we both wanted for our children. Home schooling was important to me, and Mycol was really supportive about it. We talked it over and decided this would be the best move for all of us. Mycol would buy a truck and start a trucking business, and I would have a turn at staying home with Austin and Jessie.

All these wonderful and amazing things I pondered in my heart during this transitional time: a word from God, divine revelation, personal thoughts, the awesomeness of watching our story unfold, experiencing the gifts of God opening doors as we fasted, prayed, read His Word, and listened. These were priceless treasures, a collection of awe and wonder...

The Candleholder

Everything has its story, and if you could hear my candle holder
it would tell you of a son's deep love for his mother.

Three candles in
a candle holder
Rectangular
solid granite
Three circular cut-outs
for tea-sized candles
A gift from my son
A gift—
My Son

My birthday is near the end of October,
And the black granite with orange candles probably caught his
eye from the store shelf.
I forgot about it once when I changed jobs
and didn't take it to my new office.
He found it at home and forgave my complacency toward him
and his gift,
gently admonishing me to take it to my new desk,
its intended home at the time of acquisition.
Somewhat damaged in the flood,
it now bears white scars of dingy lake water.

Everything has its story, and if you could hear my candle holder
it would tell you of my son's deep love for his mother
and how important is its duty to continuously broadcast his love
while I am away from him at work.

Chapter 8

What's Spiritual Warfare Got to Do with Me?

David Lino was the pastor of Forest Cove Baptist Church in Kingwood, Texas, where we were members. We so appreciated him as our pastor, and I can honestly say that few pastors have ever had as strong and committed a spouse as our pastor's wife, Barbara.

The Linos had recently celebrated thirty years of marriage, as well as twelve years at that same church. At a time when some pastors are given large gifts–boats, cars, or European vacations–for their anniversary, when asked what they would like as a gift, David and Barbara replied that they wanted the good news of the gospel of Jesus Christ to be delivered to the people in the 10-40 Window. It was their desire to see Bibles in the Persian languages provided for the Middle East–Iran, Iraq, Afghanistan, and other countries situated between the tenth and fortieth parallels north of the equator. Though the 10-40 Window is the very cradle of civilization, it is also one of the darkest and most non-evangelized regions in the world. More than 90 percent of those who have never heard the message of salvation, and many of whom are also among the poorest people in the world today, live in this relatively small but volatile section of our planet, yet fewer than 10 percent of all missionaries live and operate in the region.

Most of the countries located in this area are considered "closed countries," meaning that Christian activity is illegal and often unsafe, due largely to the predominance of the Muslim faith, communist governments, and dictatorships. Evangelization can be dangerous work, even when operating thousands of miles away from this 10-40 Window.

And yet, contrary to what some may believe, sending Bibles and proclaiming the Christian faith to those who live in those closed countries is not a matter of forcing our beliefs on others. Rather, it is a matter of obeying the Great Commission, to go into all the earth as Jesus commanded, to share testimonies of faith, and to offer the Truth of God's Word, which will set people free and give them everlasting life, and then leaving the choice to them.

If these people never hear the message or read the Bible, how can they have the opportunity to make the choice to receive salvation and to serve the true and living God? The prophet Joel delivered God's message that "whoever calls on the name of the Lord shall be saved," (Joel 2:32) but how will they know to call upon Him?

Romans 10:14-15;17 ¹⁴How then shall they call on Him in whom they have not believed? And how shall they believe in Him of whom they have not heard? And how shall they hear without a preacher? ¹⁵And how shall they preach unless they are sent? As it is written: *"How beautiful are the feet of those who preach the gospel of peace, who bring glad tidings of good things!"*…¹⁷So then faith *comes* by hearing, and hearing by the word of God.

In order to make an informed decision, people must first hear the message. Jesus never forced anyone to believe in Him, but He came and offered His love and His life to anyone who would willingly receive it.

When Pastor Lino told the congregation about the idea of sending Bibles to the 10-40 Window, he did so with great seriousness. "Pray about this before you decide to get involved," he warned, "because Satan will attack."

Christian missionaries serving in that part of the world confirmed his warning. Satan, the anti-God power, will come against us for invading his territory where the Word of Jesus Christ is outlawed and persecuted.

Spiritual warfare is very real, and our pastor wanted us to make our decisions with a clear understanding of that fact.

After hearing the pastor's idea and admonition, Mycol prayed about whether or not to get involved, but once he sensed God's direction to move forward, he did so without hesitation. Still, throughout the months we and others in the congregation engaged in this project, Pastor Lino continued to caution us.

And he was right to do so. Within months the church began to experience friction within the leadership which, of course, is always the place the enemy attacks first. Once leadership begins to polarize, the followers are apt to do the same.

Mycol and I, however, wanted no part of the polarization of our church. Rather than get involved with the disagreements and side-taking, we, along with others in the congregation who shared our feelings, chose to distance ourselves from the arguments. We chose instead to support our pastor and the entire congregation through prayer, taking the vertical approach of talking to God about the problem, rather than the horizontal approach of talking to one another about it.

The real issue, of course, was spiritual warfare. We had invaded the enemy's territory with the only thing that can defeat him–the Word of God–and he was mad. My family prayed daily for our pastor, the deacons, the church staff, and all who attended and considered Forest Cove Baptist Church their home. We knew the most obvious way for Satan to attack the body of Christ was by sowing seeds of division, doubt, and discontent, resulting in un-Christ-like behavior. Mycol was adamant about praying for the health of our church, for we took seriously the concerns that the anti-God force would be attacking.

Our Personal Involvement

And yet, in spite of the very real danger involved, we as a family chose to purchase Bibles to be sent to the Middle East. Some people have since asked me why I would want to "push my religion" on others. I answer that I don't do that at all. First, this is not about religion–it's about relationship. A religion can be made of anything, and anything can be its god. Religion is nothing more than a set of traditions, strongly-held beliefs, values, and attitudes that people choose to live by. A person's religion could have little or nothing to do with God Himself.

I choose to live by my convictions, but those convictions are based on my relationship with a very real and very personal God, established by my faith in Jesus Christ and the sacrifice He made to pay for my sins. That personal relationship is available to everyone. Each of us has the choice whether or not to enter into a relationship with God, but our acceptance or denial does not change or affect God or His Truth one bit.

So what does this have to do with spiritual warfare and sending Bibles to the 10-40 Window? Opposing forces work in both the spiritual and physical realms. The anti-God force fights against God and seeks to enrich its army by winning the devotion of God's own creation–you, me, and people everywhere. The spiritual realm is as real, or more so, than the physical. More importantly, it lasts forever.

Perhaps one of the most dangerous things a person can do is to ignore the force of evil in this world in the name of "religious tolerance." If we recognize evil for what it is–a force that opposes God– then we can offer the alternative, which is the way of love, the way of Christ as Savior. The choice is always there, and sending the message of Christ's love provides people the opportunity to choose to believe in the promises of God.

Mycol and I saw this as our opportunity to participate in giving that choice to people who had never heard the good news or received the hope that lies only in Jesus Christ. This was the basis for our decision to contribute to sending Persian language Bibles to the people of the 10-40 Window. We would simply have to pray and trust God to protect us in the midst of the spiritual warfare that was bound to come, even as we continued to prepare for our move to the log house.

Ephesians 6:12

For our struggle is not against flesh and blood,
but against the rulers, against the authorities, against the powers
of this dark world
and against the spiritual forces of evil in the heavenly realms.
(NIV)

Chapter 9

Becoming Grandparents

Angie called us as she went into labor on June 6, 2002, and we hurriedly packed up and drove north to Indy. My first grandchild, Myles Thomas Temple, was born as we were en route. Missy, soon to give birth herself, rode along with us. We stayed in Indy a couple of days before going back to Texas, but in that time it was as though the Holy Spirit was telling Angie to be very careful with Myles. I say that because she was even more protective than most new moms. Her sense of his fragility seemed to me at the time more obsessive than I had felt with my children, but I never questioned her because I believe parents often get a "gut feeling" when something is out of the ordinary with their child. Once home from the hospital, she was quite selective about who could be around him and hold him. She insisted that everyone use hand sanitizer before touching Myles. So soon after his birth, although she felt badly making this decision, Angie felt it unwise to let Austin and Jess hold Myles because they had been coughing, so Mycol stayed outside with them and welcomed baby Myles to our world through the window.

Four months later we welcomed grandson number two into the family when Missy gave birth to Kody Wayne Henderson. Grateful for the opportunity to enjoy parenting and grand-parenting while we were still fairly young, Mycol and I soaked up every moment possible with family.

Serious Health Issues for Myles

By November, after things had settled down a bit and we had sanitized and repacked the belongings affected by the October flood, we received some troubling news. Myles, then five months old, was having difficulty breathing. Myles and his parents, Justin and Angie, were living in Indianapolis at the time. They had taken him to a doctor, who prescribed a medication for breathing problems, but he wasn't getting any better. The next day they took him to the emergency room, where he was admitted and started on more intensive treatment for an upper respiratory infection.

Mycol and I stayed in close touch with them over the next week, and then Angie called and said they were putting Myles on a ventilator and moving him up to the pediatric intensive care unit. The infection had turned to pneumonia, and Myles was getting worse. It was obvious Angie was scared, and I told her I'd be there in a few hours. I immediately boarded a plane, and as I prayed for direction, I felt strongly moved by the Holy Spirit to read the Book of Job in order to give sound counsel to Angie and to help her turn to God in total trust–regardless of the outcome–even if we didn't understand. I sensed a need to be prepared for something tragic that would require great strength.

My younger sister, Barbara, also lives in the Indianapolis area, and she would help Angie as much as she could. Barbara, along with her four home-schooled children, picked me up at the airport and took me directly to the hospital. When we arrived at the receptionist's desk at the pediatric intensive care unit, Angie was called and informed she had visitors. When she walked through the ICU doors and saw me, her entire countenance changed, as an almost tangible sense of love and strength passed between us. Barbara described it this way:

> In that moment what I saw was a worn-out young mother of an ill child, who has been round the clock caring for, worrying about, and interrogating physicians on behalf of, who sees her own mother in the hallway of the pediatric intensive care unit

waiting area for the first time since learning of her son's unknown illness. Her mother, my sister, having just flown in from Texas, leaving behind work and a young family of her own… there was an instant change of countenance: from a face that may have portrayed strength to some, but to others an outward "surviving on adrenaline" appearance, to a little girl wanting just to be cradled by her mother and forget about having to be "the grown up in charge" for just a second or two. As an aunt, I almost melted in my own tears at the tender sight of the two of them: Their hug seemed to last forever. I felt like it was such a sacred moment I shouldn't be looking at them. It was a private moment that didn't have the luxury of being private. If you could "see" the emotion of love between mother and daughter, I did that day. I felt unworthy but blessed to be a bystander; and grateful to be a part of this family.

Over the next ten days, I sat at Myles' bedside, studying the Book of Job and praying for God's peace, wisdom, and guidance, and doing what I could to comfort and encourage Angie and Justin. I left the hospital only once during that time to attend a Bible study class with Barbara. The message from the guest speaker, whose name was Terri Camp, was, "Even though we don't understand, we still trust You, Lord," as told through her own family's story of grief. It was exactly what I needed to hear, for at that time the doctors were giving Myles a fifty-fifty chance of surviving.

When I attended that Bible study, I was not yet familiar with the music of Terri's son, Jeremy, who was just then capturing the attention of the Christian music world and would later earn several Dove Awards and be voted "Singer of the Year." Terri shared with us about how the death of Jeremy's young wife–Terri's daughter-in-law, Melissa–had affected Jeremy and the rest of the family, and we were overwhelmed with the incredible faith that had emerged from this heartbreaking situation. Melissa had died of cancer just one year prior, and the family faced confusion and grief as they tried to make sense of it. And yet, though they struggled, they remained faithful.

When I returned to the hospital, Terri's testimony was still working its way into my heart. Not knowing the ominous impact this teaching could have on me personally, I wondered, *Did God lead me to that Bible study so I could help prepare my daughter for the difficult times that lie ahead? The message is that I am to trust the Lord with Myles' health, regardless of the outcome. It's a good thing I decided to go to that study tonight. I need this strength to draw on.* I felt sure the Lord wanted me to hear this to help Angie as I'd been studying Job since arriving in Indy, hoping I could be some encouragement to her, regardless of the outcome. This would be very helpful.

Other family members were also at the hospital during those long days of waiting, and we took turns in the intensive care unit. I used the time to pray and study God's Word, preparing for what I hoped would not happen.

"Trust God," I advised Angie, time and again. "Trust Him that He knows what He's doing."

We talked about Job, about trust in our sovereign God, and about keeping faith even when we don't understand what's going on around us. Finally, on Thanksgiving Day, though we still had no confirmed diagnosis or cause, the doctors said Myles was doing well enough to be removed from the respirator. Angie had been faithful, even under such extreme duress, to pump her breast milk for her baby. Whatever was wrong with Myles, it would be better for him to have her milk than to have formula, as long as she was able to provide it.

We had no idea at the time how important Angie's milk would prove to be. Myles' health still seemed fragile, but he appeared to have recovered from his pneumonia, and so Justin and Angie took their baby boy home. I flew back to Texas the next day for a late Thanksgiving dinner with Mycol and the kids.

Matthew 10:29-31

"Are not two sparrows sold for a copper coin?
And not one of them falls to the ground apart from your Father's will.
But the very hairs of your head are all numbered.
Do not fear therefore; you are of more value than many sparrows."

Chapter 10

The Move

December had arrived, and because our move was scheduled to happen over Christmas, we decided to celebrate a week early. We planned to go to the home of Mycol's sister, Lynna Blue, and her husband, Rusty, for dinner, fellowship, and a gift exchange with the rest of the family, but unfortunately I came down with the flu that day. This was unusual for me, as I seldom catch stomach flu, but Austin had been down with it the day before, and I had slept downstairs on the sofa-bed with him that night. Though Austin was recovered in time to go to the celebration, I wasn't, and so I ended up missing what we all knew would probably be the last Christmas get-together with the Texas part of our family for quite a while.

Lynna, the oldest of Mycol's five siblings and the one who most resembles him, is a tall, slender woman–beautiful both inside and out. Despite the ten-year age difference, Lynna and Mycol have similar personalities–gentle, kind, patient, and always cheerful and smiling. There's an old saying that opposites attract, and that is definitely the case with Lynna's and Mycol's spouses. Though Rusty and I are the in-laws of this foursome, we too are a lot alike, and we are grateful for our wonderfully patient spouses who make us better than we are. In spite of himself, though, Rusty is a generous man, a man with a really big heart who is eager to serve and help others. As a result, Lynna and Rusty enjoy hosting the family Christmas celebrations at their home each year.

This year was no different. When Mycol and the kids returned from the event, they were bursting with excitement and happy from their fulfilling visit with aunts, uncles, cousins, and grandparents. Austin amazed Uncle Rusty with how much steak he could eat, and when asked if he was ready to move away from the warm weather of Texas, he delighted everyone with his oft-repeated response, which quickly became famous within our family circle: "I'm made for the cold!" True to form, Austin's wit, mature beyond his years, made him a joy to be around.

December breezed by quickly, as we completed the last of our packing and prepared to leave on our new adventure. Since we had kept a considerable amount of our belongings packed from the temporary move into the town home and then again when we re-packed after the flood, packing wasn't nearly as big an issue as saying our goodbyes and finding a way to load up everything that needed to go with us.

The last time we attended church at Forest Cove in Kingwood, we exchanged lots of hugs and received many well wishes from longtime friends and fellow parishioners, and promised to return for visits whenever we were back in Texas to see family. As we headed toward the church exit, Pastor Lino came up to Mycol, gave him a hug, and told him he would miss us. But then he assured us that moving on was a good thing because it meant God had work for us someplace else "Something big is going to happen in Virginia," Mycol told him. "I don't know what it is, but I can feel it."

Even as Mycol responded to all the well-wishers with his usual big, confident grin, I wondered what that "something big" might be.

Avoiding the Storm

We rented the largest moving truck available, but we still couldn't quite get everything to fit. We had a large swing set–more like an entire playground, actually–a huge wooden structure sectioned off with every imaginable piece of equipment: a yellow slide and swings, a merry-go-round, rings, and places to climb and play. We had some other large items as well, including a washer and dryer and an old refrigerator, all of which we decided would have to come on a second load.

As we packed up the truck with help from family and friends, a winter storm began to blow its way into town. This is an unusual occurrence for South Texas, an area known more for nine-month summers, high heat and humidity, and hurricanes, but this storm was reportedly packing a serious punch and would bring lower than normal temperatures and possibly violent weather.

It wasn't long until the temperature dropped and the wind was gusting at near tropical storm force, slowing our packing and loading and causing us to run a day behind schedule on our departure. But at five o'clock in the evening on December 24, 2002, we finally said goodbye to the life we had built in suburban Houston and headed east on I-10 toward Virginia.

Mycol had been concerned about driving the twenty-six foot moving truck during the previous day's fierce windstorm, but our one-day delay gave the damaging storm time to pass, leaving only a cold and gloomy feel to the otherwise exciting day. True to his optimistic and upbeat demeanor, Mycol announced, "God is watching out for us. Had we left on schedule yesterday, we would have been right in the middle of that storm, and that could have been a disaster for a truck this size."

Well equipped with snacks, drinks, coloring books, Matchbox cars, pillows, blankets, and walkie-talkies, we set out. Mycol led the way in the big yellow moving truck, and the kids and I followed behind in the minivan. The walkie-talkies were a big hit with the kids when they discovered they could still talk to Daddy as we rode along. They also found a lot of interesting things along the way that inspired questions, conversation, and laughter.

By midnight it was time for a gas stop, so Mycol exited the freeway in Picayune, Mississippi. It was cold and windy as we pulled into the gas station, renewing Mycol's concerns about the storm that had passed through Houston the day before. He wondered how fast or slow the eastbound storm might be moving and whether or not we would catch up with it. He went into the station to pay for the gas and asked the clerk if she knew how far we could get that night before running into the storm. She didn't know, but just then another customer walked in–the only other person out at midnight on Christmas Eve–and, having overheard Mycol's question, said, "You can get all the way to Nashville."

That was much farther than we would have driven that night anyway, so we knew we were safe. Mycol came out of the store beaming, as he described what had happened. "God is looking out for us," he declared again. It seems the customer who gave him the information was the chief meteorologist for a local network affiliate, and he had been tracking the storm. I remember thinking how ironic it was that he was there at exactly the same time we were, with the exact information we needed. And then I noticed the sign in the gas station's store window: "Jesus is Lord of Picayune." *That is so cool*, I thought, smiling as we pulled back onto the road.

We made it as far as Meridian, Mississippi, that night, and managed to find a hotel room. The only place open for breakfast on Christmas morning was an old smoke-filled short-order restaurant on Virginia Avenue, so that's where we ate before heading out once again.

Later in the afternoon, as we traveled through Alabama, Austin requested that we take the lead. He said he was "tired of looking at the back of that yellow truck," so we called Mycol on the walkie-talkie and told him we were going to move in front of him for a while.

Around midnight, with only about four more hours to drive and against Mycol's wishes, we stopped in Tennessee to spend the night. Mycol had wanted to finish the drive, but the kids were restless and weary after two long days of driving, so we pulled into the parking lot of a hotel. Sparkling fresh new snow was falling and beginning to accumulate on the ground. Although our children had been in Indiana one winter when they were babies, they didn't recall ever having seen snow, so as far as they were concerned, it was their first real snowfall.

Not knowing what to expect, they climbed cautiously out of the minivan, but soon they were laughing and cheering and waving their hands in the air as they saw their footprints in the snow. We showed them how to make snowballs and throw them, and how to stick out their tongue and catch snowflakes. There was so much laughter and excitement that night, and so much newness in this adventure. *Things seem so right,* I thought. *Surely we must be in God's will.* I would soon learn the fallacy of this thinking.

After a good night's rest and a warm, hearty breakfast, we set out again, this time with only a half-day's journey ahead of us. At some point along the way Mycol radioed us and pointed out the mammoth white cross outside a church near the freeway. He gave it a thumbs-up and his usual remark when he was impressed with something: "That is so cool!"

Arriving in Roanoke

We finally arrived in Roanoke on the afternoon of December 26. Mycol suggested we stop at a store to buy coats, hats, gloves, scarves, and long underwear–things we didn't own because we hadn't had much use for them in Texas–before going on to our new home. Jessie had a hard time choosing between a Dalmatian-patterned coat and a waterproof Scooby-Doo coat. After we explained that it would be okay to roll in the snow in the Scooby-Doo coat, she decided the Dalmatian coat could wait until another time.

Before long we were loaded up with all our winter necessities, and we drove the last few miles to our historic 212-year-old log house, arriving about four in the afternoon. Soon after we got there I wrote in my journal, *This is SO exciting! There is snow, and the kids are having a blast exploring our new digs.*

There wasn't much daylight left by that time, but we made the most of it as we explored our new home. At last I was in my dream home, filled with my childhood memories, the one place I had always wanted to live. Then, unexpectedly, I found myself overwhelmed with feelings of unworthiness, as I thought about how I already had the best of everything important. I was married to a wonderful man who loved me so very much and who was an exemplary husband and father. He was an encourager to so many others through his involvement in our Bible study class and in a weeknight men's Bible study. I fell in love with him on our first date. His eyes, dark brown and sparkling full of fun, his bushy eyebrows, which Missy called "eye beards" and full head of thick, dark hair to match, first attracted me to him. His fun-loving personality, his tendency to almost dance when he walked, in a bouncy sort of way, full of life and love, made me hang on to find out more. I loved how compassionate he was whenever someone came to him in need. Being a "home father" as he called himself, he was often available during the day for other moms on the cul-de-sac when they needed help. Whether it was fixing something on a car, unstopping a toilet, or helping to catch a loose dog, Mycol always jumped at the chance to help someone. Our children–my two grown daughters, as well as our two "babies"–were the light of our lives, along with our grandsons, Kody and Myles, who now seemed to be doing well. Mycol and I could look forward to being grandparents here in the old log house, which I now realized was just the icing on the already perfect cake.

And yet, in the middle of all that joy, I felt tense and uneasy. The earlier excitement I had shared with Mycol and the kids began to be replaced with a feeling of heaviness, so much so that Mycol commented on how he thought I would be happy about moving into my dream home. I would have thought so too…but for some reason, I just couldn't shake that heavy feeling.

Later that night I carried a box from the truck down the slope of land to the walk-out basement. As I stopped beneath and just about even with the front door on the first floor above, something happened that is very difficult to explain. I heard something from outside of me–not with my physical ears, but a spiritual kind of hearing. It may have been something like when Mycol heard God say, "Go to Alaska." I don't really know, but I do know the experience was unusual, and I will never forget the sense of the words I heard: "You will get to enjoy this house for one month." I felt a chill pass over me, as I looked up from the basement level to the front porch and stared straight at the front door.

One month? The first thought that came to me was that I was going to die in one month, so I didn't tell Mycol because I didn't want to scare him. So I kept the words to myself, as I wondered who had spoken them. *Is it true*, I wondered, *or am I going crazy? What does it mean?* I was scared, confused, and very upset, and I spent a lot of time over the next days and weeks thinking about the strange message, even as the unexplained heaviness I had felt since soon after our arrival continued to grow. And yet I knew that God is not the Author of confusion, so why did I feel this way?

Then, on December 27, the day after arriving in our new home, Mycol left to drive back to Kingwood to pick up the things we had left behind, including the kids' giant playground set. He would return in a few days; meanwhile, our children and I would begin unpacking and setting up house. I wrote in my journal that *the kids are really enjoying the property.*

Austin and Jessie were busy getting acquainted with the nearly eight acres that probably seemed like a hundred to them. I readily joined them, rolling down the huge slope of ground that made up the four-acre area of hayfield, and giggling with them over the newness of it all. I showed them how to do the log roll all the way down the slope; we played and ran and kicked a ball around, and ended up deciding we needed to buy a kite to take advantage of all the wind that blew so close to the divide between the mountains.

As we surveyed the land our little Jessica declared, "We'll have to get a sheep to cut all this grass!"

I laughed as Austin replied, "Oh, no! We're going to need a cow for all this!"

There seemed to be nothing but fun and happy times ahead for Austin and Jessie, as they would grow up on this little piece of heaven.

"Mommy's Leaving"

Mycol returned on December 30, and were we happy to see him! He had spent the previous night at his parents' home in Humble, Texas, and as he was leaving to return to us in Virginia, our brother-in-law Kurt suggested that he spend another night in Texas before heading out, as it was late and he was concerned about Mycol being on the road by himself.

"That's okay," Mycol replied in his usual confident fashion. "When the Lord calls me home, I'm ready." I had heard that remark from Mycol often, but Kurt was struck by the oddness of such a response from a man who was only thirty-six years old, and tried unsuccessfully to convince him to stay until morning.

After Mycol's return we spent New Year's Eve doing more unpacking and more discovering. The next day I would return to Houston to work until Mycol's trucking business got going. He had applied for a business loan, and we anticipated that it should take six to eight weeks for it to go through. We didn't like the idea of this separation, but we were willing to take it on as a challenge that would strengthen us. I would be back home soon, and then I could be the fulltime home-schooling mom I so longed to be. That thought would keep me going while I was away from my family, and as soon as possible I would turn in my letter of resignation and return to the ones I loved who waited for me in our new home.

Still, even knowing our plan and how sensible it was, I was uneasy about it. That night I wrote in my journal, *I really don't want to leave Virginia right now. I want to stay here in the log house with the rest of the family.*

The first morning of 2003 we drove to Raleigh-Durham, North Carolina, because that airport is usually less expensive to fly in and out of than Roanoke, and not that far a drive. From the time I got up that morning I had felt uneasy about leaving, but I knew we had no choice. We would just have to make the best of our temporary separation, and then enjoy our reunion that much more once I returned home.

We arrived at the airport pressed for time, but we wanted to have lunch together. We bought some pizza and bottled water and sat down on the floor, right next to where I would go up the escalator and then walk through the metal detectors where Mycol and the kids couldn't go.

We rushed through lunch so I could make my flight, then hugged and kissed as we said our goodbyes. Just before I stepped onto the escalator, I confided in Mycol about my reluctance to leave, but I knew I had no choice. I turned to wave a final goodbye, and Mycol told the kids to wave back. "Mommy's leaving," he said.

"Have a hundred-sixty-ninety-forty-hundred-hundred-hundred nicey-nice days!" Austin exclaimed in his usual farewell, as Jess tried to break away and run toward me.

"No, you can't go," Mycol said, stopping her before she got to me. "Stay here and wave bye-bye."

Anyone who is a parent can relate to the feeling that comes over you when you have to leave and your children beg you not to go. But this was different. I knew I'd be separated from my family for a long time–six to eight weeks. When I saw my baby Jessie try to run toward me, I felt a stab of fear as the thought ran through my mind: *What if this is the last time I ever see her? I don't want to leave! I want to stay in Virginia!*

Forcing myself to walk away from my family and toward the gate, I tried to calm myself with the reminder that it's natural not to want to be separated from the ones you love, but I knew we were doing the right thing—the thing we had to do for the time being. But no matter what I told myself, leaving them continued to tear at my heart and burn in my soul.

John 14:1

"Let not your heart be troubled;
you believe in God, believe also in Me."

Chapter 11

Back in Texas

Once I was back in Kingwood, I spent as much time as possible with my daughter Melissa, but I stayed in the home of our former neighbor Cheryl, a single mom, and her teenaged son, Rob. They had been our good friends and neighbors for years, and I felt very comfortable and welcome there. When Mycol had become a fulltime stay-at-home dad, he kept Rob after school while Cheryl was at work. Mycol helped Rob with his homework and modeled to him the Christian father and husband the boy didn't have living with him. The two of them developed a close relationship as they went to various events together, including Houston Astros baseball games and men's church league softball games. Our move was hard on both Cheryl and Rob.

Now, as I awaited my reunion with my family, the unwanted separation dragged on, with Mycol and the kids and I talking by phone every evening and communicating through emails during the day. As we did, I attempted to hush the worry inside me that came from the thought that I would only have "one month." It was strange and scary and I could not explain it so I discharged the thought every time it surfaced. With so much time alone I found myself focusing more and more on prayer–prayer for Mycol as he worked on starting his own trucking business, as well as prayer for our move to be completed and for the issues in our church in Kingwood to be resolved. One evening, as I asked Mycol for his prayer requests, he expressed his concerns and uncertainties about beginning the business. Then he asked, "How 'bout your prayer requests?" I told him I wanted God to do something with my life, something to make it meaningful and bring glory to Him.

Mycol and I had begun researching churches in the Roanoke area before moving there, and one of the first things we were committed to doing was finding a church home for our family. We had drawn up a list of churches to visit, and on the first Sunday I was back in Texas, Mycol and the kids visited the first church on the list: Rainbow Forest Baptist Church. They called that Sunday afternoon to give me the "church report." Austin really liked the church, entertaining me every time he said the name–*Rain-bow For-est Bap-tist Church*–and Mycol remarked on how friendly the people were. He thought we would be very comfortable there, and while he knew we'd be visiting other churches, he and the kids liked this one very much. Mike Grooms, the senior pastor, was out of town the day they visited, so they looked forward to another visit in the future.

Before Mycol and the kids could try out the second church on our list, I received some very sad news, in the form of an email, only one week after returning to Texas. It read: "Linda: Rebekah died in her sleep last night. We found her this morning. Just wanted you to know. Love, Chris"

I was shocked. Rebekah was only four, the same age as Jessie. She was one of sextuplets born just one day before Jess, and the babies had a big brother named Jon Christopher, who was the same age as Austin. Our families had gone to church together, and our kids were in Bible class and children's choir together. Their family had suffered so much already, with Jon Christopher being afflicted with cerebral palsy and one of the sextuplets having been taken from the womb early, only to die soon after. Rebekah too had cerebral palsy, but her parents later learned that she'd also had an undetected and complex brain disease that had ended her short life. As soon as I read the email I called the church to get information about the funeral. *I don't know what I can offer them*, I thought. *I can't imagine the sorrow and grief they must be feeling.* I attended Rebekah's funeral and grieved for her parents and siblings.

Exchanging Church Reports

The next Sunday, January 12, Mycol and the kids gave me a report on the second church on our list, Calvary Memorial Church, led by Pastor Mark Vaughan. Mycol had met a couple there named Greg and Beth Reed, who invited Mycol and Austin and Jessie over for dinner that evening. Mycol was excited about these new friends, as Beth and I had much in common. We were both paralegals, plus Beth worked at home and I would soon be staying home to home-school the kids, so we'd probably have time to get to know one another. Mycol really liked this couple and their three little boys, and our kids had great fun playing at their house. After Mycol reported his findings on the church and said he thought it too would be a good place to go, he repeated how much he liked this family and was certain we would all become good friends.

And then it was January 19, our third Sunday apart. Mycol and the kids called with their weekly church report, and again it was good. They had visited Lakeside Baptist in Salem, Virginia, and Mycol really liked the pastor, Reverend Art Hearne. Austin and Jessie seemed content wherever they went, and seemed to understand they were "church shopping." At this point, however, Austin had a favorite: "I like *Rain-bow For-est Bap-tist Church*," he said ever so carefully, enunciating each syllable slowly and with respect.

As we told each other about our day, I shared with Mycol about Pastor Lino's sermon from 1 Thessalonians. It was about when we all go to heaven and what a glorious time it will be. "And we'll see Rebekah!" Pastor Lino had exclaimed, as he called out the names of several people in our church who had gone on ahead of us. Mycol and I then talked about Rebekah and her family, as well as Nana and others who had left this life and moved on to be with the Lord. We discussed the mystery of it all, and why Christians are sad, even when we believe in eternal life in heaven and that death has been conquered and joy lies ahead for us.

In fact, our Bible study for that week had been titled "The Promise of Heaven," and it had covered several passages of scripture, including one of my favorites:

John 14:1-4 "Let not your heart be troubled; you believe in God, believe also in Me. ²In My Father's house are many mansions; if *it were* not *so*, I would have told you. I go to prepare a place for you. ³And if I go and prepare a place for you, I will come again and receive you to Myself; that where I am, *there* you may be also. ⁴And where I go you know, and the way you know."

Doubts and Divisions

As I continued to work and endure the hardship of being away from my family, I spent as much time as possible with Missy. Since she and her husband, Steven, had just welcomed Kody into their household in October, they were busy learning all about being Mommy and Daddy, and I was excited to be a part of their new family.

Meanwhile Mycol and I were truck shopping on the Internet. When he heard I had been contacted by a recruiter with an opportunity to interview with a prestigious law firm in downtown Houston, to my surprise, Mycol began to express his concern about our decision to move.

I tried to reassure him and then told him Missy and I were going shopping for a new car seat for Kody, but Mycol's mind was on our situation, as was obvious in his next email to me: "You can take that job with the law firm, and we can move back and live happily ever after. You could be in the 'downtown crowd.'"

The thought did not appeal to me at all, and I wrote back that I did not want to live in Houston–especially not in the downtown area. Mycol's turn from confidence to doubt was fueled by his fear that he might not be able to earn enough money. Returning to the work force after so many years at home seemed overwhelming to him. As important as a man's job is to him, this new job, being self-employed, brought about feelings of insecurity, as I think any man can understand. I figured we had trusted God to that point, and I didn't want our doubts and fears to start controlling our actions. But Mycol still had doubts, and the topic continued to creep into our daily conversations.

In the midst of all that was going on in our personal lives, the divisive issues in our Kingwood church, which had begun soon after getting involved with the Bible outreach to the Muslim countries in the 10-40 Window, continued to fester and grow. Mycol and I discussed the problems, both by phone and email, and we continued to pray for our pastor as the situation worsened and the divisions deepened. Through it all we continued to love the people at our church, regardless of where they stood on this issue, for we recognized that it was a demonic attack that was causing the rift. Mycol expressed the depth of his concern when he wrote in an email that Satan "has brought down many good men (and women) and good churches." He then went on to say that we could not allow ourselves to be intimidated by that fact, and I agreed, not wanting the power of doubt and fear, or the author of confusion, to infiltrate and influence us. We didn't understand or support the division in the church, but we committed ourselves to continue praying about the situation and to trust that God would bring glory to Himself in the outcome.

It was now twenty-two days since we had been together, and the waiting was becoming more difficult all the time. We were talking with a trucking company in Ohio about the possibility of Mycol's contracting with them, as well as talking with another man in Ohio who had a semi-truck for sale. To contract with the trucking company, Mycol would have to attend a three-day orientation seminar in Ohio, so we wanted to work out the details so he could get the truck inspected, purchase it, and attend the seminar all in one trip. We still had financial details to work out, but the numbers were telling us that if Mycol's first truck was in service at least eighty percent of the time, we'd be okay; he'd get the calls and make the runs to deliver whatever was to be hauled for the customers.

I tried to encourage Mycol in this new venture. Considering the independent business owner status and the type of work he'd be doing, I didn't think the numbers we figured were too bad. And as we began to add more trucks and drivers to the fleet, he would be able to work less and be home more. When he had two or three days between runs, he could come home and be with the family. I even told him that on his shorter runs, the kids and I could follow him and meet him at his destination for a fun "field trip"–possibly in Washington, D.C., or Jamestown or Williamsburg. I knew it wouldn't happen often, but I told him we could watch for the opportunities.

We were expecting a call with recommendations for diesel mechanics for a "check-out" on the truck we found for sale in Ohio, and I was trying to help from my end, but Mycol had greater concerns on his mind. We had reviewed some online survey responses from people signing on with the trucking company we were considering, and they seemed positive, but the separation was getting to Mycol, and he was beginning to feel scared and desperate–"getting cold feet," he called it, both literally and figuratively, as it was snowing in Virginia again. He was beginning to focus on the negatives: less projected income than we originally anticipated, no health insurance or retirement benefits, and lots of time on the road. He was concerned that he would let us down and wondered if we wouldn't be better off if we had stayed in Kingwood and left things as they were.

I wrote him an email on January 23 that said, "We need to have faith in God that He, and He alone, has brought this move about. Too many unexpected things have happened to pave the way. I understand your doubt; however, I choose to trust that this is His plan for us, and as long as we remain in His will and serve Him, then I am okay with whatever happens." Later we talked on the phone, and Mycol eased up some, but his concern about being able to adequately provide for his family continued to nag at him, no matter how much I reassured him that we'd be fine. And despite my previous doubts when I left Virginia to return to Kingwood, I meant every word I said.

We had been hoping Mycol would be able to take the kids to stay with Barbara and her family in Indiana over the weekend of January 24-26 and then go on to the three-day orientation at the trucking company in Ohio. But since we didn't get the truck inspected and the business loan money was still on hold at the bank, Mycol had to postpone his trip until the following week.

Daily life concerns, church issues, the trucking company, bank loans, and schedules continued to nag at us as we endured our separation, but little did we know that all those minor annoyances would soon pale in comparison to God's big picture and what was about to happen that would change our lives forever.

Nana and Pop-Pop at the log house

Log house

Log house

Our last Christmas in Texas

Austin with football

Daddy and the Buddy

My Prince: He hung the moon

Mycol and babies

Mycol reclining with Austin

Mycol holding baby Austin

Mycol laughing

Mycol with a baby in each arm

Mycol with baseball glove at picnic

Mycol with kids in lap

PART II

...and The After

Chapter 12

The News

On the night of January 26, 2003, the fourth Sunday I had been away from my husband and children, I knelt in prayer beside the guest bed in my friend Cheryl's home in Kingwood, Texas. As I began to pray and intercede for the many needs that were on my heart, I felt compelled to do spiritual battle for the church we had attended for so many years, which was now experiencing such extensive discord within the membership that it seemed to be pulling apart at the seams. Our sinful human nature allows us to make decisions that the enemy of God desires. Of course, I knew the source of that discord did not originate with the members themselves, but from something much more sinister and evil.

"Satan, get out of our church," I declared. I had scarcely spoken the words when I sensed a heavy, oppressive presence that seemed to envelop me, pressing in from all sides.

How will you feel if you lose your family?

The words hissed from somewhere outside me, then slithered down my spine, smothering me with terror.

"Oh, God," I cried, "please protect Mycol! God, please protect Austin! Oh, God, please protect Jessie!"

Eventually the sense of terror passed, as I managed to turn the situation over to God–"Not my will be done, but Yours, Lord"–and climbed into bed, comforting myself with the thought that I would see my loved ones in just a few more days. I soon fell asleep, remembering my husband's last words to me before we hung up the phone earlier that evening: "I know that I really, really love you."

A Message from the Police

When I awoke on Monday, January 27, 2003, I hurriedly dressed and left for work, eagerly anticipating Mycol's phone message, which I knew would be waiting for me when I arrived at my office. But when I got there, the message light wasn't blinking.

Strange, I thought. *Maybe he's sleeping in.*

Moments later I got a call from Cheryl, informing me that the police had been at her house, looking for me. Before she could tell me why, her cell phone died and I was unable to reconnect with her.

I immediately dialed the police station and identified myself, then waited while the dispatcher got the sergeant to come and speak with me. *Hurry up*, I thought. My heart demanded a quick and easy answer, I felt like I was suffocating. Thoughts competed for my attention, but I couldn't focus on any one of them. *What was this about? Why hadn't Mycol called me? Why hadn't I called him back last night after praying for my family's protection?* My heart raced as I waited. By the time he finally got to the phone, I was quickly approaching panic mode.

But the sergeant couldn't–or wouldn't–tell me what was going on. The only information I was able to pull out of him was that it had something to do with a fire. He then gave me the number for the Botetourt County sheriff's office in Virginia, and told me they would be able to fill me in on the details.

Oh, why didn't I call them before going to sleep last night? Please, God, let them be all right! Please, just let them be in the hospital and not able to call. No, that's not right. What if they were badly hurt? A fire? What if they were burned? The image of my precious family being burned was more than I could bear! Would I really ask God to keep them alive if they had to suffer immense pain, just for my own selfish reasons? *Yes! I need them! No, this can't be! God, help me! This must be all a mistake!*

I forced myself to dial the number, as I felt my entire body trembling and my heart crying out in anguish. *Oh, why didn't I call them before going to sleep last night? Please, God, please let them be all right!*

Once again I got a dispatcher who was unable to give me any information. She took my number and said someone would call me right back. I hung up and waited, every second seeming like an eternity. At last the phone rang, and I grabbed for the receiver, only to find myself wanting to scream and run away–anything but listen to what the caller would tell me. And yet, I had to know...

"Mrs. Street?"

The male voice was tentative but strong. *Oh, please, God, let him tell me everything is going to be okay!*

"Yes," was all I could manage.

"This is Sheriff Sprinkle. I am very sorry to have to do this by phone. I would rather be there in person. But..."

Oh, God! Oh, God, no! I don't want to hear it!

As he spoke, the buzzing in my ears grew louder, trying to drown out the awful words that seemed to hang in the air, hovering around me, echoing, stinging, numbing, killing me with their finality...

Oh, God, make the words go away!

My silent plea went unanswered, and I knew the words–this message of death–would never go away. My life as I knew it was over.

"There's been a fire," the sheriff said. "Your home burned down last night, and your husband and children...did not make it out."

He paused. He may have been waiting for me to say something, but I couldn't speak.

"We'll...need dental records," he added.

Oh God, they were burned beyond recognition! There was no hope. I could not bear the thought of my loving husband, so full of life and laughter, our handsome, witty, loving son and our precious, adventurous, beautiful little girl, all being burned to death.

As I felt myself go numb, I somehow managed to murmur, "My babies... Why did God take my babies?"

"I don't know," the sheriff answered. Then he asked if I knew Lisa Arney. Apparently she was there, waiting to speak with me, but I didn't want to talk to anyone else right then. For some reason, the only person I wanted to talk to was Sheriff Sprinkle, the person who had just given me the news.

I later learned that Sheriff Ronnie Sprinkle was really struggling with what to say to me during that conversation, and he and I eventually developed a unique and cherished friendship. But at that moment, when he asked if I wanted to speak to Lisa, I felt as though he was trying to break away as quickly as possible by handing me over to someone else. I later learned that Sheriff Sprinkle hoped he could find comfort for me with someone I knew. Lisa was the only person he had to offer at the moment.

When Lisa took the phone she was crying, and it was obvious to me there was nothing she could do to help.

"Lisa," I moaned, "why did God take my babies?"

"I don't know, Linda," she sobbed. "I just don't know."

The Family Gathers Together

It seemed no one had any answers for me—at least none I wanted to hear. I don't remember how our phone call ended, and while time seemed suspended as Sheriff Sprinkle broke the news to me, in reality it was a brief call. I sat dumbfounded at my desk, unable to accept what I had just heard, or make sense of it. But Mycol still hadn't called. *It must be true. Gone. Dead* – the word felt like a jagged bolt of lightning, slicing through my heart. *My family – dead. No... No! No! Oh God, why did you take my family? Oh God, what do I do now?*

Mycol was always the first person I called if I needed anything, the one I knew I could depend on. Now I sensed...nothingness. *Mycol and the kids aren't here, and I can't go home. What do I do?*

As I sat at my desk I thought, *I need to call someone who will help me. The church. Someone there will help me. Pastor Lino–I need to tell him.*

After leaving a message for my pastor, I dialed my in-laws' phone number. When I connected with Mycol's mom, she said, "Linda, you have to get here. This is where you belong. You have to get here now. Come to the house. We need you." I felt a sense of relief that someone was telling me what to do next, as I could not have figured that out on my own. I agreed and hung up the phone, then walked over to tell Jean, my friend at work, that I'd be leaving.

"Our house burned down, Jean," I sobbed, crossing my arms around my waist as though I were holding my body up so it wouldn't collapse, "and they didn't get out!"

"No! Oh God, no!" Jean jumped up from her seat and threw her arms around me. "No, no, no," she cried, as she held me to herself and tried to absorb the reality of my words.

"I have to leave," I said, shaking uncontrollably.

"I'll take you," she said, offering to call John, one of our co-workers, to come along with us. "John can take you in your car, and I'll give him a ride back."

"No, I'll go myself," I insisted. But Jean wouldn't hear of it, so I finally agreed.

I went back to my office and called Missy, who was already there at Mycol's parents' home. My head pounded as she asked, "Mom, are you coming here?"

I said yes, noticing how strange our voices sounded. In fact, talking felt strange. Moving felt strange. The life had been strangled out of us, and trying to speak was like being in a dream when the words won't come out of your mouth, and everything moves in slow motion and nothing you do accomplishes what you want.

In a matter of minutes John arrived. With him and Jean on either side of me, we managed to get to the elevator, down the hall, to the parking garage, and into my car. Every step reverberated with the ache of shock running through my body, as I continued to cross my arms in front of me and hold my sides.

The ride to my in-laws' house seemed longer than usual. As I gazed out the window at the cars heading in various directions, I realized they were all people going about their busy day. Or were they? *Are they in a hurry, too? Are they going to Mycol's parents' house? They're going the wrong direction! Don't they know? Don't they understand what's happened? Hasn't someone told these people in their cars? Someone has to tell them! They need to know. They need to stop!* But of course they didn't. Cars continued to move down the highway, people continued to come and go and carry on with their everyday activities, as I sat wrapped in my shroud of grief, wondering how I could possibly go on without my family; how I could go on when my world had ended.

When we arrived at Mycol's parents' home, I was surprised to see lots of people already there. Melissa came and met me at the car, as others surrounded me and helped me into the house.

As I entered the living room, I saw Mycol's mother, Lillian, from whom Mycol had inherited his gentle, kind nature, his solid family values and Christian resolve–and that special smile. I could tell the moment I laid eyes on her that she was utterly broken. As she came toward me, I realized the familiar sparkle in her eyes and the cheerful smile I was so used to seeing were gone.

"No, no, it can't be true," she sobbed, as we held each other. "It can't be true; it's not true," she insisted, as if her words could change the way things were.

How I wished she were right. But even as I observed her agony, I couldn't deny the truth, and my heart broke that much more.

Years before, Mycol's mother had given birth to a son named Ricky, who was strangled by his own umbilical cord. Suddenly the grief she had lived with for so many years since losing little Ricky had become more complicated and intense.

Then I saw Corky, my tall, strapping father-in-law, the one who had passed to Mycol his work ethic and masculine strength. Corky is a hard-working man from a heroic generation, who learned the lessons handed down from his own father and always provided for his family–a man of the "old school," as he called it. Unable to reach back in time and stop this terrible thing from happening, unable to save his son and grandchildren, my big, strong father-in-law just stood there staring at me.

Reba, one of Mycol's three older sisters, was keeping busy with all the things families have to do at a time like that. She was organizing, making phone calls, and taking care of business–anything that would keep her from sitting idle, thinking about her beloved brother and her close relationship with him and the kids, anything that would keep her from the pain of knowing there would be no more visits to her house, as Mycol had done weekly for the past few years when I was finishing my degree at night. There would be no more Veggie Tales movie nights, no more deep conversations with Mycol, whom she trusted and loved. There would be no more chatter and laughter from Austin and Jessie, no more hugs, no more "Aunt Weba."

Mycol's younger brother, Wesley, who is deaf, arrived soon after I did. In my shock I was unable to communicate with him in sign language, as I usually did, but we managed to exchange hugs and tears.

I don't recall seeing Lynna arrive, but at some point I realized she was there–the oldest child of the six born to Lillian and Corky. Lynna was the quiet one, the studious one who looked most like Mycol, with her dark hair and dark eyes and facial features so similar to Mycol's that it seemed they had been made from the same mold.

Before the day was over, Mycol's other sister, Valeira, and her family arrived from suburban Austin. Most of our nieces and nephews had gathered by then, all of us in shock, some sobbing openly, others silently in their hearts.

From my in-laws' home I contacted my oldest daughter, Angela, who two months earlier had faced the possibility of losing her only child, Myles. Fresh from her own struggles with life's hard blows and having just received the devastating news herself, my dear daughter remembered the many hours we spent at the hospital talking about faith. She asked, her voice wavering through her sobs, "Mom, do you still have faith?"

In an automatic response to the daughter whose faith I wanted to protect, I answered yes, but I'm honestly not sure if I believed what I said. However, her question is one of the few clear memories I have of the time immediately following the fire. In fact, I have only partial memory of anything that happened over the next few weeks. For some of that time I was in a near-catatonic state, unable to hear or think or follow a sentence. My mind seemed to have been wiped clean except for the clear and urgent thought that I needed to get to Mycol, Austin, and Jess.

Prior to that horrible, life-changing day, I had been waiting uneasily to be reunited with Mycol and the children. Now I asked myself over and over again how that was going to happen. How would I get to them? The sense of urgency was so strong and my mental state so fragile, with only brief intervals of coherency, that it would be a very long time before I moved past my ongoing state of shock and confusion. The only thing that changed in the immediate days and weeks after the fire and the two memorial services was that I added anger to that shock and confusion.

I later learned the clinical term for what I was experiencing: post-traumatic stress. My senses were magnified. Everything around me seemed too loud, too busy, too confusing, so much so that I actually experienced physical pain as a result. I couldn't handle bright lights, fast movement, loud noises, or a lot of activity. These things caused me to feel confused, nervous, and anxious. It was as if I had ultra-sensitive antennae protruding from every millimeter of my body, the tips raw and sore from overexposure. I often wondered if that was the way I would spend the rest of my life, though I couldn't imagine an alternative.

But on that awful day, as I gathered with the rest of Mycol's family at his parents' home, I didn't know any of that. I was conscious of only one thing: I had to find a way to get to my family.

By the next day, while still in that state, my daughter Angie arrived, as did Aunt Marge, a cousin, Don Glover, and my sisters, Diane and Barbara, and Barbara's husband, Mike. Among the many other visitors to the house was Kelly Hartman, who just two months earlier had held my children as he showed them around the fire truck. He entered the house in tears, not wanting to believe this had happened. As we embraced, I cried and said, "Kelly, my kids loved you. They played 'Mr. Kelly' with their little fire trucks." Kelly loved my family too, and like so many others, he was heartbroken.

The next thing I knew people started asking me questions about a memorial service. Battling the attack on my mind and body, I had to work extra hard at trying to communicate to others the things Mycol and I had talked about, the things that would be important and appropriate decisions for a memorial for him and the children.

Evidence of God's Presence

If the house had burned to the ground, then I had nothing left except what little I had brought with me to Kingwood, which was a week's worth of clothes for work, one outfit to sleep in, and one to wear when I exercised. I would soon begin to experience the depth of what it meant to lose my home and all the tangible evidence of the life I had shared with Mycol and our children. With the exception of Mycol's baseball glove, which he had previously given to Missy and she later brought to me for comfort, I had nothing–no photographs, no videos, no toys, no clothing, no drawings–only my memories.

Because of that, Angie and my good friend Mary Morris decided to go shopping for me. Only a year earlier Mycol and I had discussed death, not realizing, of course, that it would happen so soon. He had told me he didn't want anyone to dress up at his funeral. He wanted everyone to be comfortable, to come in jeans or shorts or whatever they preferred to wear. He had also been adamant that he wanted no tears. It would be a celebration, he insisted, because he would be with Jesus. And so I asked Angie and Mary to please find a Veggie Tales t-shirt for me to wear with my jeans. The kids loved Veggie Tales, and we had every Veggie Tales video in existence at that time. I also wanted a necklace with those little charms made as children with the birthstones on them.

Angie and Mary had their assignments, and they started their search. One of the first places they went was to a Christian bookstore, and there on the counter was a display rack where that type of birthstone jewelry would normally be sold. However, it appeared empty, so Angie and

Mary asked the salesclerk if there might be a February boy and a November girl charm stored away somewhere. The clerk first checked all sides of the display mount, and much to everyone's amazement announced, "These are actually angel pins, not charms, and I only have two left. Let's see, I have a…February birthstone boy and a…November birthstone girl!"

Angie and Mary came back from their shopping trip, excited about what they believed was an evidence of God's presence and care in the midst of this disaster. It was only the first of many "faith boosters" that God would use to help carry us through those immediate days and weeks of life without Mycol, Austin, and Jessica.

Hebrews 11:1

Now faith is the substance of things hoped for,
the evidence of things not seen.

Chapter 13

First Memorial Service

The memorial service was held at our church in Kingwood, Texas, on Saturday, February 1, 2003, the very weekend Mycol and I had planned for all of us to be together. The church was packed–not an empty seat anywhere.

I requested the music from Promise Keepers be played as people were arriving because Mycol had joined that wonderful organization after experiencing one of their events, and he truly loved being a part of it. I also requested the children's song "Zacchaeus Was a Wee Little Man" because it was one of Austin and Jessie's favorites. Every time we sang that song, the two of them would act out the story that went with it. Jess especially related to the part about Zacchaeus being up in the tree because she so loved to climb up and jump off anything and everything.

Mycol's parents asked Lee Garner, a family friend and acclaimed Opry singer, to sing "The Midnight Cry," a song of hope and of the promise of eternal life. This was very important and meaningful to them, especially Mycol's dad.

Loving Words from Angie

Angela and Melissa both had the courage to speak at the service, though I can't imagine how they were able to do so. They said that no matter how hard it would be, they just couldn't imagine not doing it. And so, when the music ended, my two grown daughters walked to the front of the worship center. Angie, my precious firstborn, who was twenty-two years old at the time and a new mother facing her own struggles with an ill infant at home almost a thousand miles away, stood before thousands of people and, from her heart, brought those people a little closer to our family's world as she saw it:

> One thing–though there are many–I remember about Mycol is the wrinkles in the corners of his eyes. You know, the wrinkles people have from smiling so much. Mycol always had a smile on his face. He was such a sweet, happy guy. He always had fun. He was like a big kid. I just watched an old video the other day of him at Christmas time in his cowboy attire, singing and dancing along with a George Strait Christmas song to the camera. He was so into it.
>
> I remember last summer we were riding jet skis at my grandmother's, and I pulled up to the shore to see if Mycol wanted a turn. You could tell he was itching to try it out. His eyes lit up so big, and he was like, "Yeah!" Like a kid in a candy store. He never lost his youth or his ability to always have fun. I guess he had even told my mom he didn't want anyone to cry at his funeral. He would say that. But I think I'll have to disobey him again…like I did a hundred times as a teenager.

Her voice was wavering by then, and it was obvious she was struggling as she continued, looking straight at me as she spoke her next sentences.

> I just want to thank him for sticking with my mom and us after my horrible behavior as a kid. I couldn't have picked a more wonderful man for my mom to marry. He was a wonderful husband, son, brother, uncle, and father. He loved his family, and he loved God. And boy, did he love those kids!

As Angie continued, I found myself thinking of how she had been living in Indiana the past few years and had missed the day-to-day life with "the babies," as we called them, but we did our best to include her through phone calls, photos, and videos.

Austin Chad Street was such a funny, sweet, and sensitive little boy–and adorable too! My mom and Mycol did such a wonderful job teaching the Word of the Lord to the kids. At Christmas they wanted to make sure Austin and Jessie knew what Christmas meant, that it wasn't about Santa or reindeer, but Jesus' birthday. So I remember–I think it was last year–Austin and Jessie wanted to make a birthday cake for Jesus and have a birthday party. So while they're sitting there, Austin wanted to know when Jesus was going to show up for His party they had planned for Him. And boy, was he upset when he found out that wasn't going to happen! So, Austin, now you can have all the birthday parties you want, and Jesus will be there. I love you, Buddy.

Jessica Logan Street, with the biggest and most beautiful blue eyes I've ever seen–they went along great with her beautiful personality. She was so funny and ornery. I remember at Missy's graduation, Jessie running, being friendly to everyone, even people she didn't know. She had one pretty big piece of cake, then another, then another. Every time someone would ask her, "Honey, have you had a piece of cake yet?" she would say, "No," as she was licking icing from her lips. She was so funny like that. I was also watching a birthday video they had made for my twenty-first birthday, and they had made a chocolate cake for me. When the camera turned to Jessie, there she was, so focused on eating her cake, with chocolate all over her face. So, Jessie, in heaven you can have your cake and eat it too–all of it! I love you, Jessica.

It was obvious that even in her pain, Angie wanted to leave everyone with a message of hope, and she did so quite beautifully.

Before all of this, I thought my faith was pretty strong, but after this, not only did I question God's motives but I also questioned His existence. I prayed Monday. I said, "God, if You exist, You have to show me somehow. Please, show me a sign that You're real, and I need for it to be a sign that I know for sure it's You, not something I'm making up in my head or thinking, "God, is it You?" So Tuesday morning my fiancé woke me up at about six a.m. and said, "Angie, you have to see this." It was an article a man named Zeke wrote about our family, the move, and the whole incident. And at the end it said, and I quote, "On Monday the minivan was a mass of charred, twisted steel. On the front seat lay the only possession that remained identifiable in the burnt heap: a Bible, singed around the edges." So, if that wasn't my sign, then I don't know what is.

Indeed, it was Mycol's Bible that was found in the rubble, exactly as described in the newspaper article. Finally, Angela concluded with the message we all needed to hear.

Well, then I was angry. Why would God save the Bible and not our family? And Justin said, "Angie, that's what He's trying to tell you. God did save your family."

I hope all of you in here were blessed enough to have met these three angels. They will be missed, but I want to thank God for bringing them into our lives. So in the words of Austin and Jessica, "Have a hundred-sixty-forty-hundred-hundred-sixty-ninety nice days!"

A hundred-sixty-forty-hundred-hundred-sixty-ninety nice days. How many times I'd heard some variation of that before! It was something Austin started and Jessie soon joined in on–their way to wish someone a nice day. Our little prince and our little Jester always wished a farewell with many, many nice days ahead.

Missy's Turn to Remember

With that, Angie stepped back a bit as Missy, who was just nineteen, took her turn remembering.

I'm Missy, Linda's daughter. This has been the hardest week of my life, but as my mom and I have been reflecting on these three precious lives, we realize how lucky we were to be close to them. My mom loves her family very much. The last conversation she had with them was filled with both excitement and sadness. Mycol told her how much he missed her and how much he was looking forward to seeing and hugging her this weekend. Austin promised her knock-down hugs and to do what he calls "fingers," where he would make his fingernails go under hers. Jessica promised to give her what she called "elbows," when she would pinch the skin around the elbows. Both "fingers" and "elbows" were unique expressions from Austin and Jessie.

My mom's favorite story of Austin was when he was four. He was lying with his feet up against the window of the van, and he closed his eyes and prayed, "Jesus, come into my heart." He was so peaceful, and he repeated himself over and over again. He shared with Jessie that you have to ask Jesus into your heart. Even at their young age, they understood and had faith.

Jessie and her pure and innocent heart didn't always understand how life worked. She knew people could move to different locations and thought of heaven as a location. One day she asked, "When we move to heaven, will I get to see Jesus?" These are precious memories my mom will never forget.

I have so many memories of Mycol. He was a wonderful father. He was always at soccer games and Tae Kwon Do tournaments. He never treated my sister or me any differently than he did his own children. One time he took me to the father-daughter banquet that the church holds. As part of the banquet every father-daughter couple writes a small note to each other. I have never shared this note with anyone before this week.

Then Missy looked down at the piece of paper she held in her hands and began to read:

"Missy: Thanks again for being there and not complaining about the babies. Thanks also for making me a stronger Christian. Watching how you love the Lord is an inspiration to me. Always keep the faith, and you will always have peace. I love you and want to wish you the best as you approach adulthood.
Love, Mycol—Bonus Dad"

Now choked up, Missy struggled to continue.

Bonus Dad. He wasn't my step-dad; he was my Bonus Dad, and my sister and I were his Bonus Daughters. He put up with us when most people wouldn't have. He will never be replaced.

Indeed Mycol had never referred to my daughters as step-daughters. He thought that sounded void of the love he had for them. No, he insisted they were, in fact, a bonus gift from God. I was grateful not only that I married a man so gentle and loving, but one who could also express himself so that my girls knew they were loved, knew they were bonuses.

And then Missy went on to talk more about Austin and Jessica, the beautiful children born to Mycol and me.

My baby brother, Austin—he was our buddy. He was my mom's little prince. He made such an entrance into this world! February 26, 1997, I sat in the living room as my mom looked at a baseball card I had given her to use as a focal point during labor. It was J.T. Snow of the California Angels. I picked that card because it was his birthday too.

Soon Mycol's mom came and picked us up, and before we got to the hospital Austin was born in the front seat of the car. I believe it was right as we went under I-45 on FM 1960. I saw Mycol in traffic and was trying to remember the sign language he had taught me to let him know, but I was so excited and scared that all I could do was shake my hands. He thought I was just excited until we got to the hospital and he walked up to the car and saw my mom had already had him.

Austin was so perfect—not a typical boy. He didn't like the beach because the sand was dirty. He noticed details—the speed limit signs and if you had your blinker on when you were turning. One of my favorite memories is how he and Jessie used to pray before dinner. "God, please bless this food so we can grow big and strong and jump real high."

Jessie was our "Baby Girl." She was my "Jester." She loved to climb on things. Jessie never met a stranger—she loved everyone. One of my favorite stories is one Mycol told me. The kids were throwing pillows down to the bottom of the stairs, and Jessie was coming down when she fell. She landed on the pillows, and Mycol couldn't see her from where he was. He said he waited to see if she would cry, and all of a sudden an arm popped out from the pillows and she said, "I'm okay!"

She was so funny. At dinnertime, if we were eating chicken and beans, she would have a few bites and say, "I'm full." But when we all went to IHOP, she ate the whole happy face pancake, which consisted of a chocolate pancake, chocolate chips, whipped cream, and cherries.

At the age of four, Jessie was still working on diction, but she was proud to be in "The Yord's Army."

I was never able to leave the house without hugs and kisses. They loved all their family, from Indy to Texas, and their family will never forget them.

With that, my daughters returned to their seats, leaving all present in awe of their strength and courage. I am so grateful to them for going beyond themselves that day, and countless times and in immeasurable ways since then.

Loving Testimonies

My brother-in-law, Kurt Bullinger, spent three days immersed in creating a gift of love, a video put to music, which we played at the service. From other family members Kurt collected photos and video of our family and synchronized them so beautifully with two Mercy Me songs, "I Can Only Imagine" and "Spoken For." The video began with a quote from Mycol, something he said to Kurt the last time they saw each other. It was something he had begun saying often in the six months leading up to the fire: "When the Lord calls me Home, I'm ready." After Mycol's quote, the video goes on to show the words, "Mycol, Austin, and Jessie…are Home." Somehow Kurt had come across a video taken during Christmas time that captured Austin opening a gift of Matchbox cars and saying, "This is so cool!" Kurt was so moved upon seeing it and felt it would be an appropriate comment to include at that point in the video, as if we could all imagine the three of them saying those very words–"This is so cool!"– about being Home. The video also included dozens of photos and video shots of my beautiful family, and at the end was part of the video we had sent to Angie, the part she had mentioned earlier that showed us all eating chocolate birthday cake to celebrate her twenty-first birthday. At the end, the kids are saying, "Good-bye!" There was so much love and devotion put into making that video, and I have no doubt that it had to be very difficult for Kurt to do. It's a really difficult video to watch, and there wasn't a dry eye in the sanctuary by the time it ended.

Other people wanted to share their memories too. I had asked some of the children's Bible school teachers to speak, so they, as well as Wes, Mycol's younger brother, imparted stories of my family. They also testified as to how they had been strengthened in their faith through the lives and witness of Mycol and our children–Mycol's willingness to be an example of a husband and father who walked in obedience to God, and Austin and Jessie because of their purity and trust in the Lord.

As I sat there, listening, I realized there was no greater gift anyone could give me than to hear how my family had helped people grow in their faith. I got to hear a lot of that sort of testimony during that memorial service, and I continue to hear it often today.

Pastor Lino Gives "the Message"

Our pastor, David Lino, was also hurting that day. He confessed before God and the thousands of other hurting people present in that sanctuary that he just did not understand.

"Why, God?" he asked—and then began to deliver his message, built on that very question and confirmed by a discussion the two of us had prior to the memorial service.

"They must hear the message," I had insisted.

He knew that already, and readily agreed, but I had to say it. I had to say, "Mycol wants you to preach the message." And Pastor Lino did just that.

Why? That's the question that's probably on all of our hearts. Why? You heard about Zacchaeus earlier because that was Jessie's favorite story. Why would God go to all that trouble to seek us out like He sought out Zacchaeus? Austin's favorite verse was John 3:16: "For God so loved the world that He gave His only begotten Son, that whoever believes in Him should not perish but have everlasting life." Jesus Christ didn't come to condemn the world; He didn't come to condemn you. He came to save you and make you part of His family. If He loves us that much, if He seeks us that much, like He sought Zachaeus, why,

why would He give you, Linda, a husband and two little children? Why? And then you're told to trust God.

Everything within you says, "I don't want to trust a God like that. Why would I want to trust a God like that with my family?" How many times did you and Mycol pray, as you were going to Virginia? How can you trust a God like that?

He paused and looked around the vast room, directing the question to all who were gathered there.

Who wants a God like that? Do you?

Well, it depends. You see, most of us trust a concept called trust, and whatever you understand as trust is what you're really trusting in. What we're really trusting in is not Jesus Christ. What we're really trusting in is our understanding of how life should work and what is best. So we trust, not understanding; we trust what we think is best. We trust our common sense. So when God doesn't fit our definition, we don't want to trust God.

You see, we predispose who God is, and we have a predisposition as to how God should act and behave. When we pray we come with certain presuppositions of how God should answer my prayer and take care of me. When we say to God, "Keep my family safe," what we really are saying is, "Do it my way." It's very difficult for us to understand that when you and I talk to Almighty God that He is in fact Almighty, that He actually sees the big picture, and you and I tend to live in a little cocoon and think that what we can perceive in our little cocoon is the total understanding of what life is really about.

Mycol's favorite verse was Romans 8:28: "And we know that all things work together for good to those who love God, to those who are the called according to *His* purpose."

And even though you and I don't understand, we have created an idol we call God, and that's what we want to trust in our understanding of who God is.

Mycol got beyond that. He came to the realization that even though he may not understand Almighty God, he may not be able to work through what it is that Jesus Christ is actually doing, that his trust wasn't in a concept of a false god. His trust wasn't in a concept; his trust wasn't in his ability to understand why. His trust, his faith, wasn't in the ability to give you an answer as to the question why. His trust was actually in a Person. That's why Romans 8:28 was his favorite verse: that in each and every situation, God is at work for the good of them that love Him.

You've heard testimony here today on how Mycol would talk about death. What a strange thing for a young man like that, to talk about death. But why? Because he knew that no matter what, whether it was his death or Linda's death or the children's death, God was actually at work for the good of those who love Him. Do you understand that?

He paused once again, looking out at us as he let the words sink in before answering his own question.

Nor do I. We don't understand. Our brains cannot assimilate it. Our emotions are devastated, and we cannot put it together. Don't just give us words to try and comfort Linda; give us a Person called Jesus Christ, who has all the authority, who knows the end from the beginning, who has Mycol and Austin and Jessie in His presence forever and ever. We do not have the big picture; God does. Pray that God will help us trust Him when we're feeling so scared.

He stopped again and pointed to me before continuing.

Give this lady, this wife, this mom, the comfort of a Person who has all the authority to be able to carry through His promises. Because if you're like me, I cannot even begin to relate to what Linda is going through. Not just the loss of her best friend, her husband, her buddy, not even the loss of her two children, not even the loss of her home and every single thing that is familiar. She can't even go into his closet and smell his clothes. And for those of you who have been bereaved, you know how important that is, just to take that person's pillow and smother your face up against it and just smell them. She doesn't have any of that. No photographs, no pictures. Not only has she lost all of that, but she's lost her identity too. Not only has she lost her identity, but she's also homeless. Is God doing it? Can you trust a God like that, who would allow a person to go through so much pain?

I don't know why God would allow something like that in this lady's life, and I don't know why God allows a lot of things in our lives, but you and I know that if you and I would not allow our hearts to become hard against Jesus Christ, He can bring good out of any situation whatsoever.

And because He is Almighty, He doesn't need a little bit of good to start with so He can bring good out of it. He doesn't need any good whatsoever. He can take an absolutely and totally hopeless situation and bring hope into it.

He then implored all present to remember beyond that day, to take the time and effort to encourage me for the days to come, even the birthdays, holidays, and anniversaries I could not celebrate. And then he posed this question to them.

One day, when we're having your funeral, I hope your family knows where you are. You see, you don't become part of the family of God by osmosis. What that means is that if you sit in church long enough, you have church membership, you have churchy things done to you, that you somehow think that makes you a Christian. Not according to what God says.

Mycol humbled himself before Jesus Christ and confessed that he had no rights, no claims, nothing to barter with when he came to God. He acknowledged that he was a sinner. He humbled himself before God and said, "Lord, forgive me. Thank You for dying on the cross for me. Please take what You did on the cross and apply it to my life."

So when we say Mycol is in heaven, we're not just giving false comfort, just talking a lot of hot air. We're talking the promises of God. You too, sir; you too, ma'am. If you would humble yourself before Jesus Christ, if you would confess you are a rebel, you're stubborn, you're stiff-necked, you're arrogant, you're prideful—ask Him to forgive you. Ask Him to take what He did on that cross and apply it to your life. Would you ask Him to make you part of His family so that He can start preparing a room for you in heaven? That's His promise: You become part of His family, you get your own room, and He's going to prepare it for you. When it's ready, you're on your way. You coming? You coming home when Jesus comes to get you? I'd like to give you that opportunity today.

Yes! He did it. He said what most needed to be said. Because of Mycol, because of Austin, because of Jess, Pastor Lino was presented with an opportunity to invite every person there to accept God's offer of salvation. This was all that was important to me, for this was all that was left.

I'd like you to ask the Lord Jesus Christ to take what He did on the cross and apply it to your life. Is God preparing a room for you at home? Because this is not home. Will you ask Him to do that for you? To come and live His life in your life?

Help me pray for Linda, Mr. and Mrs. Street, the family.

The Father of all comfort, would You put Your arms around Linda, Mr. and Mrs. Street, and do for them what none of us as human beings can do? Supernatural grace. Peace that passes all understanding. Strength when they feel so weak. They trust in You when they are so numb and in so much pain.

Linda, may the Lord bless you and keep you. Linda, may the Lord make His face to shine upon you and be gracious to you. Linda, may the Lord turn His face toward you and give you peace. Through our Lord Jesus Christ, amen.

In the Palm of His Hand

There were so very many people present that day that once the service had ended, it took a very long time for everyone to make their way toward me to offer their love and encouragement. And yet they stood patiently, even when the line extended out the door, and I appreciated it so much. I thanked each one of them, though I was in such a fog at the time that I remember very little of what was said. The primary message was a simple one: "I'm so sorry, Linda." For most, it was all they could say–and it was all I could process. I also knew there were those who found it too difficult to come up and speak to me that day, but their presence at the service told me they were willing to go through at least part of the pain with me, and that meant a lot.

When Rudy Hargis, my boss, came through the line, it struck me that I hadn't yet turned in my resignation, and I felt badly that it was in such a setting that he had to learn of my intent to leave the company. I opened my mouth and started to apologize, but Rudy stopped me. "Shh," he said, wrapping his arms around me. "Don't talk."

People from all areas and periods of our life came to that memorial service, including the Collins family, whose daughter, Rebekah, had just "moved to heaven," and the Mallettes, whose daughter Savannah, one of seven children, was the one special girl our young son had his eyes on. It pained me greatly to see the children–my children's friends–as I didn't want the little ones to hurt, and I felt so sorry for them.

And then it was over. As we headed back to Mycol's parents' home, I felt completely empty. I had no idea what I was going to do next. The pastor was right–I didn't just lose everything, as far as family, home, and personal possessions. I had also lost my identity. I still felt like a wife, but I couldn't act like one. I was still a mommy, but I couldn't do mommy things, as my only remaining children were grown. I simply wasn't able to think beyond the moment.

After that I often sat on my mother-in-law's couch for days at a time, staring silently, or curled up in a fetal position on the bed in Mycol's old room. The only thing I could really feel was this powerful, commanding, potent anxiety of need to get to my family. It was much like any parent or spouse might feel when a loved one is away and needs help. I felt driven to go to them–and yet, of course, I knew there was no possible way for me to do that. Still, knowing it was impossible didn't make the feeling go away. I knew it wasn't cognitive thinking, but rather anxiety and bewilderment, but the thought that echoed through my mind every waking moment and even in my sleep was, *I need to get to them!*

Even after attending the memorial service, I still couldn't comprehend that I wouldn't be with them in the next few days. We belonged together; Mycol and the children were part of me, and I was part of them. They were the very essence of my identity! And yet I could sense the Holy Spirit directing me: *Just live in this one moment. Just be, right now. Just be...* I imagine God was truly holding me in the palm of His hand, day after day, week after week, month after month, for there is no other explanation for how I made it through.

Psalm 147:3

He heals the broken-hearted
And binds up their wounds.

Chapter 14

Second Memorial Service

I soon learned that the people of Botetourt County, Virginia, were also planning a memorial service. I was so moved by the fact that they would want to do such a thing for a family who had only lived among them for one month and whom most had never even met. But their hometown had been strongly affected by this tragedy, and they too were grieving, so they felt they had to do something.

Humbled by their generosity and wanting to attend the service, I made my desire known to family and friends surrounding me. Suddenly, in a flurry of activity, phone calls and plans were made, and the next thing I knew I had a reservation on the first flight to Roanoke in the morning. People from our church and elsewhere were donating funds and frequent flyer miles so that anyone in the family who wanted to go to the service in Virginia could get there at no cost. One very generous man, who had been saving his flyer miles for years for his dream trip to see the Tour de France, gave up all his miles and donated them for our trip to Virginia. His wife told me his trip to France meant nothing to him when compared to his compassion for our family.

Jim and Christin Pivero had been friends of ours for about six years and had lived for about four and a half months in Lynchburg, Virginia, before moving to Texas. During that brief time in Lynchburg, they had made connections that would have lifelong effects, including blessing us as we worked out the details for our trip. Upon hearing of our plans to go to Virginia, Jim, whose career is in radio, spoke with his friends and former employers, Barry and Linda Armstrong, of Spirit FM, a Christian radio station that broadcasts to the Lynchburg and Roanoke areas. Barry and Linda had heard all about the fire, and though we'd never met, they had prayed for us and wanted to do anything they could to help. Jim explained to them that several family members wanted to come to Virginia for the memorial service and that we'd need transportation, food, and a place to stay. Barry said he'd get to work on it, and in a matter of minutes, Jim received a return call from Barry, telling him everything would be covered. In that brief space of time, Barry had contacted Don Eckenroth and his wife, Kim, owners and operators of Gentle Shepherd Hospice, which serves all of Southwestern Virginia, and told them of our situation. They quickly agreed to help. Now, in addition to all the others who were actively working to help us get to Virginia, the Eckenroths got involved. As it turned out, this unselfish couple opened their home to us–twelve strangers from Texas–arranged for food and transportation, and most importantly, offered loving compassion and prayer. We later learned that this was "standard operating procedure" for Don and Kim, who make it a habit to give themselves to others for the glory of God.

Eleven family members from Texas, including me, made that trip to Virginia, along with a pastor named Dr. Jim Clemmons, who I later learned had been a firefighter before becoming a pastor. Brother Jim, as he preferred to be called, was the pastor of North Main Baptist Church in Liberty, Texas, where Mycol's sister Lynna and her husband, Rusty, were members. In his typical and most gracious and humble way, Brother Jim decided he would accompany us at his own expense because, as he put it, "This family should not for one minute be left in need of a pastor at this time." Brother Jim was not a man who seeks recognition; he was a man who serves. And he did a lot of that for our family.

Looking back, I see so clearly how the Lord was at work in all of it. He has promised never to leave or forsake us, and He was true to His promise. In addition He brought us together with a pastor who had previously been a firefighter, as well as a couple who had dedicated themselves to working compassionately with grieving families through their hospice company. God cared enough to walk through every finely detailed moment with us.

A Precious Messenger

One week after the fire, on Monday, February 3, we arrived in Virginia for the second memorial service, where we were met at the airport by Don Eckenroth and his friend, Steve Musselwhite, a member of the Methodist church in nearby Vinton, Virginia. The Methodist church donated the use of their fifteen-passenger van to cart us all around the entire time we were there, and Don and Kim opened their beautiful home to twelve complete strangers, resolute in their belief that we should stay together, that the family not be separated.

They took us first to their home, where we were met by some of their hospice staff who were prepared to assist with grief counseling and prayer. That was when I first met Mary Lynn Barrett. As I was guided into the house and offered a seat on a couch next to Mary Lynn, she introduced herself, and that was the beginning of a lifelong friendship with one of the most compassionate people I have ever met. A hospice nurse accustomed to grief, Mary Lynn put her arm around me and prayed.

It was also then that I first met Sheriff Ronnie Sprinkle in person. He and one of his deputies arrived at the Eckenroth's home shortly after I did. Sheriff Sprinkle needed to ask me a lot of questions, and he knew it was going to be a painful ordeal for both of us. Barbara and Rusty accompanied me in the library and comforted me as I began the ordeal of providing information to assist the investigation.

As sheriff, he needed to find out if we had any enemies-if the scene of the fire could also be a crime scene.

"No," I answered, wishing he knew my family so he'd know how ridiculous the thought was.

He then asked about smoke detectors and candles, and our habits at home. He asked about our last conversation and wanted to know as much about Mycol as I could tell him. I did my best to provide the information, understanding that Ronnie was doing his job, but some questions I couldn't answer because I hadn't been there. Did Mycol light a fire in the fireplace? I didn't know. We had talked about it, but I didn't know whether he had done it. What kind of heaters did we have? Had Mycol purchased a space heater? Since I had been in Texas the past twenty-six days, I couldn't answer whether he had or not. There were so many questions asked, but I also had questions of my own.

"I need to know something," I said–urgently and painfully. I swallowed and took a deep breath, wondering if I would be able to get the words past the lump in my throat. "Did they know?"

"You mean did they know there was a fire?"

"Yes," I replied, my voice and body shaking. Rusty and Barbara each put an arm around me, wanting to protect me from the answer. "I need to know."

There is something soothing about Ronnie Sprinkle. He's a big man, over six feet tall, and in good physical condition. Prematurely grey, his deep brown expressive eyes exude compassion, while his very posture confirms he will fight for justice. He speaks with authority and confidence, but in a calm, reassuring tone.

"No, honey," he said. "They didn't know anything. I am confident of that."

Ever since his first phone call to me I had worried over whether they were awake and knew what was happening. The idea was so sickening that I wanted to push it away. I was haunted with visions of my family trying desperately to escape out a window, Mycol trying to throw the children out, as they screamed in fear. I was inundated with visions of them huddling together, Mycol consoling the children as he knew they would die from the fire. These thoughts prowled around me like venomous snakes, waiting to devour me at every waking moment. I cringed at the way my imagination attacked me, and while I wanted answers, I didn't want to hear that my family was scared or felt any pain.

"They were found near their beds," Sheriff Sprinkle explained. "I feel confident they were asleep." His answer was as comforting as it could be under the circumstances. "If you have any other questions, you call me at any time, okay? I mean that. Any time."

Before he stood up to leave, this man with a passion for justice and a heart for people said, "Keep praying, honey. Keep your faith. And I will be praying for you."

God's hand in the midst of my pain continued to be evident in so many ways. People from several area churches donated so much food the Eckenroths' home began to resemble a combination grocery store and cafeteria. We were being taken care of, both physically and spiritually, and there was yet another big message of faith waiting just around the corner.

People from the small farming communities of Troutville, Daleville, and Fincastle arranged a dinner at Aunt Teen's house—the very place we had gathered for a similar meal following Nana's funeral just four months earlier. And now I found myself walking into the same place where I had announced to the extended family that we were buying the log house.

Aunt Teen's farm is just three-quarters of a mile from the property where the log house had stood for so many years. When I walked into my aunt's house, I spotted Lisa Arney, the lady who, along with her husband, A.J., had bought the log house from Nana and then eventually sold it to us. I made a beeline to her, and we embraced and cried. She felt horrible about the entire situation.

"We tried, Linda," she sobbed. "A.J. tried. He tried to get in. I'm so sorry."

A.J. Arney had risked his life by running across Catawba Road to the burning log house, hoping to rescue Mycol and the kids. He managed to find a window at the back of the house where the freezing wind was blowing the flames away from him, and he was in the process of trying to climb through that window when Tim Geiger, a neighbor who had been on his way to work, stopped A.J. from what would surely have been an act of suicide. He pulled A.J. away from the burning building and told him that even if he got inside, he would never get out again. A.J. stood outside, watching the flames and crying and screaming for Mycol and the kids, but of course it was already too late. I will forever be grateful to A.J. for his willingness to put his life on the line for my family.

After a few moments, through her tears, Lisa told me she had walked the property after the fire, looking for anything that might be salvageable. "I looked everywhere, Linda. I wanted you to have something—something to hold on to. Out in the yard, this is all I could find."

She reached into her purse and pulled out a tiny Matchbox toy–a U-Haul trailer–and held it out to me.

I could scarcely breathe. Blinking through a blur of tears, my eyes, already swollen from days of crying, focused on this precious gift of hope. As I took it from her hand in what felt like a moment frozen in time, oblivious to all else around me, I recalled the memories of coming home from work while we still lived in Texas, of stepping over long lines of Matchbox and Hot Wheels cars. And then, as I continued to stare at this miniature U-Haul, I heard my little Jessie speak to my heart: "Mommy, we moved to heaven."

Lisa, of course, had no idea how significant that little Matchbox toy was. She was not aware that Jessie had talked about moving to heaven, nor did she realize what this little memento meant to me. After all, it was just a trailer. There was no truck with it, no cab–just the trailer part with the hitch sticking out. And when you think about it, a child doesn't play with a trailer by itself because a trailer has no motor. What's more, when you consider the fact that this one toy was all that was there, out of the hundreds and hundreds of little cars we once had, the significance increases because I knew our children's routine. I knew they had taken a bucket of cars outside to play with, as was our custom, and when it came time to clean up, they "accidentally" left one out. But I knew it was no accident. God planned for Lisa to find that one little Matchbox toy and give it to me to reassure me of the truth of Jessie's words, spoken softly but distinctly to my heart: "Mommy, we moved to heaven." It was one of the most personally significant "faith boosters" I have ever received. The message came through, loud and clear–and from a very precious messenger.

Compassionate Virginians

I requested that the service be held at *Rain-bow For-est Bap-tist Church*. As much as my family loved that place, and I loved hearing my son say the words, I knew no other place would be right. This would be the closest I would ever come to being at *Rain-bow For-est Bap-tist Church* with them. So after the meal at Aunt Teen's we drove to *Rain-bow For-est Bap-tist Church*. As we rode through that beautiful countryside that evening, I couldn't even bring myself to look out the window. What had once held such a rich and special place in my heart now filled me with pain, darkness, and confusion. It seemed I was surrounded by a huge, black hole, and all I wanted was to vanish inside it.

When we arrived at the church, we were amazed at the vast turnout–family, acquaintances, neighbors, townspeople, law enforcement and fire department personnel–some we had met, most we hadn't. Tom Meritt, funeral director of Rader Funeral Homes, escorted me to my seat. Tom is a rare kind of person who goes way beyond the call of duty, as he did in assisting with many details for our family. The tragic death of his best friend in high school brought Tom to his life's devotion to assist grieving families. His work fills the need he has to care for those left behind when someone dies. Today I am thankful to call Tom Meritt my friend.

Four pastors from different churches also attended, and each participated in the service. In addition, an administrator from First Baptist Roanoke, the last church my family attended, and the Sunday school teacher who taught Mycol's adult class that day were also involved.

I was especially touched by the Sunday school teacher, who spoke of the brief time he had spent with Mycol and how impressed he had been with him in that encounter. And then this sensitive and caring gentleman slowly and respectfully read the prayer request Mycol had written on a piece of paper and turned in that last Sunday morning of his life here on earth. It was a request concerning my return to Virginia and the reunion of our family. When the gentleman was finished reading, he walked over to me and, obviously understanding that this was one of the few tangible pieces of my life with my family that I would ever have, carefully handed me the piece of paper with Mycol's handwritten prayer request, as well as the visitor registration forms Mycol had filled out when he dropped off the kids at their classes. I gratefully took the sacred items, my heart aching that these were but remnants of my family, yet grateful for anything I could get.

The administrator from First Baptist Roanoke then went to the microphone and recounted his meeting with my family. One week before the fire, Mycol and the kids were returning home from having visited Calvary Memorial Church. As they passed by First Baptist Roanoke, Mycol decided to stop in and tour the place, as he was planning to visit the following Sunday. This man lovingly talked about what a positive and powerful impression Mycol and the kids had made on him during that time. He said he watched Mycol interacting with the children, and it was obvious that he was a loving, faithful husband and father.

I remember wondering, should the situation have been reversed and it were Mycol sitting there listening to others eulogize me, if Mycol would have been as proud of me as I was of him at that moment. It's a thought worth considering–for all of us. When we leave this life, what will be our legacy? Mycol used to say he was "ready" whenever God took him, and the faithful way he lived his life is his legacy to those of us who love him.

The administrator then went on to describe what he saw in our children. "Austin was quiet and polite. He just sat right there with Mycol and was very well behaved." *Yes*, I thought, *that was Austin, contemplative–a really good little boy.*

The man paused, as a hint of a smile danced on his face before he continued. "And then there was Jessie."

This brought a brief smile to my own heart, as I knew exactly what he meant. Full of spunk, curiosity, mischief…and then my heart sank. Her *life*. She was no longer full of that life as I knew her…

"Jessie was climbing all over everything," he said. "She was climbing on the chair. She was climbing on Mycol. She was just a happy, beautiful little girl."

Yes, I knew exactly what he had experienced, and I so wanted to say I could feel their presence…but I couldn't. At that moment I couldn't feel anything but my heart being ripped apart yet again.

On Holy Ground

At the end of the service Brother Jim, our Texas pastor who had accompanied us, stepped up as the family spokesman and thanked all the wonderful, loving people of Botetourt County who had been willing to come out on such a cold, cold Monday night to honor a family most had never met, to offer their love and comfort to a woman they had only heard about, and to share in the grief of the rest of the family. Brother Jim told those precious people how our family members and friends back home had wondered why Mycol and I had wanted to leave Texas, but now, seeing the love and commitment of the people of Botetourt, he understood.

"When we return to Texas," he told them, "we will all have a little bit of Virginia in us. I hope…" His voice wavered, and he paused for a moment before saying, "…that you will have a little bit of Texas in you."

As I had at the first memorial service, I stood and received the guests, thanking each one for coming. Most of them had to introduce themselves to me, as there were so many I didn't know. But there was one in particular who, though we had not met face-to-face, felt like an old friend the minute she introduced herself.

"Hi. I'm Lyn," she said, and then mentioned how I would know her. "We met online one night."

I was stunned. Some time after Mycol and I knew for certain that we were going to buy the log house but before we had moved out of our home in Kingwood, Mycol decided to go online and see if we could find anyone from Troutville who might be online at that very moment. We found someone and sent an instant message. She responded, and we quickly began a two-way communication. We told her we would be moving up there soon and wanted to get to know some people. She was quite friendly, wished us well in our move, and told us to get in touch with her when we arrived. And now, here she was, standing in front of me.

To say I was touched would be an understatement. But there was more. After introducing herself, she turned to the man standing behind her in line and said, "And this is my husband." Her sentence echoed in my ears, as I looked at him and realized he was one of the firefighters who had tried to save my family, and who had now come to honor them.

As the line continued to snake along, we shook hands with, hugged, and thanked countless people. Afterward, Lane Hasson, the minister of education at the church, offered to take us to the classrooms where Mycol and the kids had been when they visited *Rain-bow For-est Baptist Church.* As we walked toward the kindergarten room, Lane glanced at the poster hanging on the door. It was a picture of Jesus, surrounded by children.

That poster would have been a warm and open invitation to any child to come in and learn about Him, and instinctively Lane knew that Austin's eyes had seen this very poster. I could imagine his noticing the poster and saying something like, "Jesus sure loves all the children, doesn't he Daddy!" I could imagine Mycol bringing him into the classroom, talking with the teacher, taking the time to be sure Austin was comfortable before leaving the room. As my happy little evangelist had prepared to walk through the very doorway I was now about to enter, that poster would have been his personal greeting, and Austin is one who would have noticed it and recognized its meaning. Lane, obviously understanding how much the poster would mean to me, asked if I would like to have it.

Speechless and nearly overwhelmed by the enormous grief that accompanied walking into that room, I could only nod. In response, Lane carefully removed the poster from the door, rolled it up, and handed it to me with what I can only describe as great reverence. "Austin saw the poster; I'm sure of it," he said.

I took it, realizing how much Lane and others wanted to be able to give me something–anything that would be a tangible representation of my family's life, their love, and their presence. And then Lane found the nametags, with the safety pins still attached, that Austin and Jessie had worn–another *something* for me to hang on to.

As we toured Austin's, Jessie's, and Mycol's classrooms, I felt as if I were walking on holy ground, just knowing I was in the same places my family had so recently occupied. Those were sacred moments, filled with confusion and grief…but most of all, with great love.

Through the long night when nightmares are vivid
And all the memories come back to haunt us,
He takes our hands, leans close to us
Whispering gently and softly in our ear,
"I Love you and I will never leave you."
What amazing tenderness from the heart
Of our blessed Saviour!
He is a friend beyond compare.
—*Anonymous*

Chapter 15

"Why...?"

For weeks after the fire our Bible study leader and friend, Dane Parish, came every day to Mycol's parents home, where I was staying, to pray with me and for me. Dane loved Mycol and was a faithful friend to all of us. During that awful time immediately following the tragedy, I asked Dane over and over again, "Why?" And then each time he asked me in return whether I'd asked God that question. I said I had, but I wasn't getting any answers. Then, patiently, Dane would remind me, "Have you been reading your Bible? Have you prayed? Have you asked God and listened for His answer?"

I knew he was right, but I just didn't seem to be able to follow through on that knowledge. I guess I just wasn't able to function on that level yet; reading and comprehending takes much more concentration and focus than I had at that time. An excerpt from the Book of Job offers some similarity to what I was feeling and dealing with:

Job 30:15-20, 26-27 ^{15}Terrors overwhelm me; my dignity is driven away as by the wind, my safety vanishes like a cloud. ^{16}And now my life ebbs away; days of suffering grip me. ^{17}Night pierces my bones; my gnawing pains never rest. ^{18}In his great power God becomes like clothing to me; he binds me like the neck of my garment. ^{19}He throws me into the mud, and I am reduced to dust and ashes. ^{20}I cry out to you, O God, but you do not answer; I stand up, but you merely look at me... ^{26}Yet when I hoped for good, evil came; when I looked for light, then came darkness. ²⁷The churning inside me never stops; days of suffering confront me. (NIV)

And so I continued to ask why. Why did it happen? Why wasn't God showing me a reason? Why didn't I get to "move to heaven" with my family?

Dane finally said, "Linda, you keep asking God to speak to you, but you aren't praying and you aren't reading His Word. You have to do that. You have to try. I've been praying Psalm 23 with your name in it every day, several times a day, as have so many other people, but you have to pray too. If you want God to answer you, you have to talk to Him; you have to open His Word. 1 Peter 5, verses 6-11. If you don't know what to read, read that."

Another Faith Message

I call Dane my "Hammer Man" because he isn't the gentlest friend I have, but he is definitely one of the most loving. He just really insists on what he believes is right. And throughout that time he was sending emails to everyone he knew, asking them to pray a personal prayer of Psalm 23 for me. God had another faith message to give me, and Dane was being obedient to help deliver it.

It happened exactly two weeks after the fire, as I was going to bed in Mycol's childhood bedroom. Dane's persistence finally drove me to pick up my Bible. I had no idea where to open or what to read, but then I remembered Dane had told me he was praying Psalm 23 with my name in it, and to read 1 Peter 5:6-11. In fact, he had read the passage in 1 Peter aloud to me many times over the past two weeks, and so, since I didn't know where else to begin, I turned there and began to read. It was difficult to focus, to concentrate, to read, but I managed to get through those six verses:

1 Peter 5:6-11 ⁶Humble yourselves, therefore, under God's mighty hand, that he may lift you up in due time. ⁷Cast all your anxiety on him because he cares for you. ⁸Be self-controlled and alert. Your enemy the devil prowls around like a roaring lion looking for someone to devour. ⁹Resist him, standing firm in the faith, because you know that your brothers throughout the world are undergoing the same kind of sufferings. ¹⁰And the God of all grace, who called you to his eternal glory in Christ, after you have suffered a little while, will himself restore you and make you strong, firm and steadfast. ¹¹To him be the power for ever and ever. Amen. (NIV)

Shaking inside and out, with tears running down my cheeks, I urgently prayed for the first time since before the fire: "Okay, God, You made me this way. You made me human, with all my human limitations, and You know what my limitations are. So I need You to tell me two things, God. I need You to tell me in my own limited human terms, in a way I will understand, that number-one, they really are okay, and number-two, I really will be with them again."

I was crushed and I was weak, and I needed to know these two things with clarity. I so desperately needed to hear Him! I was honest with God about my hurt and confusion. I needed Him to speak to me so personally that I would know it was Him, so personally I would not later doubt or begin to think, *Maybe that wasn't really God.* I needed to know personally that He would unmistakably answer my most urgent questions in a way I would understand, in such a personal way that it could be no one but God speaking to me.

And then I went to sleep. Sleep, so long as I didn't have nightmares, was the only break I had from the pain.

The next morning my brother-in-law Rusty called to say he and Lynna would like to have me over for dinner that night. He asked if he could pick me up after work and take me to their home. Lynna and Rusty live about an hour from Mycol's parents' home, and Rusty's office is an hour away in another direction. This was a Tuesday, so I declined his invitation, thinking it better to wait until the weekend because I was not willing to spend the night anywhere but in Mycol's bedroom. That bedroom was the closest I could be to my family. If I had dinner with Lynna and Rusty, I would have to be back at Mycol's parents' home to sleep. All that driving would make a late night for Rusty, and I knew both Lynna and Rusty had to be up early for work the next morning.

But Rusty continued to insist I come for dinner that very night. I resisted a little longer, maintaining that I had to sleep in Mycol's old bedroom. We went back and forth a bit, but finally I gave in when Rusty promised he would return me to Mycol's parents' home that night and said he didn't mind the drive at all.

When Rusty picked me up I was thinking that it really was a waste of food to invite me for dinner because I wasn't eating much those days. But after dinner Lynna got up from the table and said she had something for me. She went into the bedroom and came back with a little plastic pouch that had something wrapped in tissue paper inside.

Carefully, curiously, I opened the pouch and unwrapped the tissue paper. When I saw the contents, I could scarcely breathe, let alone speak. There, in the midst of the rumpled tissue paper, lay Mycol's wedding ring and his high school class ring. I knew immediately it was God's specific, personal answer to my prayer.

At last I managed to squeak out, "Where did you find these?"

And then they told me that while in Virginia our twenty-one-year-old nephew, Daryl, had gone to the site with some of our other family members before the memorial service. Daryl was walking around the area that sloped down by the walk-out basement, and something glimmered just long enough to catch his attention. He looked over through the hole that had once been a window in the basement and saw something shiny. He tried to get closer but had to stay behind the police and fire line. But when he leaned in as far as he could for a better look, he saw what appeared to be a ring. Immediately he called for his father, Kurt. Kurt and Rusty, along with Lynna and Kurt's wife, Reba, hurried over while Daryl, gently poking the ashes with a stick and then reaching in with his hand, managed to grasp the rings and pull them out of the remains of the house.

When I later had a chance to ask Daryl what the area looked like when he found the rings, he said it was amazing he had found them. The wedding ring was set atop a pile of wet ashes, nearly invisible, and the class ring was hidden in ashes. It wasn't until he reached in and picked up the wedding ring that he found the other ring beneath it. The roof had blown apart over that spot, the second story had caved in, and the main floor was mostly caved in as well. Everything had dropped to the basement level and had become a heap of ashes. Daryl said it looked like someone had gently placed that wedding ring on top of the ashes where its gleam would be noticed.

Miraculous Discovery

The miracle of this discovery went deeper than Daryl or Rusty or Lynna realized, for Mycol's wedding ring had been lost for two years–since long before we moved to Virginia. Mycol and I thought it had been left behind somewhere in Texas. In fact, when we were in the midst of moving into the log house, Mycol had said, "Well, I guess my ring is going to stay in Texas forever." But no one else in the family knew any of this.

Neither did Rusty and Lynna know that I had just prayed for the first time the night before, asking God to give me His answer in human terms that I could understand. The wedding ring is a human symbol of eternal love, an endless circle of precious gold. The fact that it was Mycol's lost ring answered both questions for me. The lost ring found: my family really is okay; the fact that it is a wedding ring: we really will be together again.

I know what the Bible says about there being no marriage in heaven, but that's not what this is about. This is about a personal relationship with God. This is about how He speaks to us personally if we will seek Him and listen. What better human symbol of love and eternity could God have used to answer those two specific questions asked out of the depths of my grief and pain? Mycol's ring is as personal as it gets, and that's what I mean when I refer to a personal relationship with God. The ring would not have meant the same thing to anyone else. Indeed, this was a personal answer from a personal God, answering my specific questions with impeccable timing.

And yet we can't know what God's timing will be. Sometimes answers come quickly; sometimes they don't. Dane, being a faithful servant, continued to pray and persist with me, and God was just waiting for me to open His Word and come to Him. When I did, He answered me so personally that I can never doubt His presence, His love, or His compassion for me.

I now keep Mycol's gold nugget wedding ring with me at all times, as another huge faith booster from a personal God. I have since given Mycol's class ring to his mom, as he was "hers" at that time in his life.

Once I had those rings in my hands and realized what they meant, I couldn't wait to share the news with Dane. All our friends and family were waiting, hoping, praying for something good, some sort of encouraging news to come forth. So when I told Dane about the rings, he sent out an email to the many faithful family members and friends who were praying for me and told them that I had started reading my Bible again, that I had prayed and asked God for a tangible, personal answer to reassure me that my family was okay and that I would be with them again, and that God had answered in a miraculous way.

God's Perfect Timing

God's timing is always perfect–not only with the rings, but with everything, including some cards Mycol and the kids sent me on January 18, just nine days before the fire. Though I had received them a few days after they mailed them, I had no idea at the time what they would mean to me in the weeks and months to come.

Now, about three weeks after the fire, I read those cards over and over again, trying to absorb their handwriting through my eyes and into my heart. The card from Mycol said, "I'm Missing You" on the front, and inside was printed "I wish we didn't have to be apart, but I'm trusting the Lord to keep us close in spirit until we are together again." Underneath Mycol had written, "It's not a home without you here. I love you. Mycol Bebe."

Each time I saw his signature I could feel the corners of my mouth trying to turn up in a smile, even in the midst of the pain. Mycol Bebe. Bebe. That's what we called each other. Not "baby" or "bee-bee," but "beh-beh," with the accent on the first syllable. And no matter how anyone tried, no one could say it like Mycol because he was the one who made it up.

At the bottom of the card was stamped "2 Timothy 3:1-12," a passage of scripture that is an encouragement to be faithful…no matter what. God knew how much I would need to hear those words, over and over again, as I walked through this seemingly endless, dark night of my soul, and how much more it would mean to me coming from Mycol.

Austin and Jessie's cards were Tweety Bird cards that said "I Miss You Wots" on the front. The kids had signed their names and written messages inside: "I love you, Mommy," "I miss you," and Jessie's one-word message: "Cookie."

I stared and stared at their handwriting—the ink in lines and curves guided by their hands—and I longed to hold them, to act on my natural feelings as a wife and mother, but I couldn't. All I could do was hold the cards that had been in their hands, and feel the pain of missing them.

My maternal instincts were to protect my children. When thoughts of fire crept into my mind, it took a lot of energy to overcome them and to envision my children happily playing and laughing in heaven. I had to relinquish my motherhood, as their protector now is Jesus, and my role as Austin and Jessie's mommy is finished.

Not yet ready to accept the end of my mommy-hood, one of my driving emotions during that time was the urgency to be with them, to go to them. I asked God several times what I still needed to accomplish here in this life so I could be done with it and move on. I didn't want to be left behind any longer.

I tried to keep reading the Bible, but some days I just didn't have the strength. Most days I just stared at it, not knowing what I was reading. Then, about a month after my family "moved to heaven," I was praying, asking God to let the truth be known about the cause of the fire. The police and fire marshal still had a lot of questions as the investigation continued. But I was confused and grief-stricken and couldn't always think clearly. Dealing with the cold, hard facts of this enormous tragedy would have been impossible to do on my own. Thankfully, certain family members and friends filtered as much information as they could to protect me. As it turned out, the cause of the fire wouldn't be determined for eight weeks.

While the various investigators queried and searched, my own questions were reserved for God. Sitting in Mycol's old bedroom, I closed my eyes and prayed that God would lead me to something in the Holy Scriptures that would help me. I didn't know where to turn, but I had determined to search His Word for answers. When I opened my eyes I saw immediately in front of me a card on the desk. It was an old card that had been there for some time, and on it was written "Luke 12:34." When I saw it I decided to go to the twelfth chapter of the book of Luke.

"Lord," I prayed, "please speak to me." I read verses 24 through 34, which told me not to worry, to seek first His kingdom, not to be afraid because God has been pleased to give me the kingdom, to lay my treasure in heaven, for where my treasure is, there my heart is also. What seemed to stand out to me was the message not to worry. Was that what God was telling me, not to worry about the cause of the fire?

I decided to read on, and the next verses told me to be prepared—"dressed and ready"—so that when He knocks I can open the door. He will come, the Bible told me in verse 40, "at an hour you do not expect."

This is so true, I thought. But then I wondered if God had considered that I was not ready on January 27. Is that why He didn't come for me too? Is that why I didn't get to go with them?

I turned the pages back to Luke 12:4-5 and read that I should not be afraid, even if what happened was done by human hands, because God cares for us. Fear only God, the scripture said. I didn't need to fear human hands against my family, I realized. I needed only God.

In my despair I wondered if God was guiding my hands through the pages of Luke. I stopped in chapter ten and read verses 25-28, focusing on the last two: "…'love the Lord your God with all your heart, with all your soul, with all your strength, and with all your mind' and, 'your neighbor as yourself'... Do this and you will live."

I knew these verses well and had already accepted Jesus' sacrifice for me, but now, drowning in desperation, I thought, *Somehow I feel Mycol and the kids just have a better grasp, a deeper understanding than I do. I'm afraid God will judge me by my motives; I want to go to heaven now because I want to be with my family, yet I should want to be in heaven because of God, because of His promise.*

I would say all I could think of was being with my family, but I wasn't doing much thinking; I was just being. And I needed to be with them.

Back to the Site

About a month after the fire I asked Rusty if he would accompany me if I went back to Virginia...back to the site. I hoped to find some personal items in the rubble, and despite the pain I knew it would cause, I wanted to make the search.

Rusty agreed, and during the week we were there we sifted through wet, snowy ashes and mud, looking for any piece of something to hold on to. We stayed again with Don and Kim Eckenroth during that time, and also spent some time with Sheriff Ronnie Sprinkle and my cousin Bill Potter.

Bill is Aunt Teen's son, a chemist and a farmer, and one heck of a great cousin. I soon learned that Bill was the last person to see my family alive when he stopped by the log house on his way home that Sunday evening. It was cold, and he wanted to check on Mycol and the children to see if they were warm enough or needed anything. Bill and his son, Jon, were chatting with Mycol out on the front porch when Bill asked for some phone numbers of family in Texas, just in case of emergency. Mycol gave him Reba's phone number and Cheryl's too, since I was staying with her.

At 2:21 a.m., when the first 9-1-1 call came in, Bill was awakened by a phone call from Lisa Arney.

Lisa cried through the phone, "The cabin's on fire!"

Before she could say another word, Bill hopped out of bed and into his truck, then sped down Catawba Road, but by the time he arrived there was nothing he could do. As Sheriff Sprinkle approached Bill's truck and climbed in, Bill wept. "That's my cousin's house," he said, and he filled the sheriff in on who we were and provided the emergency phone numbers Mycol had given him just hours before.

Ronnie Sprinkle and Bill Potter go back a long way. Their fathers were good friends and ran for sheriff against one another back when Botetourt County was all farmland and Catawba Road was a one-lane dirt road. Now Ronnie would head up an investigation by several different agencies, including local, state, and federal authorities, in what would prove to be the most heart-wrenching incident of his career so far.

Cousin Bill, Ronnie Sprinkle, and Don Eckenroth spent a lot of time with Rusty and me that week, helping us dig through the rubble and just generally being there for us.

People Willing to Hurt with Me

As the days and weeks passed, people returned to their families, their homes, their routines. I still received visitors, cards, phone calls, and donations of clothing and household items from precious people who realized I had lost everything–not just my family but all my material possessions besides the few clothes I had with me. I also know there were so many prayers being offered on my behalf. But the loneliness, the confusion, and the ache for my family grew more intense as time passed, and being gracious became difficult at best. It seemed I was entering an even darker time. Anyone who has ever lived through such tragedy knows that darkness all too well. It's terrifying. It swallows you up and refuses to spit you out, despite your cries for deliverance.

But God hears those cries. Even when all we see is darkness, the Holy Spirit is working out His plan. The Lord encouraged me to keep a journal during those days of utter darkness, though I had no idea of why at the time. I had kept journals at other times in my life, but not for the same reason or in response to the Holy Spirit's urging. I did not know then the importance of journaling, or how so many pastors and counselors recommend this for its value to spiritual and mental health. All I knew was that I felt an undeniable urge, an absolute certainty that I needed to keep a journal, that God was going to use it somehow, and that I wouldn't want to have to rely on my poor memory later. And so I began to journal everything. What I wrote was raw and at times very ugly, but it was also very real, and when I share excerpts from it, it is with the hope that it may help someone else and show that God has compassion.

One of the many things that stands out as I re-read those journals and reflect on that time of darkness and pain is that God was teaching me something about human nature: We have a propensity to "fix" things, simply because we want to avoid pain and the sense of powerlessness that goes with it. This doesn't apply just to ourselves; it extends to our desire to help others, to make them feel better, for then we are comforted because we still feel some sense of control.

Now I'm not in any way suggesting that those who reached out to help me did so to meet their own need for comfort and control. I believe people reach out to others to console, to love, or to help carry a burden because God moves them to do so. But it truly is a strange phenomenon that in reaching out to help someone else, we are sometimes motivated by a need within ourselves to *do* something–to offer a solution, to fix the problem, to regain control. And for all those who came to me to offer solutions or explanations in an effort to comfort me and to get past their own feelings of powerlessness, I understand completely. I would no doubt have done the same thing had I been in their shoes. Ultimately, however, because the focus of this book is faith, I must explain a few things about grief and the needs of grieving people.

What I needed most at that time were people who were willing to do nothing more than hurt with me–as many of them did, either because they understood the importance of doing it and how to go about it or because the Holy Spirit prompted and directed them. But there were others who just didn't know or understand about ministering to someone in such despair and anguish. The story of Job in the Bible is similar to some of what I experienced. Job's friends were quiet at first, but when they spoke they were not able to give him what he wanted. None of them could solve his problem, answer "why," or relieve his pain.

At times I wondered why some of the tears I cried were brought on by things people said in an effort to comfort me. Some even suggested that maybe I would marry again one day. I can't even begin to explain how painful this was to hear at that particular point in time. It felt insulting to my family, and a minimizing of our tragedy. From experience I can affirm that the best way to minister to and support a grieving person is to carefully consider and pray about your words before speaking. The Lord may very well direct you to say nothing but instead to be willing to enter the grieving person's pain. It was such a comfort to me when someone sat silently beside me and held my hand and even cried with me. That meant so much more than empty words and meaningless phrases. The worst, without a doubt, is "I know how you feel." It takes great restraint on the part of a grieving person not to cry out, "No, you don't! You have no idea how I feel or what I'm going through because you haven't been through it!" Each person is unique, and each person's relationships with others are unique. It's insulting and offensive–not to mention untrue–to say we know how someone else feels.

More than once I heard people say, "Time heals all wounds." Not only is that statement untrue, but it sounds disrespectful by failing to acknowledge the moment and the feelings that are *now*. Now is all we have, and we must seek God in this moment. My father-in-law, Corky, said it better: "Time doesn't heal wounds–in time, you learn to walk with them."

Faith...and Encouragement

At Lynna and Rusty's church, North Main Baptist, they had just begun an eight-week Sunday school study on *The Case for Faith*. In this excellent book author Lee Strobel is on a journey, looking for an explanation, a defense of God, for why He lets bad things happen to innocent people. Strobel takes a copy of a photograph of a young mother living in a drought-stricken part of the world, holding her baby daughter's lifeless body, and tells a prominent theologian, "All she needed was rain." Then he presses the scholar for answers and asks, "What would you tell her?"

The theologian, Dr. Peter Kreeft, responds, "Nothing." The conversation then proceeds like this:

"Nothing?"

"Nothing. I wouldn't say anything to her. At least not at first... I would be Jesus to her. I would enter the pain with her."[i]

Enter the pain. Bingo! That was it. Dr. Kreeft was right, and he put words to what I was experiencing. Because of our human nature to want to fix things, to comfort and control, Dr. Kreeft's suggestion is an extremely difficult one. To enter into pain with someone else, to refrain from the natural tendency to fix things and make them better, is a great challenge.

For me, as for others who are grieving, there is no comforting anyone can do by trying to fix things, because *there is no fixing to be done*. I hurt, and I needed people who were willing to be Jesus to me, willing to acknowledge and validate my pain and to just love me right where and how I was. This is exactly what my brother-in-law Rusty did and continued to do for me. He is a vessel of God's love and an incredible example for others.

As we studied *The Case for Faith*, one man in our class talked about when his wife was dying of kidney failure, and her hospital roommate was dying of the same thing. As a result the two husbands became friends. When the wife of the man in our class died first, the other man came to the funeral. Afterward he came up and just hugged his friend; he didn't say a thing. Three weeks later the situation was reversed, and the man in our class attended the funeral for the other man's wife. Our classmate later explained the quiet response and sharing of one another's grief as "feeling like the arms of Christ," a total acceptance and validation of the other's pain, as though they had been standing in the pain together without having to say a word, relieving one another, at least for a moment, of the loneliness so heavy in grief.

This is how Rusty has supported me, and this is a good point to tell about all I have received through and from this brother, for he has been my human anchor. Lynna and Rusty, as a couple, have walked together with me through this entire tragedy, from January 27, 2003, to the present. Thank God they have a solid marriage! I can see how Rusty's ongoing support for me could have been a problem if their relationship were less than it is. In addition Lynna has been every bit as important as Rusty because she has never complained about the amount of time he has given me: the countless hours he sat with me, listened to me, ministered to me, held me when I needed to cry, and just let me *be*–but not alone–accepting my pain and allowing it to hurt him too. Because of the selflessness of this amazing couple, they were able to walk right alongside me through this tragedy.

I didn't have any brothers when I was growing up, though I always wanted at least one. The day of the fire, the day that separated the "before" and "after" of my life, Rusty sat down next to me on the couch at our mother-in-law's, and somehow–maybe without really knowing what was happening–he let God use him in a profound way. God had provided the brother I'd always wanted and now needed so desperately. And it was only the first time of many that Rusty would share my pain. Many times he sat with me when he was tired and had to get up for work the next day, even when he didn't feel like it or when he was busy and had other obligations. If I had put in a custom order with God for a brother, I could not have come up with a better one than Rusty Blue— not because he's perfect, but because in faith, obedience, and love, he has been willing to let God use him. We often turn to trusted friends for answers, and I am no different. There are many important men and women in my life, but it was God who worked through them to provide the answers and guidance I needed.

My mother, of course, was another one who supported me with unconditional love. She was concerned about me, as any mother would be in such a heartbreaking situation. She also knew how impatient I can be and that I needed encouragement to hang on and keep putting one foot in front of the other. This was especially important at a time when my primary focus was on wanting to go and be with Mycol and the kids. My parents were good encouragers when we were young, and since my dad had passed away in 1998, Mom wanted to offer the ongoing encouragement I so desperately needed. I distinctly remember one particular phone conversation we had on that very topic.

"You know I have no patience, Mom," I told her. "That's why you gave me a Polaroid when I was little."

"Oh, I remember that. We gave Diane a Kodak and you a Polaroid, and you were so disappointed."

"That was just because I thought anything she got must be better than what I got because she's older. But when you explained she'd have to wait for her pictures but I'd get mine instantly, that was all I needed to hear. I don't want to wait, Mom. I want to go now."

"I know you do," she said. She understood, but she wanted to redirect my thoughts. "I remember when you were running track in middle school, and you had a bad meet one time. You came in last in one of your events. Do you remember that?"

"No, I don't," I admitted.

"Well, I do," she said. "And I remember how you handled it. I was so proud of you. The next meet you were determined not to let that happen again, but as you were running your event and doing so well, you saw another girl on the other team who was really struggling. You knew what she was going through because it was fresh on your mind, and you didn't want her to quit. So you slowed down and ran at her pace, and you encouraged her through the rest of the race."

That surprised me, as I truly didn't remember the event, but Mom insisted it happened.

"You stayed with her and told her she wasn't going to quit because you wouldn't let her," she said. "You told her how you'd been discouraged in the last meet, and you wouldn't let discouragement cause her to quit now. And then her teammates surrounded her in excitement because she had never finished a race before." She paused, giving me time to absorb her words before saying, "She finished the race because of you."

Though the impact of what she was telling me wouldn't hit me until later, I appreciated her attempt to remind me of how I had encouraged others with my words and my actions. It was many months before I began to relate the story to the prompting of the Holy Spirit, and perhaps an entire host of angels, cheering me on in a great voice and encouraging me to finish the race.

I smiled at the memory–one of the few smiles that had crossed my lips since before the fire.

Through the reliving of childhood memories that had made her proud of me, I knew Mom was trying to encourage me in the best way she knew how. She has always believed I'm strong, but I know I'm not–at least, not by myself. And right then I was so emptied out, so lost. There was nothing left in this life that I wanted, and I still had to deal with probate and insurance. It sure didn't look like things were going to get better any time soon…

Waiting for the Glory

When all that's left is meaningless
Why did you give me these eyes?
I wish to gouge them out
All I see now is worthless
Am I to love
The lavender canvas you painted this wintry afternoon
Reflected in snow-capped mountain and purple frosted lake?
Oak is tickled over the pink horizon and chuckles from smile-shaped leaves
Pine waves winnowy fingers eager to capture my attention
But I turn away, their beauty deflected by my sorrow

When all that's left is hollowness
Why did you carve out these ears?
Take your blade and sever them
That I may never again
Waste the signals of sound on my brain
I hear no child laughing
No birthday songs nor pattering feet
Sweet nothings are nothing
As there is nothing new to hear
Let me be deafened by the silence

When all that's left is insignificant
What good is my mouth?
Perhaps your seasoning was meant to be savored
Budding spring gardens in manifold flavors
Summer's thirst for lemonade
Autumn spiced with wassail
Winter warmed by hot cocoa
Though I tasted of these none would engage my senses
My dry mouth drenched in death
The bitterness of remains leaves an incurable halitosis

When all that's left is emptiness
Why must I carry these arms?
These hands will not test warm bath water
Or catch a child jumping from the side of the pool
Nor touch the scratchy five o'clock shadow of the man I love and long to feel
Soft lamb's wool and feathers in my pillow, the gratifying feel of grain
Have no grasp on me
Fingers that want to stroke his hair, caress his chest
Provide instead a constant reminder that I could not protect
That I am armed with nothing

When all that's left is trifling
Grief is as plain as the nose on my face
No longer fondling a kiss
Unable to capture a whiff of dirty diapers and baby lotion
Soiled socks and after-shave
The fragrance of your floral hillside theater
Wafting through the valley
Searching for acceptance by my sniffer
Wastes your efforts on me, drowning in the stench of death
I can only hope heaven is as sweetly aromatic as this life is a redolent dirge

When all that's left is senseless
What purpose does my body serve?
Void of desire for your wondrous creation
Robbed of pleasure which once filled this armor
Now irredeemably shattered
I'd like to reject the abyss, overthrow the chasm
Which, numb as it is, gives my soul its only identity
Crying out for liberation from the confines of these cells
From Rome the lion's roar
Sounds as close as if my head were stuck in its mouth.

Chapter 16

Searching...and Waiting

Shortly after the fire our church did, in fact, split. It was not becoming of many Christians, but sometimes our humanness gets the best of us. Between Texas and Virginia I was in attendance at a few different churches. My life was just too unstable then to settle in any one church, but when I was physically and emotionally able to get up out of bed, I would decide that morning where to go to church.

My experiences have taught me that God does not do all I would like Him to do on my time schedule. Sometimes God's actions seem deliberate; other times His responses are subtle. Often, regardless of which church I went to, I received something pertinent, something usable and appropriate for the place I was in at that moment, and I knew it was God, continuing to communicate with me in a very personal way.

Six weeks after the fire, our pastor preached from Romans 10:14-21, emphasizing verse 21 and applying it to present-day conditions. Pastor Lino's paraphrase of the verse went like this: "God says all day long, 'I offer you My Word through the scriptures; I hold it out to you and wait for you to listen to Me, to seek Me in My Word.'"

I knew what the pastor was saying was true–that I needed to keep seeking God by continually reading His Word–and yet I was still in such deep grief, still so shaken and unsettled that I wanted God to speak to me in a way that would meet my deep need for comfort. My prayer at that time was:

Please don't stop, Lord—I'm still seeking. You promised I'd find You, so please don't stop. I want to rely on hearing You speak to me through Your words, through prayer, with the help of other believers, but then I think of Psalm 107, believing You were taking us to a city where we would settle, and Jeremiah 29:11: "For I know the plans I have for you," declares the LORD, "plans to prosper you and not to harm you, plans to give you hope and a future." Lord, please be understanding that my needs are as huge as this tragedy.

As I continued in what I now think of as my "searching...and waiting" mode, I began to spend weekends at Lynna and Rusty's house. Often Rusty and I would stay up talking till 2:00 a.m. We talked about Psalm 107 and Jeremiah 29:11-13–and nightmares. My nightmares were not about fire, but often I would dream of seeing my family and not be able to get to them. I dreamed once that someone kidnapped our infant grandson Kody while I was babysitting him. It was all my fault and I couldn't find him anywhere. I was running and screaming for anyone to help me find him before he was killed but no one helped. Somehow, in these nightmares, I'd be stopped from getting to someone I loved. The dreams never had an ending but I would awaken full of anxiety and fear to the realization once again that my family was gone–and that was not a dream. Each time we talked, Rusty prayed with me and for me. He prayed that God would wrap His arms around me, his sister. He prayed God would reveal His plan and purpose for me, that I would understand Him, and that He would protect me from any more nightmares.

I also told Rusty about my prayer on January 26, the night of the fire, and how immediately afterward I had felt that evil, oppressive presence. I asked him what he thought, but he said he didn't know what to think, and again he prayed with me. He prayed that God would comfort me and that I would know His will for me. Rusty is a good listener, and we developed a close and trusting relationship during that time. As a result, I was eventually able to leave Mycol's childhood home and moved in with Lynna and Rusty in Liberty, Texas, where I continued my journey out of the pit of darkness and despair.

Small Things—and Whoppers

I believe–no, I *know*–that God speaks to each of us in a very personal way. When Jesus healed people while He was here on earth, He did it differently each time, but it was always a one-on-one personal experience, just as it has been for me. As I watched for evidence of God's presence through those faith boosters that gave me hope, I found that evidence in small things and also in what I call "whoppers." Mycol's ring and the U-Haul trailer were whoppers. But there are so many times and so many other ways God has spoken by placing a knowing deep within, in my very core, if only just to show me the truth of His words: "I AM with you."

And, of course, one of the many ways God has revealed Himself to me, time and again, has been through the words and actions of others. On March 19 I wrote the following in my journal:

I had an idea last night (dare I say from the Holy Spirit?) to write a letter to friends and family and ask that they write down a prayer for me and mail or email it to me. Here's what I'm thinking: I'm keeping this diary and I seem to have moved from "paralyzed" to at least being willing to go to grief counseling and asking Him to reveal His plan and purpose for me. I think it would be a nice part of the diary to have written prayers from all those who are supporting me. I may even ask if I can put that request in the church newsletter, and even in other church newsletters.

When I decided to move ahead with the request, the response was incredible. I sent out over 200 letters requesting prayer, and in return I received prayers not only from those I asked but from some of their friends as well–people I didn't even know. My dear friend Mary Lynn Barrett, the hospice nurse I met at the home of Don and Kim Eckenroth, decorated a binder in which to keep all these prayer letters, each as unique and individual as the people who wrote them. I still had many difficult days ahead, days when I seemed unable to climb out of the pit, but this precious binder full of written prayers was something tangible I could use to find some comfort, as I read the words over and over again.

I wish I could reprint every prayer I received, but that would make a whole book itself, so here's just one, the prayer I received from Mary Lynn:

> You are such an awesome God. You eagerly wait for us to bring our petitions to You. You yearn to answer our requests. Lord, I come to You again on behalf of my friend Linda. I thank You and praise You for answering her requests for assurance that Mycol, Jessie, and Austin are safely in Your arms. I praise You for the gift of the wedding ring from the ashes…a symbol of their unending love and of Yours, oh, Father.
>
> Father, we cling to the truth of Mycol's favorite verse from Romans 8:28: "All things work together for good to those who love God." There is yet much we don't understand. I pray especially that Linda will feel Your peace in the midst of unanswered questions, and that the peace that passes all understanding will guard her heart and mind.
>
> Lord, my overwhelming prayer for Linda is also from Your Word. You tell us that life is a special gift, given by You, to be cherished for whatever time it is given. My prayer is that there will only be three deaths from the tragic fire. I pray that Linda will "Choose Life!" I pray that she will feel Your guidance, strength, power, and comfort for each new day. May she realize that You are there to wipe her tears, giving her a clearer vision of Your Divine Plan.
>
> Lord, I have come to love Linda, but I know You love her even more. As I think of the fact that I am usually far from her in distance, I know that You are always next to her. I give her lovingly into Your hands, knowing that You know best how to

love my friend. May Your will be accomplished in her life, and may You receive the praise and glory.
In Jesus' Most precious Name, Amen.
Prayed often, with love, by Mary Lynn Barrett

Every prayer I received brought with it incredible strength and love, encouragement, compassion, and a willingness to step outside the comfort zone and into the pain. I am forever grateful to every person who took the time to send me their prayers.

Another Faith Booster

Two months after the fire, I walked outside to my car, the one that had belonged to my mother-in-law. This was the first time I had gone near that car–the car our son was born in–since before the tragedy. I had tried once before, but I just wasn't able to make it. My arms had begun to ache and I felt sick inside, so I'd turned around and gone back in the house. But this day I was determined to go through with it. When I opened the door and looked inside, I discovered a crayon drawing on the shelf by the back window. It had Jessie's name on it. She must have drawn the picture in church school just before we moved, or it wouldn't have been left in the car; it would have been packed with all the other drawings. It is a picture of our family which has become the cover of this book, a message, and a symbol of God's desire for a personal relationship and His love for us all.

Four figures, each identifiable: one can tell a lot about a child's development from their drawing. Since I was the one who worked outside the home, it was common for Austin and Jess to put on my shoes and walk around the house. I used to do that with my dad's shoes. "Work shoes" are a detail a small child would notice, and one of the details Jessie included to identify which figure is me. Daddy, of course, is the biggest figure, and she drew herself and Austin in appropriate size for their ages. Mycol, Austin, and Jess are colored entirely purple, and they each have big smiles on their faces. I, on the other hand, have a black body and a purple head, and I am the only figure who has a yellow covering, or glow, around the top of my head. From behind me, at the top of my head and arching outward, is a rainbow.

Interpreting the colors helped me understand the message: purple is the color of royalty, the color of our King, Jesus Christ. Mycol, Austin, and Jessie are entirely purple, and they are with our King. But only my head is purple, while the rest of me is black. The head represents knowledge, and the body represents emotion. Black represents my feelings of grief, but since I do know the truth that my family is safe with Jesus, and I will see them again, my head is purple, confirming my knowledge of our King. Even in my grief, which God has acknowledged and honored, I *do know* the truth. The yellow covering over my head represents God's grace, his message, "I AM with you," while the rainbow has been the sign of God's promise to mankind since the time immediately following the Flood. Yes, there is tragedy, but even so, we are all together in the picture. To this day the Holy Spirit ministers to me through this picture, drawn through our Jessie's little hands, to show that He was there and still is, that He knows how I hurt, and He promises it will be okay in the end. This is the only drawing I will ever have from my two youngest children, and I believe God directed Jessie's hand in drawing it, and He purposely made sure it was left there for me to help me understand.

Missy's Wisdom

This was my third "whopper" faith booster—the discovery of the U-Haul toy being the first, and Mycol's rings the second. But even with all these faith boosters, the spiritual warfare continued. The church had split, despite my prayers and the prayers of so many others, and my family had "moved to heaven." The end of our pastor's leadership of this church came with a lot of hurt. It saddened me to see the church splitting, but even more, it scared me because of what I said when I prayed the night before the fire: "Satan, get out of our church." What had really happened that night? Who had spoken those words to me about my family? What was really going on in the spiritual realm?

I wanted to ask Pastor Lino those questions, but he'd been so bogged down with all that was going on that I didn't want to bother him. Now that it was his last week before leaving the church, I felt we should talk, so we made arrangements to meet at his office.

I told him about my prayers and what I had said on the night of the fire, and then I asked him, "Who said that to me? What happened that night?" But he had no answers for me; all he could tell me was to continue to trust. I was disappointed. I wanted answers, but nobody seemed to have any–not Pastor Lino, not Rusty–no one.

Then, after my meeting with Pastor Lino, I met Missy for lunch, where I posed the same questions to her. We talked about the *why* of all that had happened, and specifically about my prayer that night: "But not my will be done, but Yours." Was the fire God's will? Was it God's will for Mycol and Austin and Jessie to move to heaven that night, leaving me behind?

Missy's response settled comfortably in my spirit. She saw the bigger picture–the God picture. "Mom, you had no control over what happened, but you did have control over whether or not you were in God's will when it happened."

She nailed it, and I knew she was right. The fire, the destruction, the pain and confusion, none of that was God's will. But it is God's will that each of us put our trust and faith in Him, that we believe in Him and His Son, and that in accepting His gift of salvation and eternal life, we enter into a personal relationship with Him. It is then that we step into His will, trusting Him in His omnipotence, even when we don't understand the things that happen in our lives. Missy's words helped me more than she can ever know.

Staying Faithful

And she wasn't the only one. Everyone, it seemed, found ways to help me through this dark and painful time. Kurt Bullinger, the brother-in-law who spent long, stressful, emotional hours creating the video for the memorial service, graciously agreed to be my support and caretaker for my next trip back to the Roanoke Valley. He took time off work, something that can be expensive for a self-employed small businessman, and we left for Virginia to begin probate of Mycol's estate.

On this trip we stayed with Howard and Annette Sumpter, "Grandma and Grandpa Sumpter," as they prefer to be called.

The Sumpters lived next door to the Arneys, and their living room picture window opened up for a view that was once beautiful to them–an old log house in front of Tinker Mountain. But in the early morning hours of January 27, 2003, Grandma and Grandpa Sumpter watched in horror as the fire blazed before them and the heat penetrated their home.

The Sumpters remind me of the book of James–faith requires deeds in order to be alive. They are people who take action, who serve others with the energy of someone half their age. The night of the fire they opened up their home to every firefighter, sheriff deputy, and emergency personnel as a refuge from the bitter cold. Grandma Annette prepared snacks, coffee, and hot chocolate for anyone who needed a break. In fact, we learned that it was from Grandma and Grandpa's home that Ronnie Sprinkle first called me that morning. And now here we were, staying in that same home, as Kurt and I prepared to trudge through probate, answer more questions in the ongoing investigation, and attempt to work with the insurance company. These things needed to be done but would not be easy or pleasant.

While we were staying with the Sumpters, Grandma handed me the local newspaper, pointing to an article about my family. I took the paper from her and read the letter to the editor on page two of the *Fincastle Herald*. It was written by a teenage boy named Devin, and I wondered if God had coordinated the timing of that letter's printing so I would see it while we were there. The heading read, "Do not give up hope, stay faithful."

Editor:

Sometimes we forget just how fragile our lives actually are. We forget how quickly we can travel from the top of the chain to rock bottom.

It was Monday. Time to go back to school for another agonizing week of homework and lectures. My alarm awoke me and I began heading toward the shower. As I was walking into the bathroom, I overheard a conversation downstairs. Mom was talking on the phone about a neighbor's house. It had burnt down! Curiously, I asked whose house it was and if everything was OK. Reassured that everyone made it out, I hopped into the shower and continued getting ready for school. Little did I know what was awaiting me.

I casually walked to my friend's house, expecting him to be waiting on me in his house or at the bus stop, but both spots were deserted. As I continued to search for my friend, another one of my buddies from school arrived. He quickly informed me that there were three deaths in the house fire and my friend probably was across the street from the accident. We decided to investigate. Sure enough, my friend was at the neighbors' house, along with everyone else in his family. After getting details on what happened my friend and I made sure everyone was going to be OK and made our way back to the bus stop.

Here's what we learned: two children, one 5 and one 4, and their father had died in the fire. Their house (which was a historical landmark) was totally burnt to the ground except for a few walls and the basement. Their car was melted and everything they owned (which was packaged in cardboard boxes at the time) was burnt to a crisp. The only survivor was the wife who was in Texas finishing her job so she could join her family. Just like that, everything she owned and loved was gone. Every possession, along with her two children and husband were taken from her in a matter of a few hours.

I'll bet you're thinking, "Where was God in all this?" The answer may not be to your liking, but God knew about this and planned for it to happen. The reason is probably because it was their time to go and God may be testing the wife to see if she stays faithful to him as Job did when he lost it all. Another thing that we can be reassured about is that God lets these bad things happen because He knows some good will come out of them. Only God knows his true reason for what He does, but we can still be thankful that He has a plan for us because of His never-ending love for all of us, sinners and all.

If the mother and wife of the family doesn't give up hope after losing everything she owned and loved, then why should we give up hope just because some school bullies make fun of us for being a Christian? Why should we? Stay faithful to God in all that you do and say, and your reward will be eternity in love, life and joy with the master of the universe.

—Devin Quesenberry, Troutville[ii]

Staying faithful. Young Devin's words were an encouragement to me, and right then I needed all the encouragement I could get. As I thought about Devin's letter, I recalled a conversation with Mycol in which I told him a story about something that had happened nearly twenty years earlier, when my mom called to tell me about a situation involving her neighbor, who was a nurse.

Mom's nurse-neighbor had a patient who was dying of cancer. The patient, a young woman, with a husband and three small children, had asked to be buried in a pure silk gown. The family didn't have that kind of money, and Mom asked if I'd call the church I attended then to see if they had some kind of benevolent fund for situations like this. When I did, they told me they didn't do anything like that. I have to admit, I was shocked and disappointed.

I had to get to my class at college so I left, but the whole thing just kept bothering me. I kept thinking that this poor woman deserved to get her wish, even if it was for the sake of her family. I didn't know her, but I guess I took it personally when the church turned down my request. It just didn't seem right.

When I got to class, I was scheduled to present a speech that evening about drunk driving, but even while I was giving it, I couldn't get the woman and her last wish for a silk gown off my mind. Afterward, as I listened to the other presentations, I kept thinking, *I really have a better speech than the one I gave. I wonder if he'll let me do another one...* That little something inside kept nudging me, and by the end of class I couldn't hold it in any longer. So I asked the instructor if he'd let me give another speech, and he agreed. I told him this one wasn't for a grade, I just felt so strongly compelled to tell the story, and I didn't know why.

I then told the class what I knew about this woman and her family and what the church had said, and the next thing I knew, my fellow students were opening their purses and wallets and handing me cash. Some of them had tears in their eyes and said they didn't want to be left out of this opportunity to give. When I counted the money, there was $105! I was stunned. Here I'd turned to a traditional church in an established, upper-middle class neighborhood, and they did nothing. But God performed His miracle through financially poor but spiritually rich college students.

I hadn't even thought of where to go to find a pure silk gown, so on my way home from class I stopped at the mall. The first store I went into, about fifteen minutes before closing time, had Christian Dior pure silk gowns on sale. I *knew* this was God's work, and I was glad I had listened and acted. Everything happened so smoothly. The sale price for the gown was $109, and with my own few dollars added to what the others had given, there was just enough. So I got the gown just in time before the store closed, and then rushed over to Mom's and told her what happened. She ran over to get the neighbor and told her about it, and the neighbor delivered the gown to her grateful patient, who died a few days later.

"I can't tell you how much it meant to me to know she was buried in that beautiful silk gown," I had told Mycol.

I remember Mycol's smile of understanding as he listened to my story. We knew God was working in our lives, and this story was just a timely reminder of our Lord's faithfulness. Mycol and I had often discussed the "knowing" we had that God was at work in our lives, even though it was difficult to explain exactly how we knew. We concluded that much of it came about through listening for that still, small voice, paying attention to what He said, and cooperating with what He was directing us to do. As young Devin Quesenberry said in his letter to the editor, it's about staying faithful. It's about believing in the sovereignty and holiness of God, regardless of circumstances, and trusting that He will work all things together for good, for those who believe and are called according to His purpose, as it states in Romans 8:28, Mycol's favorite verse. In fact, Mycol had marked it as such in his Bible, along with the year–2002. Now, a year later, that verse challenged my faith, even as it offered promise to my wounded heart.

Stepping into Eternity

I needed more. I wanted so badly to hear Mycol talk to me. I wanted to hear him tell me that everything was fine and that he wanted me to be strong. Then one day, while talking on the phone with Mary Lynn Barrett, she asked me as she had before, "Honey, have you read the book I sent, *Stepping Into Eternity*?" I was sorry to have to tell her I hadn't read it yet, and I sensed she was disappointed. She really felt she was led to buy that book for me.

Mary Lynn and her husband are beekeepers, and they sell their honey through various outlets. A man had been inviting them to set up a booth at some kind of annual fair to sell honey, but Mary Lynn wasn't really interested. But the guy persisted each year, and by the third year Mary Lynn thought, *Okay, Lord, You must want me to be there, so I'll go.*

Mary Lynn and her honey jars sat for most of the day with very little attention from the fair-goers. Getting bored, she decided to take a walk and see what else was around. She stumbled upon the booth of Reverend Tom Parrish, a minister from St. Paul, Minnesota, who was there selling his book, *Stepping into Eternity*.

Having been a hospice nurse for so many years, Mary Lynn was keenly interested in Reverend Parrish's book. "What's your book about?" she asked.

Tom explained that the book is about his experience with people as they cross the threshold into heaven. In his thirty-plus years of attending to the sick and dying, he has witnessed the presence of Jesus on many occasions. Mary Lynn thought immediately of me, of my constant anxiety and desperate desire for evidence that everything I say I believe is true, and began to tell Tom of our story.

She then bought the book and sent it to me, along with Tom's telephone number and a note encouraging me to call him. She was sure the stories of his experiences would be comforting to me. But being uninterested in reading anything, I had resisted even opening the book. Now she was asking me about it again. Admitting to my dear friend that I had just put the book away and never even looked at the cover, I felt like I was being disrespectful toward her. So after our conversation I went to the bedroom and dug out the book and began to read.

Mary Lynn was right on. This book was for me! Story after story recounts the proof of the presence of Jesus at the time of death. How reassuring it was to read his personal eyewitness accounts of people encountering Jesus as they left this life. Tom's stories are real and they lift my soul and give me peace. Because Tom has put these experiences in writing, I am able to embrace the vision of when Jesus came for my family. That vision replaces the one of the sheer horror of what fire does to the human body. By the time I reached the fourth chapter I was dialing Tom's phone number, eager to hear his experiences personally.

"Hi, Tom? My name is Linda Street. Mary Lynn Barrett gave me a copy of your book, and—"

"Linda," Tom interrupted, "I was hoping to hear from you!"

From there we had a long conversation in which Tom reassured me time and again that everything I believe is true; that Jesus really did come for my family, and that they really are with Him now. His book, his experiences, have been an incredible comfort to me, and his reassuring tone and kind, gentle nature quickly made me call him my friend. Tom's personal testimony in *Stepping into Eternity* brought me renewed hope from real stories; it's a book that can renew your faith and refresh your personal relationship with God.

My next phone call was to Mary Lynn. I thanked her not only for her gift and her friendship, but for being persistent so that I would pick up that book and read it.

Evangelistic Festival and Seed-Planting

On May 2 I returned to Virginia yet again, but this was the first time I made the trip by myself. While I was there I went with Lisa Arney and her son, Evan, to the Franklin Graham Festival. As we waited in line, Evan saw several friends, but I commented that I probably wouldn't know anyone there. I soon learned how wrong I was. Once inside I ran into pastors and people from the churches my family had visited, as well as Tim Geiger, the passer-by who had stopped and tried to help A.J. the night of the fire, and who also happened to be a member of *Rain-bow For-est Bap-tist Church.*

Cody Lowe, a writer from the *Roanoke Times* who was there to cover the event, heard I was there and approached me before the festival began, asking for an interview. I agreed, under the condition that he would print what I said and not edit out things that might be "politically incorrect." He agreed.

Still not thinking clearly all the time, I did my best to manage through the interview, with Martha Furman, my grief counselor, at my side. After the festival Cody asked permission to devote an entire article just to my family. Making the interview a part of his story on the festival just wouldn't do our story justice, he said. So two days later this story appeared:

Her Family Dead, Woman Seeks Solace at Graham Festival

> The woman sitting in the second row of beige folding chairs on the Salem Stadium field didn't draw any attention to herself.

Only a handful of the estimated 16,500 people at the first night of the Franklin Graham evangelistic festival even knew who she was.

But perhaps no one in the audience Friday night felt a stronger obligation to be there—or a more intense desire to be just about anywhere else—than Linda Street.

Street had come from Texas, summoning all her courage to continue her battle against the demons of despair and doubt that have threatened her since Jan. 27.

She was in Houston that day, finishing up some paralegal work. In about two weeks, she was to join her husband, Mycol, and two children, Austin, 5, and Jessica, 4, who had already moved to their new home in Botetourt County—a historic 200-year old log house on Catawba Road.

No one knows how, but in the early hours of that morning their home caught fire. Mycol, Austin and Jessica died of smoke inhalation in their beds, investigators said.

"I'm still searching for the 'why,'" Street said Friday.

The search brought her to the Roanoke Valley over the weekend. She's met with the pastors of some of the churches her husband and children had attended after moving here. And she's confided her spiritual struggle to people such as counselor Martha Furman, who comforted her during the festival Friday night.

They are the people who have "prayed with me and for me. Who've tried to help me," Street said.

"I'm in a dark place, clinging to the light of hope I have" in her Christian faith, Street said. "The same light Mycol believed in."

Speaking with a reporter, Street struggled for just the right words.

Her slim body trembled as she fought to tame the emotions that squeezed out tears she could not stop.

Part of that reaction was rooted in her dismay with the way the media covered her family's misfortune, including the presence of cameras at the memorial service for her husband and children.

"Grief is a private thing," Street insisted.

But her struggle for control was also anchored in her desire that "whatever I say…be something my husband would want me to say."

Coming to the Graham festival was emotionally difficult, Street acknowledged, but then "getting out of bed's hard." Not that she sleeps much, she said.

"It's very hard to be around more than one or two people… It's not what I would have asked for, but I believe Mycol would want me to do it."

And, Street said, she does feel the "need to be with Christians. I've never been challenged like this before."

At the end of Graham's message Friday, when hundreds were responding to his invitation to come forward to accept Christ, Street reflected on the spiritual lives she'd already seen in Austin and Jessica.

While riding in their van when Austin was 4, Street and her husband were surprised when "on his own, we heard him say, 'Jesus, come into my heart.' It brought tears to our eyes.

"We used to have Bible study and prayer time every night. One night Jessie, who turned 4 in November, said, 'When we move to heaven, will we get to see Jesus?' And I said, 'Yes, baby girl, we will.'"

Pausing to let the tears pass, Street continued, "She never said, 'When we die.'"

"I know my baby girl is with him right now…I want people to see that I'm grabbing for the light and that I know my family is in heaven."

"I would hope that the people who have cried for me, hurt for me, would grab for that same light I am grabbing for, because Mycol would have wanted that."

"I would tell them, 'Yes, there is a path of light that is the same path I cling to. That's all that I have.'"[iii]

I probably didn't do a great job of expressing myself, but I did the best I could. The next day Don and Kim Eckenroth asked if I wanted to go back to the festival with them. We attempted the trip, but the weather was so cold and rainy that we decided against it. Instead, we went out to dinner and then back to their house, where Don and I sat at the kitchen bar and had another of our many deep conversations about God and anger and trust. He asked me how church was and I had to admit that at times I was so angry I didn't want to go. I blamed God for not waking Mycol and getting them out of the house. Being angry made it hard to go to church.

"Don, I don't really feel like I like God. I know I'm not supposed to say that, but I'm so angry. I don't want to talk to Him."

Don, a gentle shepherd, opened the door to another way of thinking. "Well how would you feel about just talking to Jesus?"

Puzzled, I looked straight at him. "What?"

"Would it be easier for you to accept that Jesus understands? Could you see around the fact that Father, Son and Holy Spirit are three in one, and just talk to one?"

I sat contemplatively as the gears churned in my brain, trying to put this puzzle-picture together. It had to make sense to me. If it didn't, I couldn't just do it because it felt good.

"Being that you know He hung on the cross," Don continued, "you know the pain He endured, do you feel He could understand your pain? Could you talk to Him?"

I pondered that thought for a moment longer. "Yes, I think I can," I answered, letting the idea settle in my soul. Over the coming months talking to Jesus would begin to melt away the anger, as I knew He understood.

"Good," Don replied. "Now, would you like to see a video of Sudan?"

"Sure," I said as we left the kitchen and headed for the den. As I watched the first of Don's videos of his mission trips to Sudan, I was fascinated with what I saw.

In addition to the many other things Don does in Christian service, he is on the board of directors of Answering the Call (ATC), an international Christian mission organization. That evening, as we sat in the Eckenroths' comfortable home, we talked about the medical mission trips to Sudan and Don's experiences there. Kim suggested I should take a trip with him sometime. She thought it could help me and would also help others to have a fellow sufferer in the faith come to comfort the people of war-torn Central Africa.

And then Kim went to her kitchen and took out a can of mustard seeds. "You know, Linda, just one of these is all you need." She gave me a small bag of mustard seeds to keep with me as a reminder and said, "I keep thinking of the verse from Job that says, 'Though He slay me, yet will I trust Him.'" Even as she spoke the words, I had to admit that the verse certainly seemed appropriate in my case.

Kim and I continued to talk about helping others in this time that I am left behind here, and she again encouraged me to consider getting involved with the mission work, either in Sudan or somewhere else. Indeed, a seed was planted that night.

Pumpy Tudors and Pinky Promises

And then, a few days later, it was time to return to Texas. Traveling through Chattanooga in the fast lane on my way back to Houston from Roanoke, I was crossing a bridge when the driver of the van in front of me suddenly hit his brakes. I immediately slammed on my own brakes–and then I spotted the cop. He had me on radar. Pulling out behind me, he turned on his lights and siren and pursued me to where I pulled over, just a few yards up. I have to admit that I hadn't been paying any attention to my speed, just to the traffic around me.

Having just attended the very moving and meaningful Franklin Graham Festival a few days earlier, not to mention that this was my first trip back to Virginia on my own, I was in quite an emotional state. I rolled down my window, and the officer began firing questions faster than I could process them. Where was I going, where was I coming from, what was I doing in Tennessee, where was my license and registration, etc. Needless to say, I was flustered and couldn't keep up with his questions or demands. Later, when I read an article in the *Chattanooga Times Free Press* about this man, whose name was Pumpy Tudors, I better understood why he had approached me as he did. The article portrayed him as an honest but no-nonsense police officer who "pumped" his words out in a rapid-fire manner and often punctuated his sentences by pumping his arms in the air–hence, living up to his name, Pumpy. The story, in fact, was appropriately titled "Hall of Fame Guests Hear Pumpyisms" by Sam Woolwine.

"He [Pumpy] probably came out of the womb talking," Woolwine wrote, "and hasn't stopped since. For a Southerner, he also talks quickly, with animation… When he played at UTC, and would begin talking and waving those arms, some of the words that came out were Pumpyisms. Nobody could quite figure what he meant, but they weren't going to ask either."[iv]

No wonder I felt so intimidated! I tried as best I could to accommodate his questions, but I just couldn't keep up. He quickly became frustrated and threw my license and insurance card back in the window on my lap. Caught off guard by this sudden action, I sat there and tried to collect myself while he returned to his car for a moment. That's when I decided to show him the article from the *Roanoke Times* so he'd understand my situation, particularly my emotional and mental state. In addition, I wouldn't have to re-tell the story because he could get it all from the paper. So I reached to the back seat, grabbed the paper I had collected to bring home to Rusty, got out of my car, and headed back to the patrol car to show the article to Officer Tudors.

Of course, I had no idea then that you're not supposed to do something like that. Apparently this kind of action is considered threatening, but I had no way of knowing that since I don't make it a habit to be pulled over by police officers. Perceiving a potential threat, Officer Tudors waited until I was just even with his car door and then swung it open so it would knock into me. I jumped back, and he jumped out and told me never to do that again.

Shaken, I handed him the paper and said in a quivering half-shout, "You asked me where I was coming from and where I was going and why I was here. Here's your answer." I shoved the paper toward his midsection, but he hesitated to take it, looking down at it as if he'd never seen a newspaper before.

"What is this?" he asked. "What's it about? What does it say?"

"Read it," I insisted–several times, as a matter of fact. I just couldn't handle his interrogation style any more, and I knew I wasn't able to read it to him myself as I was already beginning to cry.

Finally he seemed to notice my emotional state and took the paper and started to read. He hadn't gotten far when, I believe, the Holy Spirit intervened. Officer Tudors was so obviously moved by the story that he threw those big old "pumpy" arms around me, pulled me close, and then held me so tightly I could feel his badge pressing into my face. I remember one fleeting thought at that moment: *I'm going to have a star imprint on my cheek whenever he lets go!*

As Officer Tudors held me he began sobbing and praying out loud. "Lord Jesus, Lord Jesus…" he began, though I can't remember much more of what he said, except that he kept sobbing and saying, "Jesus!"

After a few moments he suggested I go back to my car and calm down, while he read the entire article. When he was finished reading, we got off the highway and drove to a gas station where we could talk. I told him about my family and about the fire, and he told me about his family and his life.

The way I see it Officer Tudors answered to the promptings of the highest authority. He handled a difficult situation, going above and beyond his call of duty as a police officer. Even after we sat and talked awhile, he was concerned that I not get right back on the road until he knew I was okay. After a phone call to Rusty I was calmed down enough to drive again, but not before Officer Tudors made me promise to call when I arrived safely back in Liberty. But he wasn't insisting on just any kind of promise–he wanted a "pinky promise."

To tell you the truth, I thought I'd heard him wrong. I mean, who would expect to hear such words coming from the mouth of this big, burly cop?

"A *what*?" I asked.

He raised his eyebrows in surprise. "A pinky promise. Haven't you ever heard of that?"

Well, I'd heard of it, yes, but...

I smiled, as I realized he was serious. And sure enough, right there in the parking lot of that gas station, we locked pinky fingers–for real–and I promised to call. As soon as I arrived back in Liberty, I kept my pinky promise to Office Pumpy Tudors and left a message on his voice mail.

But then it all caught up with me. I was so tired, and it had been a very emotional trip. I had been back to the scene of the fire–the very spot that was to be our family home–all by myself for the first time. As I had stood there, staring and hurting, all I could think of, over and over again, was, *I should have been here that night. If I had been, we wouldn't be separated now. Oh God, I want to be with my family! I should have moved to heaven with them...*

Deep, raw grief creates a previously un-trodden landscape where we can easily exhaust ourselves with a climb we don't really want to conquer. As a result, we allow ourselves to freefall, so full of pain that all desire to endure rips away in the wind, as we plummet to the bottom. I needed to let out the pressure, to fall apart in the arms of someone safe, and that someone was Rusty. When I told him I needed to talk, he made himself available.

"If I do it," I told him, referring to ending my life, "I'll do it at the house, right where I should have been found—next to Mycol." I so desperately wanted out of this life, and the waiting was getting harder and more frustrating and confusing all the time. I was exhausted by the ongoing, everyday demands of my pain-filled existence.

Again—as he had so many times before and would continue to do—Rusty entered that place of pain and sat with me. He encouraged me by listening and praying, and he showed his maturity and respect by not trying to "fix" my problems.

I believe God understands how I feel, and He even grieves with me. I believe He does not criticize or condemn us for expressing grief. Christ has compassion for our tears; they are precious to Him. Just as Christ has compassion for us, we strive to have compassion for others. When people are hurting all the words in the world won't help; they need somebody to hug them and reassure them that God loves them and understands.

But I have also come to believe that while I am ready and eager to enter the gates of heaven, God still has work for me here. I still have a purpose, as yet unfulfilled, and I want to be faithful. My motivation for living was the fact that we do not have all knowledge about death and how things happen afterward. Since my pain was caused by the separation from my family, I could not bear the thought of a permanent separation. There is no way for me to know, this side of heaven, if I had ended my own life, whether I would have faced some consequence in eternity that would keep me separated from them. That fear, along with knowing my husband so well, knowing exactly what he would say to me, "Keep living, Linda; you have to finish everything before you can come Home," has kept me here and provided the strength and encouragement to write this book. Meanwhile, it is helpful to know there are those to whom I can express the truth about my feelings as I search for answers…and endure the seemingly endless waiting.

A Bone Marrow Transplant for Myles

On May 16, just days after I returned from my trip to Roanoke, we received the first diagnosis of the illness that had plagued my grandson, Myles, since soon after his birth. It was Severe Combined Immune Deficiency, or SCID, commonly known as "the boy in the bubble disease," a rare genetic condition in which the child is born with little or no functioning immune system.

This was devastating news to Angie and Justin, as well as to the whole family, especially when it came less than four months after the fire. Myles' only chance for survival was a bone marrow transplant, and we had to find a match for his marrow type before he became sick again. Any attack on his immune system, even a simple cold or the chicken pox, could kill him, and he couldn't even get vaccines.

Since moving in with Lynna and Rusty in Liberty, I had been attending North Main Baptist Church, where Brother Jim was the pastor. I asked Brother Jim to make an announcement at church, asking for people to submit to bone marrow testing to see if we could find an exact match donor. I was overwhelmed with the response, and excited and encouraged at the thought of so many people willing to be tested.

Less than two weeks after the initial diagnosis, First Baptist Liberty held a very successful blood and marrow drive, with more people showing up than expected. The workers said they had never seen such a large response to a marrow drive, especially on such short notice. The local radio station had just advertised it the morning before, and even though the workers were willing to stay late, the blood bank had to turn people away when they ran out of supplies.

Two days later we received a new diagnosis for Myles' condition. The specific type of SCID is called ZAP70, which stands for Zeta-Associated-Protein 70, the rarest form of SCID. Myles was something like the eighth known case in the world. Needless to say, he was a very sick baby.

Angie researched all the options and decided on Duke University Hospital in Durham, North Carolina, for treatment, since the doctor on staff there–Dr. Rebecca Buckley–had more experience than anyone else in treating this particular type of SCID. Dr. Buckley does not use chemo on her patients, and to our knowledge–at least at the time of this writing–she may be the only one in the world who treats SCID without chemo. As a result, Angie and Justin felt so strongly that they should take Myles to Duke and have Dr. Buckley treat him that they left their jobs and moved to Durham. The transplant was scheduled for July 1.

Angie also learned through her research that had she not argued with the nurses back in November and insisted they use her breast milk in the feeding tube instead of formula, Myles would not have had any immunity working for him at all. The antibodies he received from her milk were the only ones he got, since his body was not able to produce any on its own. It was amazing to us that there were certain medical professionals who would argue against using a mother's breast milk to feed a baby through the feeding tube. But as scary as the situation was, Angie felt redeemed by this news, knowing she had instinctively done the right thing for her son.

Toward the end of June I drove up to North Carolina, and on July 1, 2003, Myles received his first bone marrow transplant. We knew there were no guarantees of success, and Rusty and Lynna flew up from Houston to support and pray with us. Dr. Buckley decided she would use Justin's bone marrow because she felt the marrow of a parent, while not a perfect match, if close enough could actually be safer and have less chance of rejection than the marrow of an unrelated donor of a perfect match.

I was moved to hear Justin's response when he learned he would be the donor. "Angie," he said, "you got to save his life the first time, through your milk. Now it's my turn." Justin endured the surgical extraction of marrow from both his hips and woke up in time to witness the infusion of his processed marrow into Myles' little body. But it would be several weeks before we would know whether or not the transplant was successful.

The Royal Route to Heaven

There's a royal route to heaven –
Will you travel it today?
'Tis the path of full surrender
All along the homeward way.
It is yielding every moment
To the blessed Saviour's will,
Seeking only for His glory,
And His purpose to fulfill.

There's a royal route to heaven –
'Tis the way the Saviour trod.
'Tis the path of full surrender
And the deep, sweet peace of God.

There's a royal route to heaven –
They who travel it may know
Peace that passeth understanding
Which the Father doth bestow.
Dead to self and its desires,
Living unto Christ alone,
Finding joy and satisfaction
Which the world has never known.

There's a royal route to heaven –
Which will bring a rich reward
When the last long mile is covered
And we face our loving Lord.
Oh, how small will seem the trials
Of the steep and rugged way
When we stand in His blest presence
At the close of life's brief day.

—Avis B. Christiansen

(found in the book, "Royal Route to Heaven; Studies in First Corinthians" by Alan Redpath, published 1960, Fleming H. Revell Co., Old Tappan, N.J.)

Chapter 17

Tasting the Vomit

In the midst of all that was going on with Myles, I continued to battle the grief that sometimes felt as if it would consume me. I suspect there were those who wondered if I even wanted to "get better." The truth is, there is no "better," not by my definition and understanding. What better means to me is shedding that which caused me pain; in other words, complete healing, as though I could take a medicine and the sickness would be gone, or undergo surgery to remove the tumor. My family and I are separated by a chasm that cannot be spanned in this life, and the horror and grief associated with how it happened and the fact that it happened at all will not be removed until I go to be with them. This brings up an interesting phenomenon about grief.

Many who grieve a loved one fear that with time comes distance, as in "out of sight, out of mind." I don't want that–no one does. That fear is a looming, dark cloud that I often fight. Some people may mistake my fight against "getting better" as a desire for torment, but that misses the truth. If healing comes with time, and healing is "feeling better" or coping better, then with time we are not so adversely affected by the disaster. Yet I want to be affected by it because that's what keeps my family close to me. I don't want to lose–I *cannot* lose–the closeness in my heart. That doesn't mean I don't want to cope or manage or learn to walk with what has happened, but based on my definition of "better" and on my intense desire to be with my family, I will not be better until I am in heaven. I will–*I am*–however, learning to live with this painful, ever-present thorn.

Martha Furman was the grief counselor I had in Virginia, but I needed someone local in Texas. After an exhaustive search, with Rusty beside me at every meeting, we finally found the right person. I began grief counseling with Mary Jo Lagoski, a gifted counselor who has since become a trusted friend. Mary Jo related to me a very interesting story that explains to me why I would rather feel the hurt, the pain of missing my family, than to work on "being okay" or "getting better" by traditional standards. The story is about "tasting the vomit."

This woman was at home one day when she heard a thump, so she went upstairs to see what had caused the noise. She found her son on the floor, dying of a self-induced overdose of drugs. She immediately began to administer CPR, and as she did, he vomited into her mouth. As horrible as that was, it was her last connection of life with her son. The taste was putrid and revolting, but later, after her son was gone and she could no longer experience his life, she longed for that last moment when she could feel her precious son alive. For this mother, the final sign of life was his vomit. Wanting to hold on to that final moment, she longed to taste his vomit again, just so she wouldn't have to say goodbye, for beyond the vomit there was nothing but pain.

I understand that mother's longing, as I would rather feel the intense pain of missing my family than to distance myself from them, to feel as though I'm letting them go. While some people may view tasting the vomit as idolizing grief, for those of us who have tasted it, longed for and clung to it, there is a strong yearning for life–the pain of grief we wish we didn't have.

The Faith Chapter

As the aching for my family and the pressure regarding Myles' situation continued to mount, I decided to call Terri Camp, the woman I'd heard share her family's story of faith and tragedy just a few months before when Myles was first hospitalized. She was so gracious to talk to me for more than two hours, as she told me more about her family dealing with grief and then listened as I opened up and shared some of my own grief. I was really hurting when I called Terri, and after a long conversation and prayer, she left me with the recommendation to read Hebrews 11, often referred to as the "faith chapter."

> **Hebrews 11: 1-2, 8-10, 13-16, 39-40; 12:1** Now faith is being sure of what we hope for and certain of what we do not see. ²This is what the ancients were commended for... ⁸By faith Abraham, when called to go to a place he would later receive as his inheritance, obeyed and went, even though he did not know where he was going. ⁹By faith he made his home in the promised land like a stranger in a foreign country; he lived in tents, as did Isaac and Jacob, who were heirs with him of the same promise. ¹⁰For he was looking forward to the city with foundations, whose architect and builder is God... ¹³All these people were still living by faith when they died. They did not receive the things promised; they only saw them and welcomed them from a distance. And they admitted that they were aliens and strangers on earth. ¹⁴People who say such things show that they are looking for a country of their own. ¹⁵If they had been thinking of the country they had left, they would have had the opportunity to return. ¹⁶Instead, they were longing for a better country–a heavenly one. Therefore God is not ashamed to be called their God, for he has prepared a city for them... ³⁹These were all commended for their faith, yet none of them received what had been promised. ⁴⁰God had planned something better for us so that only together with us would they be made perfect. ¹Therefore... let us run with perseverance the race marked out for us. (NIV)

"Pray it over and over," she said, "and just stay in the Word."

I was in so much turmoil at the time that I was not able to read, but I held on to her advice, knowing I would delve into that chapter as soon as I was able.

As it turned out it was late summer, not quite seven months after the fire, when I finally took a look at Hebrews 11. It was after saying good night to Lynna and Rusty, I went into my room and dove into severe depression. Curled up in a fetal position, my head at the foot of the bed, clutching Mycol's baseball glove, I simply could not reach three feet over to the table to get my Bible. I truly know what it means to be gripped by fear and pain because that's where I was that night.

And then I remembered something Rusty had said: "What's the one thing Satan doesn't want you to do? Read your Bible!" As the strength of Rusty's words of encouragement began to seep into my heart, I was finally able to reach for my Bible and open it to the book of Hebrews, as Terri Camp had suggested two months earlier. I read through all of Hebrews that night and I cried–a lot. I had to make myself keep reading, and as I did, a confusing mix of thoughts and emotions swelled. Feelings of comfort and confidence in God's Word as my weapon against attacks of doubt, fear, and depression, fought against feelings of being deceived. I couldn't make sense of it and everything felt wrong, and the stress that resulted made me sick inside. There was this undeniable sense of being deceived by the promise of Psalm 107–crying out to the Lord that He would lead us in the right way–and then reading Hebrews 11. It was as if God said, "Yes, I said I'd take you to a city, but it's not what you thought–it's heaven, and you don't get to go."

Recalling the time Barbara fasted and prayed with us, I had to compare Psalm 107, which had felt like a confirmation, side by side with Hebrews 11, searching for the answer to "Why?"

When we read Psalm 107 we thought the Lord was speaking to us to trust Him and He would take us to whatever city He wanted us in, whether in Alaska, Virginia, or wherever. We believed we were being faithful, seeking His guidance; surely He would answer.

In Psalm 107, God promised to take the Israelites to a city where they would settle. Given the facts that Barbara was fasting with us, she was in prayer when she asked God to show her His scripture, and she had no preconceived notions or plans to suggest what God would say to her–she just opened to that part of scripture–it was understandable that we would interpret that to mean that God was leading us to an actual, physical city here on earth. We could identify with the Israelites in this passage because we had been looking a long time, we had been faithful in seeking God's will and direction, and every door seemed to be open to us. Surely He was providing the way.

And then the fire happened. My thoughts tossed around as though by a hurricane. All I could see was God leading us on a death march–until Terri Camp directed me to Hebrews 11. At first I felt encouraged to keep the faith, but then I felt deceived, as if it had all been some sort of dirty trick. Hebrews 11 says that city is heaven, which is certainly not what I was expecting when we moved to Virginia.

After reading these scriptures and meditating on them, I questioned whether that was comforting to me. I wrote, *I don't really see comfort coming until I'm with my family. But it's interesting. I know I am supposed to finish the race—but I am getting awfully tired.* Too confused to understand, I finally fell asleep, but not for long. Vivid nightmares of searching desperately for my family made it a rough night. Eventually, the importance of Hebrews 11 would sink in, but for now, opening the Bible, reading the entire Book of Hebrews, was a big step for me.

Visiting the Four Churches

One of the things I felt driven to do and I hoped might bring some comfort was to visit each of the four churches my family visited in the four weeks they were in Virginia, and to meet people my family had met, people who had seen them more recently than I had. I decided to visit each church, in the same order as my family had done. *Rain-bow For-est Bap-tist Church* was first.

It was a cold, snowy day, and Rusty, as well as Don Eckenroth, accompanied me. The senior pastor, Mike Grooms, was delivering his message about pain and grief, explaining that when we are in our "winters" of life, there is hope in Jesus Christ. Pastor Grooms' sermon went straight to my heart, though he had no idea I was sitting among the congregation. He had been out of town when the fire happened and also when we had the memorial service. And yet he was talking about the very journey I was on. Afterward, Rusty, Don, and I introduced ourselves to Pastor Grooms, who responded with great sensitivity and gentleness. He shared with us how he heard the news when he returned to town, and how he had prayed for our family. He took the time to visit with us at length, to listen and ask questions, which Rusty and Don helped answer when I couldn't speak, and to offer prayer and support. There I was, meeting the pastor of our son's favorite church, *Rain-bow For-est Bap-tist Church*, but not under the circumstances I had originally envisioned.

The following month I returned to Virginia with Kurt, planning to visit the second church on the list, Calvary Memorial. Before Sunday we got in touch with Greg and Beth Reed, the couple Mycol had met at Calvary Memorial and who had my family out to their home for dinner one evening after church. When they invited Kurt and me to dinner, I quickly accepted, anxious and excited at the prospect of finally meeting them.

When we arrived at their home, we met another couple as well, Graham and Trina Stephens. Graham had been Mycol's Sunday school teacher when my family visited Calvary Memorial. Both of these couples were so gracious and compassionate in their willingness to meet and talk with us. What a gift it was to me to be in the same house and to sit at the same table and eat dinner with Greg and Beth, just as my family had done, and to talk with them about Mycol, Austin, and Jess. In true Christian example, they listened attentively and, through their compassion, willingly stepped into the fog of pain with me. They didn't try to "fix" anything; they just loved me by listening and by giving me the gift of their time and willingness to hurt with me.

Beth introduced me to two of their three sons and asked the boys to talk to me about what they remembered about our children. One of the boys told me he remembered playing Matchbox cars with them. As I listened to him talk about our children, about the things I knew they loved, about a gap of time I hadn't been able to spend with them, those moments of listening, though filled with pain, became sacred to me.

Then the younger son approached me shyly, at his mother's urging, and with a look of compassion in his young eyes, shared his memories of jumping on the trampoline with Austin and Jess. "They were good catchers," he said, referring to a game of tag they had played together.

In addition to the memories their kids shared with me, the Reeds and Stephenses also related every memory they could think of about Mycol, Austin, and Jessie–their conversations, their thoughts and impressions, the things they laughed about, the things Mycol told them. They really liked Mycol, and Graham said he was impressed with Mycol's knowledge of the Old Testament and his obvious genuine love for his family. With so little in the way of tangible things from my family to hang on to, memories like these are priceless.

Unfortunately, the night before we planned to attend church at Calvary Memorial, a snowstorm blew in, and most church services in the area were cancelled–all except *Rain-bow For-est Bap-tist Church*. So Kurt and I went back to *Rain-bow For-est*. At the end of the service, Pastor Grooms mentioned we were there and asked the congregation to pray for us.

The next trip back the following month wasn't as snowy, so I again planned to visit Calvary Memorial. I called ahead and arranged to meet with Pastor Mark Vaughan a couple of days before Sunday, and he graciously gave me his undivided attention, sitting with me in his office for several hours as we talked about all that had happened.

Pastor Vaughan remembered the night of the fire, and the flood of emotion was obvious as he recounted talking with his wife after hearing the news. He told me how the news affected them–how they held each other and cried, how they talked at length about the pain and grief they knew I would face, and about the inevitable thought, *What if that happened to us?* He offered prayer and support, and he showed genuine compassion by taking time to listen and by sitting with me. Like the Reeds and the Grahams, like Rusty and so many others, Pastor Vaughan made himself available and willing to enter my pain so that, at least for that period of time, I would not have to be alone.

Each visit to a church, and even more so, each visit to a Sunday school room where Mycol or our children had been, are emotional times for me–holy moments that I desperately needed to have and to hold on to. After the service at Calvary Memorial on Sunday, I went to each of the Sunday school classrooms where my family had gone, just as I had done at *Rain-bow For-est Bap-tist Church*. I walked into the rooms that had been graced by the presence of my husband and children, and I experienced where they had been, standing, looking, imagining, soaking those places into my spirit.

A few months later I had the opportunity to visit the third church on the list, Lakeside Baptist Church in Salem. I was at my cousin Jan's home in Marietta, Ohio, for the weekend, and Aunt Marge also happened to be visiting that weekend. On Saturday night I asked if she'd like to go to church with me in the morning, and she immediately agreed.

"In Virginia?" I asked.

She was surprised at first, but then the light came on, as if she had just remembered, *This is Linda we're talking about here, so anything goes!*

We got up early enough to drive from southern Ohio, through West Virginia, and down to Salem in time for the worship service. When it ended, Aunt Marge and I introduced ourselves to the senior pastor, Reverend Art Hearne. I had met him at the Franklin Graham Festival a few months back and told him then I'd be coming to visit in the future. Like the pastors of the two previous churches I visited, Reverend Hearne greeted us with sincere compassion and sympathy, and then asked if we were available the rest of the afternoon to visit away from the crowd that attended this large church.

We were honored by his invitation and made at ease by his relaxed and warm demeanor. I explained that I wanted to see the Sunday school rooms where my family went, so we made arrangements to meet for lunch after our tour.

As Aunt Marge and I ventured toward the Sunday school rooms, we met a lady who turned out to be one of the teachers. We told her who we were and that we wanted to see Austin and Jessie's classrooms, and her eyes filled with tears. She remembered my family well, and she took us through the kids' classrooms and explained all she could remember about what the children did the day they visited Lakeside. She pointed out where they played, colored, and had story time. She painted the picture for me of our precious little ones, sitting side by side, showing me exactly where they sat, and telling me things she remembered them saying. She remarked that they were very close and stayed together during class, helping each other whenever needed, and that it was obvious as she watched them that they knew a great love and peace in their lives.

Then she turned to a stack of papers and pulled out a small, beige piece of paper, which turned out to be the sign-in sheet from the week Austin and Jessie were there. She said she had been holding on to it for some reason, but she hadn't known why until Aunt Marge and I arrived and asked to see the rooms. Moved by the significance of our meeting, she tearfully, carefully handed the paper to me. I stood there in that children's classroom, holding a piece of paper my precious children had touched, looking at their names, written by their own hands. Bathing in yet another painful but meaningful experience, I received this as another holy gift.

After spending time in each of the classrooms we met with Reverend Hearne and his wife, Sharron, and went to lunch. They showed their compassion in their willingness to listen when I talked about painful things, and their encouragement came through their prayers and in their paying attention, listening without trying to fix anything, and just genuinely caring.

On my next trip back to Virginia several months later I visited the last of the four churches, First Baptist Roanoke. Unfortunately, the pastor was unable to meet with me, but Don Eckenroth was with me on that cold and snowy day, and after the service we toured the building, looking for the Sunday school rooms where each of my family members would have attended.

The snow was falling hard and fast. A crippling storm was forecast, and most folks were eager to get on the road before it was too late. As Don walked me down the hall to the area of children's classrooms, we looked for someone who might be a teacher or who would at least know something about where the four and five-year-old classes would be. Then we happened upon one straggler, apparently unconcerned about the weather: Linda Shelton. When Don asked if she could show us the classrooms, she cheerfully pointed out the doors and offered to walk us to the rooms, although she didn't yet know why we were asking.

Walking into each of those Sunday school rooms was as sacred to me as it had been in the other churches I visited. Thinking back on that day and that time right now, I am overcome with feelings and senses that words are inadequate to describe. As I stepped into Jessie's classroom, I turned to Mrs. Shelton and asked in a wavering voice, "How long have you been teaching here?"

Don put his arm around my shoulders in support as I awaited her answer.

"Oh, several years," she responded.

"Would you remember a couple of children who visited last year?" I asked, shaking inside with anticipation and hope.

She gave me a momentary stare, a look that made it clear she knew this was important, and then, in that moment, I sensed she had an inkling...

I was right. "Are you... Jessica's mother?" she asked.

It was obvious Don was stunned, even as I was once again overtaken by emotion. All I could think of was, *She remembers!* But not only did she remember Jessie; she also remembered Jessie's pink boots, and how Jessie and Austin were very close and stayed together, as best friends, and how they were very respectful and obedient, attentive and friendly.

Linda Shelton, it turned out, was the teacher of the four-year-olds' class–Jessie's class. "I've been wanting to find you!" she exclaimed. "I've wanted to meet you and tell you that I had them in class and that *I remember them*. I've wanted to tell you everything about our time together."

She *remembered*. She *remembered our children*. She *remembered* exactly where Jessie sat and what she did. She *remembered* her coloring. She *remembered* what she did at play time and story time, how attentively she listened and was familiar with the Bible stories and could answer all the questions.

I can't put into words how important it was for me to meet Mrs. Shelton that day. It was such a moving experience. She told me everything about the hour she had with our little Jess. She repeated how she had wanted to meet me and that she wanted me to know that Jess had come into the classroom and fit right in. She participated in everything and was such a happy little girl. Mrs. Shelton assured me through her own tears, "On Jessie's last day on this earth she was very happy."

Jess had made a huge impression on Mrs. Shelton, and I am so grateful for that meeting with her. She also took us to the room where Austin likely went to class. She said April Bates probably would have had him in her class. I wish Mrs. Bates would have been there too, and I hope some day to meet her, but I am so very thankful for meeting Mrs. Shelton.

The entire experience touched me deeply. It is so important to me that I was able to meet people who met my family while I was still in Houston. It is comforting to hear people talk about the impact my family made on them and to hear people say they remember and to share with me how my family impacted their lives.

Linda Shelton did just that. She told me everything she remembered about what Jess did that day in her class. She filled in a gap of time for me, time when I was not with my family. She shared with me a piece of their lives that I had missed. She had seen my family more recently than I. In fact, she had seen them on the very last day of their lives on earth. In telling me everything she knew of that time, she gave me a great gift, born of mercy and compassion; she laid out her memories for me to share, and in doing so, a part of my soul bonded with hers. As in each of the other Sunday school rooms where Mycol, Austin, or Jessica were present, these were holy moments for me, as I stood in those rooms and thanked God and each person who was willing to endure the pain to give me these gifts.

"God Is with You"

One of the things I've learned about grief is that each of us handles it differently. Grief doesn't come in distinct, successive, orderly stages. We don't leave one stage and enter another, neat and clean and ready to move on. Stages of grief blend and overlap and mesh, so that sometimes figuring out emotions and understanding our thoughts and behavior adds confusion to grief. For each individual, grief in all its facets takes…well, as long as it takes. Shock, denial, anger, guilt, depression, fear, and acceptance are the seven classic stages of grief through which every griever must travel, whether we walk, slide, crawl, or allow someone to carry us. I've spent long periods of time in shock, anger, and depression, often coinciding one with another. But while it's helpful to know the stages of grief and to know that it's normal to experience them in variations of time, order, and intensity, for me, seeking God's will has been paramount. Terri Camp was right: Fasting, praying, and listening for God's voice and looking for guidance from the Lord are the healthiest ways to make this journey. Over time I prayed more and more over Hebrews 11, the faith chapter. As I did, the meaning of it all began to sink in: *Even though I do not understand, I will trust Him.*

A few months later, now entering the second spring season without my family, I returned to Virginia for another visit. On Saturday I went to church with Don at the Seventh Day Adventist church where he and his family were members. The message that day was from Hebrews 11.

Now there was a time I would have considered such a "coincidence" to be more than slightly ironic. Not anymore. Since the fire I had experienced this sort of thing many times, and I had come to accept that God had purposed for me to be there and to hear that particular message. It confirmed to me the hope I have in believing the words of Hebrews 11.

The next day, a Sunday, we went to the Methodist church in Vinton. Don re-introduced me to his friend Steve Musselwhite, who was a member there and who also served as our chauffeur the year before when we all came for the memorial service. This was the church that provided use of their fifteen-passenger van.

During the worship service communion was offered. The congregation went, row by row, up to the front to kneel, pray, and receive communion. As the first row of people knelt and prayed, the second row stood behind them and placed their hands on the shoulders of those kneeling in front of them, and then prayed for that person. When the first row was finished and returned to their seats, the second row knelt to pray, again with a row of people behind them, praying for them as they took communion.

As our row approached the front, Don and I knelt, and the pastor continued in prayer. Then–and again, I knew it was no coincidence–just as Don and I were taking communion, the pastor began to quote the lyrics from Mercy Me's "I Can Only Imagine," one of the songs I had chosen for Kurt to use in the memorial video.

I think you could have knocked me over with a feather at that moment. The pastor didn't speak in reference to this song with the group before or after me as we knelt. He reached that point in his prayer *just as Don and I knelt to pray and receive communion.* Too many significant things had happened over the past year and a half for this to be a coincidence. I knew I was right where I was supposed to be, and God was with me as He had promised.

After the service Don introduced me to the pastor, who asked if I would consider returning some time and sharing our story with the congregation. We agreed to set a date later.

On the drive back, Don asked me what I thought of the service. I purposely avoided addressing the significance of the pastor's reference to the lyrics of "Imagine" because I needed some time for it all to sink in. But Don is good with helping me see the big picture. He had noticed the significance without my even mentioning it, and he admitted he was blown away by it.

"I couldn't believe my ears when he started reciting those words just as we were kneeling to pray," Don exclaimed. "Linda, God is with you, and He wants you to know that. None of this happened by chance."

The Desire of My Heart

There is nothing like the love and support of family and friends, and I had many of them in my corner. For instance, several months after the fire, Mycol's sister Reba sent me an email, in essence, acknowledging and applauding the love Mycol and I had for one another, and thanking me for making Mycol's life on earth such a happy one. Though I did my best to express the depth of my appreciation to her in a return email, my words fell short of how very much her message of affirmation meant to me.

In grief's complex mix of emotions, shock and/or numbness seemed to represent the initial stage for me. I've learned that initial numbness can actually be a gift because it helps the griever do necessary things that at a later time, after the numbness has worn off, would be too painful to endure. I attempted to express this in a letter to a friend:

Today I would not be able to do what I did back in February and March—that is, dig through the rubble. Today I shudder at the thought of it. Much of the numbness, and shock, has worn down and I have experienced severe pain. Although, at times there is still shock and disbelief. All the elements of grief come and go constantly, intermingling, making it a very difficult process to work through. And "work through" isn't really a good phrase because that sounds as though there is actually an end to it. There isn't—not in this life. The end to my grief will come when I join my family.

Struggling with being separated from them, I added these words to my journal:

There are things I need to know that only God can reveal to me. Truthfully, I hurt all the time. Everything about me has changed but I am not ready to be changed. I am still Mycol's wife and Austin and Jessie's mommy. I can't flip a switch and make that not so. Now, at every moment I am somewhere I was not supposed to be, doing something I was not supposed to be doing, so at every moment I am face-to-face with a life I don't want, being left behind, separated from my family. I want more than anything to be with them NOW; to see them, hear them, touch them, and laugh with them, falling on the ground with knock-down hugs and elbow-pinchings.

As time went on, I began managing better on the outside, but I didn't feel any differently inside. I was learning how to walk with this grief. Confiding in Rusty that I might write a book, he gently suggested that the first step might be to return to work, to get myself out of the house and around people again. As I prayed about sharing this experience through a book, I wrote in my journal:

I have no idea how this book will come together. It seems like it will take so much energy to write. I wonder if that's even the Plan anyway. Maybe not. But now I have to return to work and I do not want to do that. I have no desire for anything but to be reunited with my family. I want to be happy with them again. So how do I write a book? And what's the story, "Once upon a time there was this girl"…?

The desire of my heart was for God to use this tragedy to His glory, but I had no idea how He would do it.

Song of Solomon 2:10

"Rise up, my love, my fair one,
And come away."

Chapter 18

Recognizing the Sifting

Meanwhile, after several months of tracking and testing, Myles' transplant was declared unsuccessful in November, 2003. This meant the family would have to stay in Durham longer and plan for a second transplant. But Dr. Buckley would not give up. As a pioneer in this type of medicine, she was willing to try again. And so we continued to pray for our little Myles, even as I continued to battle with my own grief and heartache.

When I approached the first December without my family, as well as the January one-year mark since the fire, anxiety built inside me. I knew I needed to get away from the traditional American Christmas celebrations, and that meant getting away from anything that triggered painful memories. It wasn't that I wanted to leave the rest of the family–in fact, I didn't want to leave Rusty and Lynna, my daughter, Missy, or anyone else, for that matter. But I just couldn't handle being there with them, doing what everyone else does this time of year–the same time of year that just one year previous we had left Texas, hauling our belongings through the South and arrived in Virginia. Now I felt I had nowhere to turn, nowhere to go. In desperation I ran an Internet search for secluded cabins, and then sent out requests for information to various places in the U.S., Canada, and Europe.

The first person to respond was Jo-Anne Goulden, owner of Whispering Waves Cottages in Ingomar, Nova Scotia, Canada. When she emailed me with information, I called to make the reservation and Jo-Anne asked which cottage I wanted. I hadn't considered that before, but I suddenly realized the cottages might be decked out with the traditional seasonal decorations, the very ones I was trying to get away from, so I asked, "Is there anything available without any Christmas decorations?"

"There is if that's what you want," came her warm reply. I was relieved when she didn't pursue me with any personal questions; she just took down the information to accommodate me. I so appreciated her sensitivity in not pressing me for details or questioning why I would want a cabin with no seasonal decorations. Whispering Waves sounded like a safe place to be, and so I chose to spend my first Christmas after the fire in Nova Scotia.

Off to Nova Scotia

When I told the rest of the family what I was going to do, I think some of them thought I'd lost my mind. But I knew it was the right thing for me. As I said, it wasn't that I wanted to be alone–I definitely did not want to be alone at that time. But everyone else was planning to celebrate the Christmas holiday in the traditional way, so there was really nowhere for me to go. The family wasn't being insensitive; their needs were just very different from mine. Rusty did try to convince me to stay and be with the family, but I did my best to explain to him why I had to go away.

I decided to drive first to Durham, North Carolina, to spend a day with Angie before flying north, making Durham my round-trip city for the flight. Angie and I had a wonderful time together, just doing mother-daughter things. She hadn't been able to get out much because of Myles' condition, so this was a treat for her while Justin stayed home to care for Myles.

The next day I left for Nova Scotia, headed for a little cabin on the water. When I arrived Jo-Anne took me to my cottage, showed me around, and said if there was anything I needed, just call. She had made all the preparations I had requested before my arrival. I had given her a grocery list, and she did all the shopping and filled the refrigerator and pantry with everything I requested. After she left I collapsed on the bed and cried. I spent six days there in that cabin on the shore.

On the second day Jo-Anne came by to check on me, and as she stood at the door with the comfortable look of a sensitive friend, she said, "If you ever want to talk, I'm here."

When she turned to go, I said, "Well, if you really have time…" The next thing I knew, I had invited her in.

Our friendship deepened quickly, as I told her of my reason for being there, how I was hurting, and that I didn't know what to do. Jo-Anne listened compassionately and then told me her own story. Her father had been killed in a house fire, and she had been there at the time. She knew something about the kind of pain I was feeling, although her own experience was unique from mine. The smell of smoke still made her shudder, however, and she soon became another person who was willing to enter the pain and just sit with me and let me be. She has had other tragedies and struggles in her life as well, and has since emerged a wonderfully strong, kind, and gifted woman–one who has learned how to walk with pain. It was obvious it was no accident that I came to that little cabin in Nova Scotia.

I took many walks along the frigid beach during those six days, watching the lobster fishermen attempt to get their boats out of the frozen water. Sometimes they stopped to chat and educate me on the trials and pleasures of a career in lobster fishing. The smell of fish was mild, probably thanks to the cold, sharp wind on the coast, but seeing them drink coffee made me a little jealous while I fasted.

Before leaving on this trip I planned to take this significant time, the first anniversary of the time we moved, which was 5 p.m. December 24 to 4 p.m. December 26, to fast and pray. Commemorating our move to Virginia, I sought God's direction, His voice, His comfort and guidance. As I began what would be many hours of prayer over the next couple of days, I asked God to speak to me through His Word. Then I opened my Bible to the book of Luke. I hadn't planned on what to read, but I figured wherever I opened would be as good as any place. I ached to hear from the Lord again, and He clearly had more to tell me. And as you will see, it was no coincidence I opened to Luke.

As my fast ended, I delved into something I was looking forward to. On my shopping list I had asked Jo-Anne to find all the ingredients for a peanut butter and jelly sandwich and tomato soup. I hadn't had that combination since I was young, and it was a real treat after my time of fasting.

Jo-Anne, of course, stopped by to check on me every day, and that was a great comfort to me. One night she even fixed a gourmet fresh lobster dinner, and we also spent two evenings painting together. Jo-Anne is quite an artist and has incredible patience. She showed me how to paint a mountain scene from a photograph in a book, and I was quite surprised with how it turned out. I never considered myself an artist, but this thoughtful friend opened up some new doors for me to explore.

Coming Home Early

After a few days Angie called. "Mom," she said, "would you consider coming back to Durham early?" She said Justin had this feeling, a persistent urging, that I should be back in Durham, even though he couldn't explain why he felt that way. But I had fasted and prayed, and I believed God was showing me that He heard my prayers.

And so I flew back early, planning to attend church with Angie in the morning. But then Justin got sick and was unable to care for Myles, which meant Angie had to stay home from church, since Myles didn't have enough immune system function to be in public, especially in a church nursery. What happened after that was another revelation and evidence of God's presence, as I explained in an email to Rusty:

My cousin's 23-year-old daughter, Ashley, works as a director of children's activities for the Salvation Army. She took a two-month leave of absence to return for another mission trip to the Dominican Republic. She shared our story with the people there, and the ladies she is serving dropped their plans for the day to have prayer for ME. Wow! When she told me they cried and prayed, and some of what they said, I was just blown away. Ashley prays for me a lot, if not daily. Recently she shared with me the part of scripture where Jesus said to Peter, "Satan has asked for you, that he may sift you as wheat. But I have prayed for you..." I didn't recall reading this, so I asked her where that was. She didn't remember right offhand, but said she'd get back to me with the "address" of that scripture.

But before she could respond, as I was in Nova Scotia fasting and praying, I asked God to lead me in His Word. After praying this, I opened to the book of Luke, and as I read, I came across that scripture. Jesus said it to Peter at the last supper. What an impact this has had on me! First, I was hit with the fact that there was an adverse situation going on, and Jesus PRAYED for something to happen for a person–something I have not been believing. This scripture was really speaking out to me. Loudly. So while I was praying during this fast I asked God for several specific things, including understanding.

Today Angie had invited me to go with her to her church here in Durham, but Justin was sick last night so she had to stay home with Myles. I had no intention of going to church by myself, but I went out to get breakfast and passed by a small church. Something tugged at me when I looked at that church, but I went on to eat. After I finished, it was still tugging. So I called Angie and asked her where her church was. It was one block from where I had gone to breakfast! As it turns out, it was 11:30 and their service begins at 11:00. So I went. They have a traditional type of service so the pastor was just about to deliver his message when I got there. What timing...

After church I introduced myself to the pastor, Dr. Lloyd Braswell. He knows of our history and had told Angie he would like to meet me. In fact, he and I have exchanged a few emails as I have thanked him for being so supportive of my daughter while she's here.

I met with him for over an hour. I shared with him several things I don't understand and asked him lots of the same questions I've asked others. Specifically, I told him about feeling that oppressive presence and hearing that threatening voice the night of the fire, after saying, "Satan, get out of our church!" I asked him who said, "How will you feel if you lose your family?"

Like everyone else I've asked on my search, he said he didn't know, but, different from anyone else I've asked, he followed that up with a question I hadn't anticipated. He asked, "What do you think?" He doesn't even know it, but as I began to answer him, things unfolded to me as I spoke. It was as though I weren't the one talking.

I said, "God already knew what was about to happen, and its possible Satan did too. It's also possible that at that moment the fire may have already started. Satan could have seen what was about to happen and wanted me to think it was because of what I said, so he just used what was already going to happen to take credit for it. Satan could have said that in the hope that I would blame myself and turn my back on God for not protecting them." It has been working, but not anymore. Now I look at that thing as Satan taking advantage of what was going on and making it look like something else.

Then I suddenly recalled that verse: "Satan has asked for you, that he may sift you as wheat. But I have prayed for you..." It's Luke 22:31-32.

Justin is the one who suggested to Angie to ask me to leave Nova Scotia early and return to Durham for a few more days. After I fasted and prayed for God's direction, He used Ashley with Scripture; Justin, to suggest Angie ask me to change my plans; Angie to carry out that suggestion by calling me in Nova Scotia and asking if I would consider coming back to Durham early; and Hope Valley Baptist Church and Dr. Lloyd Braswell for talking it through! WOW!!!

Here's one hesitation I have about feeling celebratory about this milestone: I still hurt tremendously and am in constant pain with the thought of what happened to my family and with missing them. But I fasted and prayed and asked for answers. God knew I planned to take that time to fast and pray, and He used it to direct me to focus on what to ask for. During the fasting I also read over and over about persistence. I told God I was going to be persistent.

I was also especially moved by Micah 6:3-8: He has done so much for us, and asks so little in return.

Love,
Linda

My beloved brother who understood me so well knew just what to say:

I know from our conversations that your faith has been shattered. I also know that the God of Abraham, Mycol, Austin, and Jessie is still in control, and He has plans for you. (Don't ask me what they are; I don't know.) Continue to seek Him and His will and plan for your life. He still has something or things for you to do before your mission here on earth is finished. You are and always will be my special sis.

In regards to your conversation with Angie's pastor, Satan is the great deceiver—he never comes clearly into sight so as to reveal himself, but he works behind a veil that he himself prepares specifically for the weakness of an individual, so that individual won't recognize what is happening for what it truly is, but rather will think the deception is the truth. Lynna and I have both been praying that you would have a breakthrough while you were away. We, and so many others, just want what is best for you.

Love,
Rusty

I sent similar emails to a few others, sharing the revelation regarding "Satan has asked for you, that he may sift *you* as wheat. But I have prayed for you..." and received many wonderful and encouraging responses, particularly from Ashley, who had first pointed out the scripture to me, and from Dane, who had prayed with and for me for such a long time. They wanted me to know they were rejoicing with me, and I so appreciated their letting me know that.

Yes, that was the revelation brought to me during fasting and prayer: Satan sought to sift me, but Jesus and others have been praying for me in my time of need. I have not been abandoned or forgotten. I asked for guidance, for God to speak to me, and He did, through His Word in Luke, and through His obedient, faithful servants.

Matthew 28:19-20

"Go therefore... I am with you always, *even* to the end of the age."

Chapter 19

The Courier

On February 26, 2004, two-year old Myles underwent a second bone marrow transplant. This was the same day Austin would have turned seven.

The marrow was again taken from Justin, and after a six-month wait we celebrated the news that the transplant was showing signs of success. Lab tests were, for the first time, showing healthy reactions from his cells, and Dr. Buckley gave Angie and Justin the green light to move back to Indy, where Justin could return to work full time, and they could begin to build a new life.

Angie would have to continue to stay home with Myles, as he still would not be able to handle the exposure to germs imminent at a daycare facility or church nursery. But at least he seemed to be getting healthier, and we all celebrated that fact.

A Powerful Presence

Spring was on its way, and for the second time since the fire, I endured the date of Mycol's birthday, March 8, without him. Birthdays and anniversaries are both special and painful. This day's entry in my journal reads:

Today is Mycol's birthday, and this year in honor of him I began a three day fast, to end today; I finished reading Jeremiah, and read Romans 8:28-39, and the book of John, praying throughout reading each verse. I took the day off work and spent it doing a few things he, and we, liked doing, including getting the oil changed and car washed at the kids' favorite carwash place, and stopping for coffee from "Daddy's favorite coffee place." I prayed during this fast for God to give me direction and comfort. I sure believe in fasting. Every time I do it things are revealed to me. During this fast I got a little bit more direction and got some great comfort in the form of two very long phone conversations. One was with Terri Camp, and the other with Robert Rogers, whose family—wife and four children—drowned in a flood in Kansas City in the summer of the same year as our fire. I talked to Terri on Monday and Robert on Tuesday during my fast, and both conversations were really good for me. I only hope I offered to each of them as much as they gave me.

As Mycol has both given and left me with great strength from which to draw each day, so has this way of honoring him on his birthday. I feel God speak to me through these Bible books and verses, and I believe He guides me to specific verses that apply.

A few days after what would have been Mycol's thirty-eighth birthday, I met Jeremy Camp and his new wife, Adrienne, for coffee after their concert in Houston. They were so kind to make time to visit with me and listen to some of my stories. Perhaps because Jeremy understood better than to try to say that dreaded phrase "I know how you feel," I sensed he really could understand some of what I felt. No, it wasn't exactly the same. There are unique aspects to his pain as there are to mine, and no two people's grief is the same because no two relationships with loved ones are the same. Still, there were some things about this life and this particular kind of a thorn that Jeremy could understand.

Before we parted company Adrienne said they would like to pray with me, so we held hands and Jeremy prayed first; then I prayed, and then Adrienne. I have never before been comfortable doing that with more than one person, and usually I keep my prayer time to myself. But I was so moved after hearing Jeremy's prayer that I wanted and felt the need to pray out loud. I thanked the Lord for this time with Jeremy and

Adrienne, and asked that He continue to guide us in His way. I acknowledged His power and the fact that while we do not understand, we will trust Him. While we were there praying together, I can say I felt the powerful presence of the Lord. In all the times I've prayed with others, I can't recall ever experiencing exactly what I did that day. It was as if a healing power was present in a new strength, something that said, "I AM here."

After meeting with Jeremy and Adrienne, I called Terri and told her about the prayer time and how I'd felt God's healing presence as never before, and also how unusual it was that I would pray out loud. Terri cried tears of gratitude for her son and daughter-in-law's willingness to let God use their own pain to help others, and to be a significant part of my life.

As more significant things seemed to fall into place, I wrote in my journal, *I have been kind of obsessing over what this book is about. If the Lord wants a book written, He will have to write it through me. This cannot be of me. It clearly must be His message.* I prayed for a working title, the theme and the purpose. Shortly after Mycol's birthday, it came to me.

Reflecting on how we met–Mycol, working as a courier, coming into the law firm where I worked as a paralegal–I recalled a conversation we had about his job. He said he liked his job for the most part, but there was one thing he didn't like: he hated serving subpoenas. I asked why, and his response was that when he handed someone a subpoena he was giving them bad news, something that would ruin their day. Mycol didn't like giving anyone bad news; he only wanted to offer good. The book, I've said, must be His Message–one of Good News through our tragedy. The book itself is a courier, just as Mycol was when I met him. I wrote:

The book will be good news, but from real human experience; it will be exactly as Mycol and Jesus would want it to be, and I will use our tragedy to bring good news by telling of trust and faith and God's never ending Love for us, with the honesty of the humanness of pain, fear, anger, and doubt. I don't know why the fire happened, but as I pray and when I fast, He reveals things to me. My testimony is to encourage others, strengthening their faith so they can in turn strengthen others.

Through all that has happened and continues to happen in my life, I'm learning not to take God's timing for granted. Within days of that journal entry, during the worship service at a new church I was attending, Pastor Lino–from our previous church–preached on Isaiah 52:7, "How beautiful upon the mountains are the feet of him who brings good news, who proclaims peace, who brings glad tidings of good *things*, who proclaims salvation, who says to Zion 'Your God reigns!'"

This book would indeed be a courier, for it is a book about God's love for broken, hurting people.

Honoring Our Baby Girl on Her Birthday

Before I knew it, it was fall again, and November 12, came far too soon. We should have been celebrating Jessie's sixth birthday together, with cake and ice cream, games, and all her little friends. Instead, I searched my mind for ideas on what to do, how to spend the day. Missy and I would be taking this day off work to spend it together. The morning of Jessie's birthday, before leaving to meet Missy, I prayed, asking God to help me find a way to honor Him and my little Jessica on this very special but painful day. Missy and I didn't have any specific plans yet, other than just being together and enjoying one another's company. When Missy called to check on me, I apologized for running late and told her I'd be leaving the house shortly. But after we hung up I felt compelled to check my email. It would not have been unusual to receive well-wishes and e-cards on a day such as this. Someone might have sent some words of encouragement in honor of Jessie's birthday that I could carry with me throughout the day and also share with Missy. I opened up my email, and at that time in the morning there was just one email concerning our special day. It was from our friend Christin, who had lived in Virginia for a short time. Christin sent a very encouraging e-card, including a quote from a psalm, but that's not what got my attention. There was a banner ad along the top and bottom of the e-card that spoke to me as an answer to my prayer. The ad was from Campus Crusade for Christ, and it said, "Send Bibles to Iraq."

By now I'd had lots of those moments when I could feel something really significant, and I knew right away that this was one of them. Having sent Bibles to the 10-40 Window before, all I could say was, "Wow! Okay, Lord. I asked for a way to honor You and our baby girl today. This must be it!" So I clicked on the link to get more information.

I read up on the program and decided this is what we would do. The idea had great significance for me, which by now was no surprise because I had seen more than once that God desires a personal relationship with us and speaks to us each in an intensely personal way. As a family we had sent Bibles to a Persian-speaking area before the attack on our church. We were warned there would be spiritual warfare as a result, and we certainly witnessed it happen. Now I had asked God for the opportunity to honor Him and our baby girl on her birthday, and here was a banner ad asking me to trust Him and send Bibles to Iraq again. How could I deny Him such an obvious request?

I decided to wait until Missy and I were together to do anything, so I jotted down all the pertinent information and then set out to meet my daughter. As soon as we were in her car, I told her the exciting news. I wanted us to be together when I made the call, so while Missy was driving I dialed the number for Campus Crusade for Christ's Bibles for Iraq department. Needless to say, I was not anticipating what I heard next—a young woman's voice that said, "This is Jessie. How may I help you?" I was floored. The young lady who took our order for 100 Bibles to go to Iraq was named Jessica! I broke down in tears, and in a flood of emotion I told her all about our little "Jester." What an amazing confirmation that I was indeed doing what God wanted me to do to honor Him and our baby girl on her birthday.

Singing Praises in the 10-40 Window

Don Eckenroth pursued the idea of my joining the team of Answering the Call on their next trip into Sudan. The trip had been put off several times because of the civil war and other uncertainties that made it difficult to get into the country. After several postponements the departure date was finally set for late February, with a return date of about ten days later. As I prayed about this opportunity, I felt the Holy Spirit leading me to go, so I just went with the flow and told Don I would accompany them. I have been asked whether my decision to go to Africa was out of a desire to regain a sense of control or to "go to the belly of the whale." While my decision was not based on that, going to Africa turned out to be an important and fulfilling experience.

We left as a group from Roanoke, Virginia, on February 24, 2005. The core team, which consisted of Gus Foderingham, M.D., Elaine Frantz, R.N., and Don Eckenroth, as team leader and medical administrator, had already been there five times; this would be their sixth trip since 1999. Robert Krause, a twenty-two-year-old missionary from Virginia serving in the Congo, met us in Uganda and acted as our guide during our stay. We arrived in Africa first at Entebbe, Uganda.

Traveling by ground transportation into Sudan, a thirteen-hour drive on severely pitted dirt roads, we stopped for the night at Kai, sleeping in an Episcopal Church guest house. But even in this remote area, so far away from Texas and Virginia and all the places where I had shed so many tears, God had another revelation for me.

We'd been traveling for two days, and now it was February 26, Austin's eighth birthday. Don, Gus, Robert, and Elaine sat with me outside the guest house and listened as I spoke of our son, his favorite songs, his funny sayings, his favorite things to do. They wanted to know more about the little boy who, when I asked him, "Buddy, Mommy thinks you hung the moon. Did you hang the moon," answered with his usual dry wit, "Oh, Mommy, no. You're so silly! I hung the sun!" They wanted to know more about the little boy who captured my heart from the moment I discovered I was carrying him; the little boy whose birthday I could not celebrate in the usual way, with cake and ice cream and gifts and family and friends, because he was not here to laugh with and to hug and to sing "Happy Birthday" to. They wanted to hear all about my little prince.

Then my friends gathered around me and prayed. After that we sang, and I requested one of Austin's favorites, "Nothing but the Blood of Jesus." Their four voices carried the song when, remembering how sweetly my son's voice once sang it, I choked up so badly I couldn't get any sound out. We also sang another of our family favorites, "Shout to the Lord." Don had his laptop and compact discs with him, and he played song after song of praise and worship while we sang to our wonderful God.

Oh, how significant this was, for it was then that it all hit me. The realization was so deep and my emotions so turbulent as I let the truth sink in: As a family we sent Persian Bibles *to the 10/40 window*, and then the church came under attack, the fire happened, and Satan surely wanted to sift me. After prayer on Jessie's sixth birthday, the Lord prompted me to continue in His work by sending Bibles to Iraq–*to the 10/40 window*. And now here I was, on our son's birthday, singing praises to God *in* the 10/40 window! *I was in the 10/40 window!* I was in the very place where 90 percent of the world's population has never had the opportunity to hear the message of salvation, to be offered the gospel of Jesus Christ. God does do detail work!

As we sat outside and watched the sun set over war-torn Central Africa, Don, Elaine, Gus, Robert, and I sang praise and worship songs for over an hour, into the dark African sky. We sang and praised God with Austin in our hearts, and then my compadres gathered around and praised God for carrying me through and prayed for my strength to endure what was yet to come.

Ministering to the People of Southern Sudan

In the week I was serving with Answering the Call in Maridi, Southern Sudan, I saw and experienced many interesting things. The northern part of Sudan is Arab/Muslim. Southern Sudan, or New Sudan, is mainly Christian. *Parade Magazine* lists the top ten worst dictators in the world on an annual basis, and in 2005 the leader of Sudan went from the number-six position the previous year to the number-one position–the number-one bad guy in the world. His government has supported genocide, mainly of the black African people of the south. These precious people have been oppressed, enslaved, bombed, attacked, murdered, pillaged, raped, and abused during many years of civil war.

In January, 2005 the SPLA (Sudan People's Liberation Army) and the Sudanese government entered into a peace agreement, providing for six years of autonomy for the mostly Christian south, while leading to a referendum to secede from the Muslim-controlled north.

Southern Sudan is in desperate need of roads, clinics, schools, electricity, and running water. The peace agreement details how the two sides will share power and oil revenues; establishes separate monetary systems for each side; exempts Christians and other non-Muslims from the Muslim Sharia law; and provides for security arrangements involving the SPLA and official government armies.

Aerial bombing has left the Sudanese in the south dependent on food aid. Now people are planting crops and building houses, schools, and clinics, with the hope that peace will remain. Land mines are still buried in many areas, and travel is unsafe. At the time we were there, we were told we should not travel beyond Juba, as mines had not been cleared to that point. An estimated two million people died in the war from the time it erupted in 1983 until we were there in 2005.

Answering the Call has done a lot of work in Southern Sudan. That first year the team began by seeing patients under a mango tree, but eventually the people of Maridi built a little hut to serve as a clinic. Now they have a clinic building with concrete floors and brick walls, including a room where they store the monthly shipments of medicines sent by ATC.

In the first two trips over there Gus and Elaine treated patients, but when they had to leave, many had not yet been treated and might not be around the next time the team returned. And so the team decided it was necessary to help the people of Maridi (population about 24,000) learn to help themselves. Gus began teaching and training them to diagnose and treat the specific diseases they deal with in that area: tetanus, malaria, river blindness, diarrhea, malnutrition, and other common ailments.

On this trip, as I watched Gus teaching a select group of about eight to ten Sudanese, I was quite impressed with his level of success, given the fact that he had to work through cultural and language barriers. Gus is a remarkable person, and the Sudanese people are amazing survivors and bright, eager students.

At first Don had planned that my role would be to help out as a pharmacy technician. But when we arrived in Maridi we learned that since Answering the Call's last visit there, the people had made many advances, had educated themselves, and were continuing to see patients and run the pharmacy on their own. This was exactly what was needed, and the team was overjoyed to see that the needs from us had moved from treatment to education and encouragement. Great success stories have emerged from these medical efforts.

Telling My Story in Another Culture

Don asked if I would agree to a change in plans. Since the clinic was running well on its own, he wanted to know if I would be willing to share my family's story of tragedy and faith, and to give encouragement to the people of Maridi, who have endured years of war, famine, disease, and oppression. As a courier of God's good news I had just begun sharing our story in Texas, and so I was open to the idea in Sudan but concerned about how to tell the story, given the extreme cultural differences. I was asked to speak first with a small group of people at the home of Reverend Rhoda, a pastor and the head of the Mothers' Union, a Christ-centered organization that educates and encourages Sudanese women in their faith.

One of the things I struggled with was how to tell the story in a way that would make sense to people who have no exposure to or understanding of our American way of life; I wanted to share our story in a way that would survive cultural boundaries. I know how to tell our story here at home, but how would a Sudanese person understand the concept of buying one's "dream home," playing with Matchbox cars, cherishing children's crayon drawings, or finding a lost wedding ring? I turned to Robert Krause, the young missionary, for help.

We took some time for me to relate the story first to Reverend Rhoda, Robert, and Reverend Gersome (pronounced Gar-so'-ma), who also worked as our interpreter several times. What a tremendous help each of them was!

With Robert's assistance I began to tell our story in a way the Sudanese people could understand. Robert explained how the Sudanese are accustomed to seeing large trucks called *lorries* bring in supplies from the United Nations and other, non-governmental operations. They could also understand the concept of moving in the sense that so many of them, as their towns were under attack, had to flee to safer places, often relocating to their relatives' *tukuns* (mud huts with thatched roofs). If I explained that we put all our belongings into something like a lorry and moved to a time-honored family home that belonged at one time to my great-grandparents, they would understand.

And while their children don't really have toys, children are children everywhere and will play with whatever they can find. I could explain the little U-Haul as a symbol of moving, as a toy our children played with, as a message of God's presence and promise. In the case of Mycol's ring, Robert said, we would explain the symbolism, what the ring means to us, that it was lost, and then found again after my first prayer. We even found a way to relate the discovery of Jessie's drawing. By explaining the drawing and associating color with emotion, the Sudanese understood the significance of her picture and were moved by the gift that it is to me. Pain and loss they already understood; they needed no explanation for that.

What we ended up doing is altering the story in some ways, and explaining other things that were significant to their understanding. The point of my testimony, however, was essentially the same: Even though I don't understand, my God does. I was able to say to them that while I don't know how they feel, I do know suffering, and I do know pain. I could tell them that I, too, do not understand why, but that I came to encourage them. I testified that God speaks to each of us in ways we will understand, that He has shown me over and over that He is with me, and that He has spoken to me in ways meaningful to me. Finally, I could tell them that He speaks to each one of us if we will listen.

Robert is one remarkable young man, and we really clicked together as a team. As Gus was teaching his medical students, Reverend Gersome scheduled speaking engagements and assembled various groups of people to come and hear our testimony. I would share our story, and then Robert would follow up with scripture, prayer, and encouragement.

The response we received every time was really incredible. People wanted to touch Mycol's ring. They looked at photos of my family. Women were moved to tears. Both men and women wanted to hug and thank us for coming. Many asked us to come back.

Robert helped me immensely in finding ways to tell the story so they would understand. As we talked, I shared with him other things about spiritual warfare, such as the answer I received while fasting and praying in Nova Scotia: "Satan has asked to sift you, but I have prayed for you." Robert immediately recognized the verse as being from Luke 22:31-32. He flipped quickly to the page and read it aloud: "Simon, Simon! Indeed, Satan has asked for you, that he may sift *you* as wheat. But I have prayed for you, that your faith should not fail..." In the past, that was where I always stopped reading. But Robert read on: "...and when you have returned to *Me*, strengthen your brethren."

Robert stopped and looked straight at me. "Linda," he said, "that's what you're doing *now!* You're strengthening your brothers and sisters."

I hadn't realized it until then, but Robert was right. As the enormity of that realization hit us, we sat quietly for a moment, unable to speak. It seemed as though God was continually pointing out my life to me in His Word.

The next day, as we accompanied Reverend Gersome out into the bush to the home of Gersome's aunt who had passed away the previous night, we were asked to give words of encouragement to the extended family and friends who had gathered there to mourn. Again, I shared our story.

Later that day, following the morning worship service, Robert and I addressed a large assembly at the church. After that we spoke to another large group at the new school, where 502 children were enrolled, and then later at an adult school, with several hundred adults eager to learn more about God.

One day Reverend Gersome even took us all out to the open market, an area where there are several shade trees, where he managed to get the attention of hundreds of folks, and set us up to share our message of faith and encouragement right there in the marketplace. Speaking in the market (we called it "The Maridi Mall") was quite an experience, and I was a bit nervous. First we walked around and observed all the people trading their wares (what little crops they had, some soap, and various other items), and then Reverend Gersome asked if we were ready.

I had no idea how to start, and honestly, it was a little intimidating, standing in an outdoor market with thousands of people milling around. But Reverend Gersome started talking and getting everyone's attention. Once a large crowd had gathered, I tugged on Robert's sleeve and whispered, "You go first." Brave Sir Robert–I don't think he'd ever done anything quite like that before either–valiantly jumped right into it, which helped me tremendously because, as he was talking, I was able to think about how I would share our story in this unique situation.

Each time I spoke with a different group, the message came out a little differently. I believe that's because God wants to reach people in very personal ways. There in the market the theme turned out to be what Mycol kept saying in the last year of his life: "We are not promised tomorrow."

The people of Southern Sudan have suffered great losses for many years and are desperately in need of encouragement and hope. They are peaceful, loving people, who are hungry to know more about God. They want to hear about the gospel, about the love of God and the promise of heaven. They identify with stories of pain and grief. They hunger for comfort and reassurance. Their responses are, "Come back and encourage us again! We want to know more about God's love for us!"

James 1:17

Every good gift and every perfect gift is from above, and comes down from the Father…

Chapter 20

A Firefighter's Gift

We returned to the United States, to Roanoke, on Sunday, March 6, and before coming back to Texas, I stayed in Virginia a couple of days to visit with my aunt and cousins.

The next day Aunt Teen and I thought we'd venture out to Cracker Barrel for lunch (as soon as her favorite TV program, "The Price Is Right," was over). I was getting hungry, and right at noon, as the credits were rolling at the end of the show, I said, "Okay, ready to go?"

"Well," she said, "let me just see the first few minutes of the news, and then we can go." So I waited through about ten minutes or so of the local headline news.

One of the news items in that first few minutes was a follow-up story on the condition of a firefighter who lived in Buchanan, Virginia, a small town just outside Roanoke, near Troutville, in Botetourt County. His name is Don Keller, and he came home one night to find his house on fire. His parents were inside, so he rushed in to get them out. Of course, he hadn't had time to get any oxygen, but he was successful in ushering his parents out of the burning house. Then, knowing his fellow firefighters were on their way, he turned back and re-entered the home, thinking he could get a start on extinguishing the fire.

The TV news story was following up on his condition, reporting that he was still on a respirator at Roanoke Memorial. Here is the fire department's press release:

Troutville Firefighter Seriously Injured in Fire Involving His Own Home

Botetourt County—On Thursday March 3, 2005 at approximately 9:20 p.m. Troutville firefighter Donald Keller arrived at his home in Buchanan to find an alarming site... As soon as Donald recognized that his home was on fire he radioed the call in to the Botetourt Communications Center who immediately dispatched the local fire and rescue departments, which responded from Buchanan, Troutville, Blue Ridge, Fincastle, and Glasgow. While responding to a fire involving one of their own brothers, no one knew what lay ahead.

Before the first fire and rescue units arrived on scene, off-duty State Trooper D.R. Lambert Jr. arrived from his home nearby after hearing the cries for help over his scanner. When Trooper Lambert arrived he found firefighter Keller inside the residence trying to put out the fire with a fire extinguisher. Trooper Lambert yelled for Donald to come outside and when Donald attempted to do so, he collapsed in the doorway. Being pulled to safety by Trooper Lambert, Donald was found to be in and out of consciousness and barely breathing. Trooper Lambert provided lifesaving ventilations to Donald until the first Rescue units arrived.

While the fire was being extinguished, firefighter Keller was battling for his life. Donald was transported by Buchanan Rescue Squad to Roanoke Memorial Hospital, where he remains in serious condition.

As of Sunday morning, March 6, 2005, Donald's condition continues to improve, but he remains in serious condition.[v]

The news reported that Don Keller had developed pneumonia and that he had also had a heart attack–his second one. As I listened to the report, I knew I wanted to see him. I wasn't sure, but I thought there was a good chance he had been to our home to fight the fire two years ago. After all, Troutville isn't that big. So I went by the Troutville Fire Department, the station where Mr. Keller was a volunteer, and inquired. One of the guys there gave me Don's mother's cell phone number. I called her and asked permission to visit her son in the Intensive Care Unit. I had only given her my name, not the story behind why I wanted to see him, but without questioning me, she gave me the code word, his room number, and permission to see him.

With all the right information to be considered family, I was allowed into his room in the Intensive Care Unit. Don wasn't responsive at all, but I stood there and held his hand and talked to him. I told him who I was and that I didn't know whether or not he had been to my house two years ago, but I just wanted to thank him for his service to the community and for risking his life for others, and to encourage him to keep fighting and get healthy. I had felt led to bring in a copy of Jessie's drawing, so I did, but then I felt kind of odd, talking to someone who didn't know me and wasn't responding, so I wasn't sure what to do with the picture. After about fifteen minutes or so I figured I'd talked his ears off enough–if he could even hear me–so I said I'd be back in a month, since I was already planning a trip back anyway, and I told him I wanted him to talk to me then.

Feeling awkward as I turned to leave and fighting a persistent tugging at my heart that said, *Leave the picture*, I decided I'd learned enough to know better than to ignore that still, small voice, that prompting by the Holy Spirit, and so I turned and stepped back over to his bedside. Taking his hand again I said, "One more thing before I go, Don. My daughter drew a picture, and I want you to have a copy." I told him that as soon as he was able to open his eyes, I wanted him to look to his left, toward the window, and see the drawing Jessie had made, which I then taped to his hospital room window. I didn't know why I felt so strongly that I should do this, but I did.

After I left I thought that out of courtesy I should just touch base with his mother and let her know I had been there and also explain who I am and why I wanted to see her son. I called her, and after I explained everything she began to cry. "Oh, Linda," she sobbed, "I'm so glad you called. I'm so glad you went to see him. Linda, Don carried one of your children out."

I have no words for what I felt at that moment; her statement took my breath away.

Then she told me how her son had sat with her for many days after the fire, crying and telling her how much it affected him. She also told me he kept a copy of a photo of my family, which had been displayed at the memorial service, in his truck so he could always remember why he does what he does.

I was so touched. Tuesday morning after breakfast, before heading to the airport to return to Houston, I went back by the hospital and talked to Don again. He was off the respirator but still not really responsive. As he lay there, eyes closed, coughing from the irritation of smoke and the respirator tube that had been down his throat, I told him I now knew he had indeed been there at our home. I told him his mom had told me all about it, and I looked forward to hearing him talk and seeing him with his eyes open. I later explained the significance of Jessie's picture to Don's mother and asked that she make sure he got it.

Meeting One of My Heroes

In just one month Aunt Teen, by now ninety years old, was planning to take one last climb up the mountain that stood behind her home, and I was planning to return to Virginia to take that trek with her. I hoped Don would be fully recovered by the time I returned the next month so he and I could talk.

I spoke with Don Keller by phone the following Saturday afternoon. I had called his mother to check on his condition, and she said he had been released from the hospital and was, in fact, over at the fire station visiting his crew. I immediately called the station, and had a brief but encouraging chat with him. He still had lots of smoke in his body, but the doctors expected it to be out in two to three weeks; if not, they had a way of getting it out. In the meantime he was recovering and sounded great. I couldn't wait to see him, just to sit and talk together.

I asked if he knew I had come to see him, and he said he knew it only because his mother told him, but he had not been aware of it at the time. I assured him, "That's okay. We had a great conversation." He then said he did get Jessie's drawing, and we agreed we were both looking forward to our meeting.

On March 31, 2005, I joined my ninety-year-old aunt, cousins Bill, Nancy, and Jan, and several other family members for Aunt Teen's hike up the mountain, which later made the front-page news of the *Fincastle Herald*. The next day, I officially met Don Keller and found out that he had been to our memorial service in Roanoke, though I didn't remember meeting him at the time. For me, this was our first meeting–at least, the first one I remembered and in which we had a two-way conversation.

Don picked me up at the home of Grandma and Grandpa Sumpter, the couple who opened their home the night of the fire and served coffee and snacks and hot chocolate to the firefighters, and who also provided a place to warm up from the sub-zero wind chill. Don remembered being in their home that night, so coming to pick me up there must have been a strange experience for him.

We went out for a bite to eat, but neither of us was very hungry. We had lots to talk about, though: our fire, his fire, and how we were coping.

We talked for hours, and I don't think he will ever be able to fully understand the depth of the gift he gave me. Don took time with me. He answered my questions, while respectfully avoiding graphic details I did not want to know. Then, when we realized neither of us would finish our lunch, Don asked if there was anything else he could do for me. With some reservation, not wanting to push him if it was too painful, I cautiously asked if he would go "back there" with me. He agreed.

Don took me on the very route he drove from the fire station to our place, describing how things unfolded from the time he got the first call, and pointing out the spot where he first saw the glow in the sky–about four and a half miles away.

From the initial 9-1-1 call, the dispatcher radioed that the residents were believed to still be in the home. Don said when he heard that it was as if the rest of the world came to a halt and he became a speeding bullet, rushing to the scene, intent on saving lives. He went a long distance from his home to check in at the fire station, and then on to our place in only sixteen minutes.

Being a Level 1 firefighter and EMT, Don was handed a fire hose and told to go inside. So in he went, hoping to find an area without flames and to find people to rescue. Instead, as he crawled in through the same window A.J. Arney had tried to get in, his feet touched the floor and it gave way, sending him down toward the basement, the inferno surrounding him, the fierce winter wind spreading the flames and freezing the water from his hose. Fellow firefighters had to pull him back out while he clung to the fire hose.

Don literally took me back to his experience that night, narrating for me what was going through his mind and heart at the time, as he now chauffeured me along the same route in his truck as he had taken when he got the call. We weaved our way though the shortcut, the one where he wasn't supposed to take a big fire engine because the roads were narrow but had taken it anyway because it was faster. He spoke of his drive, his urgency to get there, his hope for rescuing the people inside. But for a moment he was appropriately and respectfully silent, as he pulled down his visor to show me the picture of my family. With a glance in my direction, just long enough for me to catch the meaningful look in his eyes before they returned to the picture, we made a connection that needed no words. If a fireman can be graceful–and he was–Don was graceful in the way he gently lowered his visor, paused long enough for us both to look at the picture, and then just as gently lifted the visor back up. There was respect for my family in the way he did it, and I got the sense he handled them with this same kind of honor and respect the morning after the fire.

We arrived at our property, and it must have been nearly as difficult for Don to revisit that scene with me as it was for me to be there with him. In spite of Ronnie Sprinkle and others having assured me that my family "moved to heaven" peacefully, now that I was here with the man who had found my family and stood guard over their bodies until the coroner came, I had to ask the question again. "Don, can you reassure me that my family didn't know what happened to them? Did they really go in their sleep?"

"Yes, there's no doubt in my mind," he answered. "They were found here," he said, pointing to an area that was our living room, directly beneath the upstairs bedrooms.

"I heard they were found *near* their beds," I pressed.

"Yes, near them. As the roof blew off and the top floor came down, they dropped down with their beds and it appeared they just fell off the beds." He paused and looked far off. This was hard for him. "They were already gone by then."

I knew I didn't have to worry about their final moments, but it was comforting to hear it again, especially from Don Keller. They weren't found huddled together in a corner or near a window trying to escape. They were in sleeping positions, each exactly as they would have been aligned with the location and position of their beds.

"They never knew anything. I'm certain of it," Don said.

The medical examiner's report confirmed what Sheriff Sprinkle, Don Keller, and others had told me. My family was first put to sleep by carbon monoxide, then breathed in smoke, and finally went from a sound slumber straight to heaven, into the presence of Jesus.

I had originally believed ours was a four-alarm fire, but Don explained that eight fire stations were called. Seven responded, and one was on stand-by. At any given time throughout the night and the following day, there were forty-five to fifty firefighters on the scene.

I will be forever grateful to Don Keller and to each and every firefighter who responded, coming to our home in the hope of rescuing my family. I am well aware it was a traumatic event for each person there, as Don told me that most were not able to sleep through the night for four to six months afterward, and each received counseling to deal with the trauma.

The men and women of fire departments all over the world, who put their own lives on the line every day to save others, are some kind of special people. Most of us have jobs, and some of us may have careers, but it has been my experience that for firefighters, what they do is their life. It is a level of dedication that few can understand, but the glimpse I got of that dedication the day Don Keller told me about the fire at our log house helped me in more ways than he will ever know.

As for the official cause of the fire, eight weeks of investigation by local, state, and federal authorities brought inconclusive reports. No one was ever able to tell me for certain how or where the fire started. Most likely it was either caused by a faulty heating system or something in the electrical wiring. Neither the mortgage company nor the insurance company required an inspection before we bought the house. Several electrical shorts were found during the investigation, and it appeared the breaker failed to shut off the electricity. With no working smoke detectors, my family was never awakened from their sleep.

The media had pursued Sheriff Sprinkle for answers, but before contacting them with the results, he had first called me and said, "Linda, I promised I'd let you know what we found out. We're going to have to make the official announcement that the cause of the fire is undetermined, but you and I know that's not really what matters. I'm going to call the media and let them know, so you might be getting some phone calls soon." I told him I understood, and I agreed: It didn't really matter how it happened.

Moving Out on My Own

I lived with Lynna and Rusty for eighteen months, as they cared for me, fed me, prayed with me, and supported and encouraged me in every possible way. During that time, they helped me prepare to return to work. My employer, McDermott, supported me during the long time I was away and held my job open until I was ready to return. Then, in September 2004, Rusty came to talk to me about a situation involving their daughter, Kelli, who was facing circumstances that would force her to move back home for a while.

"Linda," he said, "we're not asking you to leave; you know you can stay here as long as you want. But I want you to know that Kelli will be moving back home soon, and things will be different around here. We won't have the adult atmosphere, and we won't be able to have the privacy and intimate conversations as freely as we have lately."

Kelli wasn't immature, but just much younger than the rest of us. She had been renting a house from her parents, and it was located just down the street from their home. Now that the rental house would be vacant, I felt a nudge that it was time to take the first step toward living on my own, even though I didn't really want to come out from under Rusty and Lynna's protective wings.

My initial request was a bit tentative, but I sensed it was right. "Rusty," I asked, "could I rent the house from you, and just see how it goes?"

"We're not asking you to leave," Rusty repeated. "If you truly want to do this, fine; we'll help you out. But don't feel like we want you to leave, because we don't."

I had never lived totally alone before, and while the idea was a bit frightening, I knew I'd only be a few houses away from Rusty and Lynna, and they continually reassured me that I could return any time. And so, the next weekend Kelli and I sort of traded houses; she moved back home, and I moved down the street.

That Saturday night, as I was getting situated and preparing to spend my first night in a house all alone, Rusty was there for me. He helped me move, unpack and put things away, and even stayed late into the night and helped me make the bed.

"Do I have to tuck you in, too?" he joked.

I was doing my best to maintain my composure and mustering every bit of courage I could find. "No," I said, shaking my head. "I need to do this, Rusty."

"I know," he responded. "But just remember, you can come back any time. We don't care if it's in the middle of the night. And if all this turns out to be too much, just come back. Even if you're only here one hour, it's okay. You have a key, and the door is always open to you. You are always welcome back."

I so appreciated his reassurances, but despite my fear I made it through that first night–and the next, and the next. Many times it was difficult, and many times I stayed at Lynna and Rusty's house until time for bed. But then I went home for the night–and made it through until morning. I was taking those first forward steps.

And then, about a month after moving out, I discovered both Lynna and Rusty were going to be gone for an entire weekend, and I began to feel some panic. Nervous about being alone and not having them just down the street, I searched the Internet for ideas of things to do that weekend, hoping I would find activities to keep my mind busy.

Sure enough, I came upon an ad for an air show at Ellington Field in southeast Houston. *Well,* I thought, *I don't really know anything about airplanes or air shows, nor do I care, but this for sure will take up one of the days this weekend and will get me out of the house so I won't be sitting here alone.*

I told Rusty about it, and he thought it was a great idea. Going to an air show would be something new and different for me, with no painful memories attached; it's not something Mycol and the kids and I ever did. So Rusty gave me directions to Ellington Field.

That Saturday I spent the day at the Wings Over Houston air show. I watched the World War II re-enactments, the aerobatic pilots, the show of strength from our own Texas Air National Guard, and the world-famous U.S. Air Force Thunderbirds. At some point during the show, as I gazed up at the airplanes, I thought, *I wonder what it would be like to do that.* A little later in the day that thought came to me again, but when an F-16 fighter jet surprised the crowd with a low approach from behind and the thunderous roar of the jet engines made everybody jump, that thought returned with as much vigor and conviction as the F-16's power and force: *I wonder what it would be like to do that!*

Monday, two days after the air show, I began researching flight schools in Houston. When I found one at Ellington Field, I decided to visit. Within two weeks I began flight training with Anthony Schreiber at Cliff Hyde Flying Service, and within six months I had earned my private pilot license. Lynna and Rusty hosted a celebration in honor of my new license, and it was two and a half years after the fire, over Galveston Island and out over the Gulf of Mexico, that I flew my very first passenger, Brother Jim Clemmons. While not many words were exchanged during the flight, our bond was strengthened in sharing the unspoken understanding of what this flight meant.

Flying has been one of those gifts that dropped into my lap. Piloting an airplane began to do something good for me. It's not a euphoric or "closer to God" feeling, but a new adventure that challenges me to keep my mind sharp. Perhaps because I am adventurous the thrust and speed of the engine and learning to control the airplane make flying a source of satisfaction. The thrill for me is the technical challenge, being busy in the cockpit and knowing that "you're only as good as your last landing." To up the challenge, I began working on an instrument rating and commercial license, and began taking up aerobatics.

Since it was at an air show where I was first inspired to learn to fly, I was honored to meet the 2005 U.S.A.F. Thunderbird team, as they toured a hospital where Myles was receiving treatment, and I thanked them for their inspiration. The following year I was honored and grateful to spend some time after an air show with Major Nicole Malachowski, the first female Thunderbird. During our discussion about airplanes and how we each were introduced to aviation, she told me, "It's an honor and a privilege to be the first female Thunderbird, and a great responsibility, but this does not define who I am." She reminds herself daily so that this one accomplishment does not steer her life to stagnation, as would happen if she rested on this admirable feat.

Flying is an amazing experience. Who would have thought a simple Internet search would lead to something like that?

Mycol with baby Jess

In front of the fireplace at Kingwood house

Austin and Jessie at Jessie's 3rd birthday party

Jessie blowing out candle at 3rd birthday party

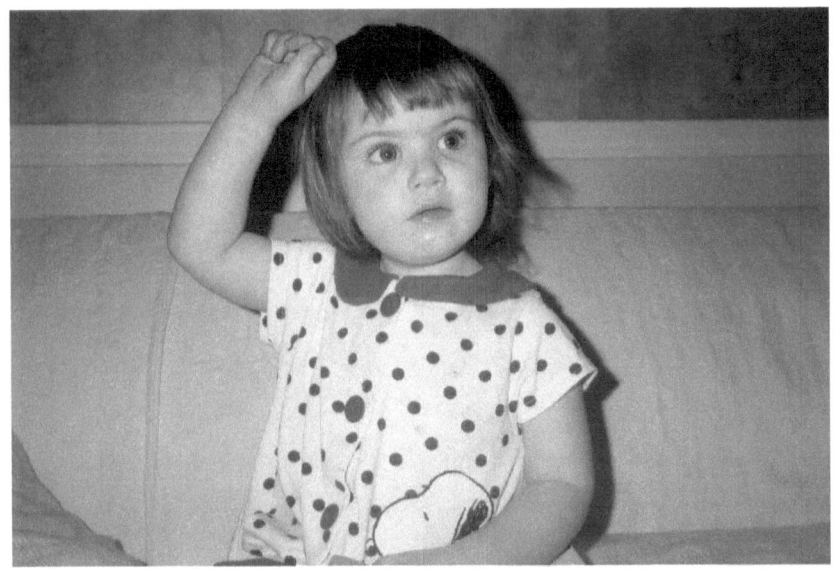

Jessica Logan Street

Cowboy and Cowgirl

Jessie petting goats at rodeo

Austin and Jess on a tractor

The U-Haul

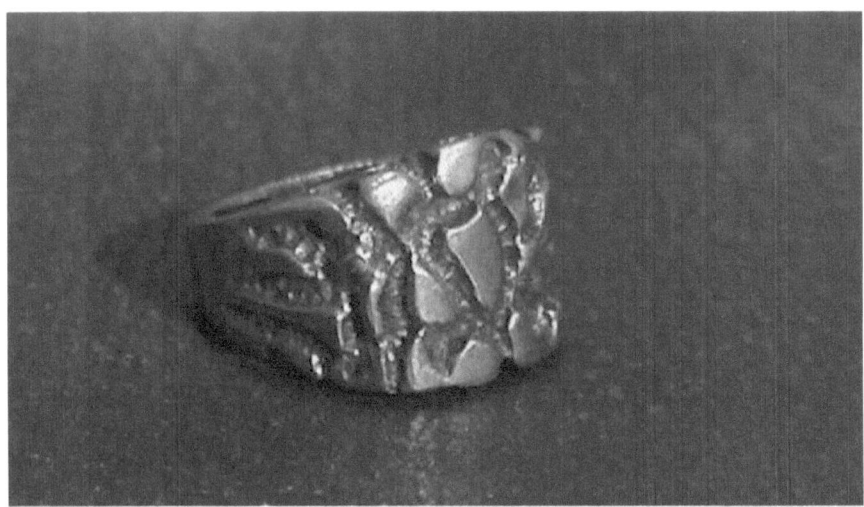

Mycol's ring

View of log house in snow

Jessica in the snow—one of the last pictures taken of her

Austin in the snow—one of the last pictures taken of him

Austin and Jess on the porch of the log house—one of the last pictures taken.

Part III

The Eternal

Acts 1:8
"But you shall receive power when the Holy Spirit has come upon you; and you shall be witnesses to Me in Jerusalem, and in all Judea and Samaria, and to the end of the earth."

Chapter 21

A Second Trip to Sudan

April 5, 2005, would have been Mycol's and my wedding anniversary. In honor of that day I planned to fast and pray throughout the morning, seeking a revelation from God. Then I would drive down to Galveston Island, ride a horse along the beach, which was something that appealed to me on this day of solitude, and then break my fast by eating lunch somewhere along the island seawall. Or so I thought.

As I prepared to leave, I called the people who rent horses on the beach to let them know when I'd be there. When the morning ended I drove south to Galveston, looking forward to a contemplative horse ride just out of reach of the waves that played tag with the shore at the edge of the Gulf of Mexico.

Upon arrival, however, I was met with a disappointing reality. The horse renters had not received any business earlier that day, and despite my phone call that I was on my way and unaware of the significance to me of that particular day, they put the horses up. All my begging and pleading could not change their minds, so I returned to my car, aggravated at the disruption to my plans.

Feeling cheated, I began to half-talk, half-cry to God: "I really wanted to ride a horse along the beach today, Lord. Why couldn't I do that–the one thing I wanted to do for *me*?" And then I sighed, tears of remorse wetting my face. "Okay, I know I set aside this morning to fast and pray, and now I'm about to break my fast. God, whatever it is You have to tell me, Lord, please, just speak to me."

At that very moment, literally, my cell phone rang. It was David Fuller, the director of Answering the Call.

"Linda? This is David. How ya doin', Buddy?"

"All right," I answered, not feeling like going into detail.

"I have a question for you," David said. "You don't have to answer me right away; you can take some time to think about it, but I want to ask you now."

"Okay."

His question was straight to the point. "Would you go back to Africa?"

Immediately I knew exactly what was going on. I'd seen it too many times before to think this could be a coincidence. I was fasting and praying; I had just asked God for a revelation, a message, some direction–and now here was David, asking me if I would go back to Africa. It was God's timing–again.

"I don't have to think about it," I said. "I already know. Yes, I'll go."

David's excitement nearly buzzed through the airwaves. "Really? Are you sure? That's great, Buddy! Thanks! I'll be in touch later with details."

Sharing My Story in Central Africa—Again

And so, in August, 2005, I made my second trip to Central Africa, this time for two weeks–one week in Gogrial, Southern Sudan, and one week in Bukavu, Congo, where we attended pastors' conferences. It was amazing–an experience I wish everyone could have at least once.

As a member of Answering the Call's team of eleven–eight missionaries and three media people–I had the opportunity to share my testimony of faith many times, striving each time to encourage people who felt they had so little hope. The trip was taped for television and aired first in Roanoke, Virginia, on the local ABC affiliate, Channel 13, for five consecutive Saturday evenings. Viewers saw five half-hour shows in reality-show format, similar to *Survivor*, but without the element of competition. The mini-series showed how eight ordinary American Christians survived two weeks in war-torn Central Africa, sharing their faith and encouraging others through the gospel of Jesus Christ. For the safety and security of the people who live in Africa, as well as some who travel there often to serve, I will change the names of many of the people involved, as I relate some of my memories of that life-changing trip.

My teammates were Dr. Jon Gudeman, an optometrist, who brought along a couple of cases of donated eyeglasses; three pastors: Dr. Charles Fuller, David Fuller, and Robert Krause (the young missionary I'd met on my last trip there); Phil and Rochelle House, a missions-minded couple (Phil is a musician, and Rochelle has her own personal story of hope to share); and Jamie Swann, a dula, which is similar to a midwife, without the direct involvement in the delivery itself. A dula is more of a patient advocate who stays with the new mother during labor and delivery and makes sure she is aware of all her options, which often the doctors don't do, so the dula's services are much appreciated. Finally, there were the three media folks: Steve Mason, the producer and host of the reality show; Kirk Wray, a camera man; and Melanie Blanding, an award-winning photographer who shot incredible life-touching photos for a book about the people and the work being done in Africa. Melanie is clearly gifted with an eye for photography and is able to bring pictures to life, honoring and glorifying God with her many blessings.

We began our two weeks in Liethnohm, which is in Gogrial County, Southern Sudan, with a three-day pastors' conference. As we made our approach to land on the dirt runway in a Cessna Caravan, we saw a large gathering of people, greeting us with songs of praise and dancing, one of them waving a white flag with a cross on it. These people had eagerly awaited our arrival and were showing us such great hospitality and welcome.

The residents of Liethnohm have little means of support. In fact, this was one place the war had prevented us from visiting when I was in Sudan the first time. Now, upon our arrival, we were shown to our rooms–mud huts, with two of us to a hut–and then we began meetings and planning for the conference. The conference was held under a large shade tree. Many pastors, as well as men who wanted to be pastors and evangelists, came to the conference, some making long journeys on foot, just because they wanted to know more about God and wanted to be encouraged in their faith.

In addition to the three days our group spent with these pastors, we also spent time with a group of women from the region who had been affected by rape, war, disease, famine, and terror. These women needed comfort, strength, encouragement, and hope.

On the first day I was asked to share my story with this women's group. Since there is a shortage of well-trained translators in the area, we had quite a bit of difficulty, but eventually the story was told. As I spoke to the group, a tall, slender woman from the Dinka tribe, dressed in yellow and carrying a wooden cross, arrived at the meeting. She was late, but her friends immediately made room for her, and many watched as she slowly, sorrowfully, made her way to her seat.

Although her reserved manner was typical for a Dinka, I could not help but notice there was something different about her. She appeared to be numb with grief, and I was immediately overcome with the memory of how I too had walked into rooms without feeling a thing other than disconnection with life. I thought, *she looks as disconnected as I have felt before*. Her demeanor was personally familiar.

Then one of her friends stood to speak, and through the translator asked that we pray for this woman in the yellow dress. What the translator was able to tell me was, "She believes God has damaged her three times, and she needs your prayers."

Without anything further from the translator, we moved toward her to pray. I knew in my spirit that she and I had something in common, even if I had no details. I placed my hands on her shoulders and prayed that God would reveal to her that whatever bad had happened, He had not brought about damage to her, but He grieved with her and loved her deeply; she was precious to Him, and He wanted to comfort her. As I continued pleading with God to help me with translation so I could be of service, tears streamed down my cheeks as I sensed God's compassion for this woman and continued to believe we had much in common to talk about.

The news spread fast that there was an American woman there who had been through hardship and heartache, and that she had come to bring a message of hope. Later that day I was scheduled to speak to the pastors and evangelists. Before that time came, however, I located the pastor who had organized the entire event. This pastor was the only experienced translator there, and he had been working at the pastors' conference that morning while I was ministering to the women. I asked if he could arrange for a private meeting between me and the lady in the yellow dress, and I also asked if he would accompany me as my translator. Despite being exhausted from a long morning of translating for the other pastors, he readily agreed. Once we had located the Dinka woman, the three of us found a place to sit and talk.

"I feel God has damaged me," she said, "and I am confused. I want to believe, but I do not understand, and it is so confusing to me. I don't want to believe the things of witch doctors and the traditional tribal spiritual beliefs, but I don't know what else to believe. We keep our cattle in a barn, and the barn was struck by lightning and burned, killing all our cows." The cows had been their only source of livelihood, and, of course, there is no insurance there. The barns are dried clay-mud huts with thatched roofs, just slightly bigger than their mud-hut homes.

The lady continued with her story. "Then our daughter was outside playing, and lightning struck and killed her." And then she told me of strike number three. "Soon after, our other daughter, our only other child, was also struck by lightning and killed."

How well I knew the confusion and fear that woman felt, how the world becomes a blur and nothing makes sense. I knew the experience of shock, and I saw it in her.

Gently I took her hand and shared my own story with her to open the door for her to understand that God was not damaging her. Then I told her I had been praying for her and that I had a message for her: "God loves you," I said. "You are His. He is not damaging you, He wants to comfort you." I went on to tell her that horrible, terrible, heartbreaking things happen and we don't understand why, but God is here, extending His compassionate love to us, and He grieves for us in our pain.

Through the work of the Holy Spirit, she knew we were kin. She knew what I said was true, but most of all, this proud, lovely Dinka woman accepted the love of God, saying she would bring her husband the next day.

Later that afternoon I presented our story to the pastors and evangelists, tying it to Isaiah 52:7: "How beautiful…are the feet of him who brings good news." I asked them to look at their feet and to know that God could use those feet to spread His Word. As they looked down at their dirt-covered feet–some with sandals, some without, some with open sores, infections, swelling, and various diseases–I told them God saw those feet as beautiful when used to share the love of Christ and the hope of eternal life, just as my own feet had traveled thousands of miles to get to Sudan so I could tell my story to encourage them in their faith.

During each of the three days of the conference we were given the gift of music, wonderful songs sung from the heart of these worshipful people, who are known for breaking out in praise songs, clapping and shouting, and singing to the Lord in the unique African way. Witnessing that is always such a blessed experience!

One Dinka man, whom I will call Joseph, led the conference in song each time we gathered together. Joseph is full of the Spirit, an incredibly dedicated Christian who has suffered severe beatings by Muslims because of his witness for Christ. Even after being beaten and left for dead a couple of years ago, Joseph recovered and asked for donations of bicycles so he could equip more pastors and evangelists to go out to the bush and share the love of God with people who have never even heard of Jesus. Watching and experiencing the atmosphere when Joseph led worship was an experience I will never forget, but what followed my testimony was something so great, so moving, that words can never do it justice.

I had just finished sharing my story when my dear friend Rob stood up and issued a powerful inquiry and invitation: Who would be willing to be soldiers for Christ?

"You who live here," he said, "you who have black skin and can go places where I cannot go, what are you willing to do for God? Will you go? Will you go and share the gospel? Even if it means you could be killed for your faith, are you willing? Who is willing? Who is willing to put his life on the line, to join this army of love, to share the news of the saving grace of Jesus Christ? Who is willing?"

Then Rob asked those who were willing to stand and come forward so we could pray for them. He said there was no pressure, and that if God was telling them not to go then he completely respected that and did not expect or want people to come forward just because someone else did. He asked only those who believed God wanted to use them as evangelists and who were willing to come forward.

Every seat was emptied, as people poured out into the aisles and streamed forward for prayer. Among the pastors and evangelists who had come to be encouraged, the very ones who had met us at the dirt runway with cheering and singing, waiting in anticipation of visitors who were willing to travel a long way to share the love of God with them, among the very ones who had suffered so much, not one remained seated.

As each one boldly stood and stepped forward toward Rob, all of us Americans ignored the tears that welled up and overflowed from our own eyes, and joined in prayer for these brave people, who know on such a deep level the importance of Christ in their lives. Rob was so moved he could no longer speak, so Dr. Charles Fuller took over, and we all prayed and rejoiced at the people's commitment and the movement of the Holy Spirit. In my spirit I could hear angels rejoicing, as I stood in awe of these people who wanted Christ more than anything. I was taken with the vision, and found myself thinking that one day I would be singing and dancing with my family–and with all these precious and courageous people–around the very throne of our God.

At the closing ceremony on the third day of the conference, our hosts put on a wonderful show for us. They brought in their youth group to dance and sing Christian praise songs in captivating African style, which was a real treat. Then they put on a skit. The youth portrayed a husband and wife and a critically ill teen-aged son. In the skit the parents had summoned a witch doctor who, after much chanting and dancing around, declared the son was cured and demanded payment (in the form of cows, their most common medium of exchange). When it turned out the youngster was not cured, the couple summoned another witch doctor, who claimed the first one wasn't any good and didn't really know what he was doing. The actors mocked the witch doctor, and the entire audience found comic relief in laughing at the ridiculousness of the whole mindset of trust in witch doctors. The second witch doctor couldn't heal the child either, but still demanded payment (more cows). Then a pastor happened by the family's home and came in to pray with them. He shared the message of the gospel with them, and together they prayed for healing for the son.

Now I personally believe prayer is for changing the hearts and minds of those who pray and for bringing them closer to the Lord, so advocating outcome-based prayer only sets us up for disappointment and confusion when prayer isn't answered in the way we want. However, the skit put on by this youth group was to show how they no longer have to put their trust in witch doctors; they are freed from that bondage and will trust only in God for all things. In that way, this youth group performed such a great skit that I know the angels in heaven must have been rejoicing and laughing right along with the rest of us. How excited and proud I felt that these people who barely have food to eat and clothes to wear still have adults who are willing to be youth leaders and to bring up their children with the teachings of Christ!

After three days of conference we prepared to leave for Nairobi, a stopover where we would catch another charter flight to Kigali, Rwanda, where in 1994 the Tutsi-Hutu massacre took place. If you've seen the movie, "Hotel Rwanda," you might imagine what its like to actually visit those killing fields. It was a haunting feeling and I was glad we were moving on, boarding a bus for a six-hour road trip across the border into Congo (formerly Zaire). We were headed for Bukavu, Congo, a port on Lake Kivu, which borders Rwanda and Congo, but before arriving for our stopover in Nairobi, I had developed an infection from an insect bite just below my inside ankle bone on my left foot. Overnight the infection spread, and in spite of oral and topical antibiotics given to me by a couple of my teammates, it got worse. I ended up unable to put any weight on my left foot, and soon the infection had spread down to my toes and up to just below my knee. My lower left leg swelled, and it was bright red, hard to the touch, and hot. I had shooting pains whenever I tried to put weight on my foot, or even with just the weight of gravity pulling on it, and I experienced a constant, severe ache all the way to the bones. During the long ride through Rwanda, my neck began to get stiff and achy, and soon I had chills. In addition, I could no longer walk on my own, due to the pain.

When we finally arrived at the Swedish guest house in Bukavu, Congo, one of the two missionary women who runs the guest house and who happens to be a nurse looked at the infection and said I would have to stay in bed that night–the very night we were scheduled for an all-night prayer vigil with our hosts. I really didn't want to miss this because earlier, when we had arrived at the Congo border, I saw so many people who had traveled for miles to welcome us. But by now I had a high fever and realized I would have to miss the prayer vigil.

Bukavu was one of the towns where Rob had stayed during his time as a missionary there, and the people were so excited to see him return. At the Rwanda-Congo border they broke out in song, shouting and clapping, happy to see Rob and Dave and the rest of us. Rob had often told me there's nothing like the vocal music of these gracious people, and I finally found out firsthand what he meant. They are so gifted in song!

I had also heard that over 600 pastors had registered for this two-day conference in Bukavu, and we'd be kicking it off with the all-night prayer vigil. I whined and complained about missing it, but Nurse Maggie insisted I could pray from my bed there at the guest house. Reluctantly, I obeyed.

The following morning it took me about thirty minutes to get my left foot from an elevated position to where I could stand on just my right foot, but even standing that way was quite painful. Gritting my teeth, I hobbled out to the van, which took us to the conference, where we began with praise songs like I've never heard in the U.S. After several minutes of praise and worship, each of the ATC team members, including the media personnel, were introduced to the conference attendees, who responded with a warm welcome. The rest of our time in Congo provided me with some of the most incredible, touching, deeply spiritual experiences I have ever had.

A separate program had been set up for women who were victims of rape and had HIV/AIDS; I was asked to spend the first day with those women. Having had no personal experience in these areas, I wasn't sure I could be of much help to them, but God showed me He could use my witness, despite the differences in culture, language, and experience.

As I limped to the front, a very helpful young man scooted a chair in my direction so I could prop up my injured foot as I stood to speak. Immediately I recalled a song by Jaci Velasquez called "Speak for Me." The song is sung to the Holy Spirit, asking Him to speak in a way others will understand, so that they will be blessed. I thought about how I had asked my niece Kelli to sing that song for us when Rob came to visit me in Texas during the summer break. The message of the song certainly seemed appropriate for my two visits to Africa. As I silently prayed the words to the song, I began to tell our story. With the help of a very gifted interpreter I shared my compassion for the people, but even more, God's compassion for them, His anguish over their hurt, and His unending love for them.

And then something amazing happened. My teammate, Rochelle, who was scheduled to speak after me, had told me before we began that she had no idea what to say and that she hoped I would take a long time. But as I spoke, God revealed to her exactly what she was to do and say. When I finished speaking, Rochelle asked the 300-plus women in that room to divide into four groups and to share with each other, in pairs, how God had helped them through their trials. We could never have been prepared for what we were about to see.

Because these women came from different tribes in areas all around Bukavu, many different languages were being spoken all at once. Some needed the assistance of others in their group, who could translate from one of the tribal languages into Swahili or French. As we watched and listened, our interpreter was able to pick up some parts of the stories and let us know what they were saying. They were all relating their experiences of rape and terror. Then the noise became louder and the activity busier in the center of one of the groups, as some of the women acted out the things that had happened to them. One child was stripped from his mother's arms, tossed to the ground, and the mother attacked. The women acted out killing the child and terrifying the mother before dragging her off to the bush to be their slave for however long they wanted to use her. The next step became very clear to us; we wanted to hear their stories spoken to us through their own lips. After a short break, we asked some of the women to come up front and, through their interpreter, tell us their stories. Over and over, we heard their personal accounts of unimaginable horror and atrocities.

"The soldiers came to our home," one woman said, "and killed my husband and my children. I was taken out to the bush for nine months and passed around from one soldier to another every day. I was beaten and hardly ever given food, and I wanted to die. They raped me many, many times, sometimes with guns. And now I have this baby, and I don't know who the father is."

Another woman with a similar story said, "Now my husband will not allow me back in the home because I have been with another man."

"They cut up my children and cooked them in front of me," one woman poured out from her grief-bound soul.

"They raped my sister with a bayonet, and she died," sobbed another.

"I am only thirteen years old," said a young girl, her voice barely above a whisper.

"I am sixty-seven," said another.

The heartbreaking stories continued.

"Because of what happened to me, I have no place to sleep and no food, and I cannot find work, and there is no help."

"Because I am now homeless, I have to live on the street, where I am a prime target for the soldiers…again."

The soldiers. When the women used that term—which they did time and again—they were referring not only to Rwandan soldiers but also to UN soldiers, supported by U.S. tax dollars. Those UN soldiers are still there; we saw them. And their atrocities continue right alongside the atrocities perpetrated by the Rwandan soldiers as a result of the Hutu-Tutsi conflict and the civil war in Congo. All of these soldiers, of course, are just tools of the real killer, Satan himself.

The following day, as I worked with Dr. Gudeman, the optometrist, two of my teammates, Jamie and Rochelle, prayed about how to continue the ministry to these women, how to help them overcome the fears that haunt them and to view themselves as worthy and valuable to God. The plan God revealed to them through prayer is truly awesome. If you too will prayerfully consider their plan, I believe a part of you will be forever changed, just by reading this.

Facing the tortured women of Congo, Jamie and Rochelle began with "A Letter from Jesus," reading from appropriate parts of the Song of Solomon, explaining to the women that each one of them is precious and beautiful to God.

> **Song of Songs 1:2, 3, 4, 5, 8, 10, 11, 15** ^{2}[Y]our love is more delightful than wine. ^{3}Pleasing is the fragrance of your perfumes; your name is like perfume poured out... ^{4}We rejoice and delight in you; we will praise your love more than wine. How right they are to adore you! ^{5}Dark am I, yet lovely, O daughters of Jerusalem, dark like the tents of Kedar, like the tent curtains of Solomon...^{8}most beautiful of women... ^{10}Your cheeks are beautiful with earrings, your neck with strings of jewels. ^{11}We will make you earrings of gold, studded with silver... ^{15}How beautiful you are, my darling! Oh, how beautiful! Your eyes are doves. (NIV)

Then Jamie and Rochelle showed them the comparison: Satan tells them they are worthless, nothing more than trash, but God tells them they are beautiful and valuable. One is a lie; the other is the truth.

Jamie and Rochelle then had the women write on a piece of paper the lie, whatever they had believed about themselves that was a result of their horrible experiences and the things others believed about them. On another piece of paper each of these beautiful Congolese women wrote the truth, what they had heard God say about them from the Song of Solomon.

My dear friend Dr. Charles Fuller often says, "The gospel is not meant for private consumption." Imagine hundreds of women, with whom the truth of God's Word was being shared, taking those pieces of paper on which were written all the lies and tossing them into a fire, releasing the lies and clinging to what was left: the written proclamation of the truth of who they are in Christ. The great rejoicing, the light of the omnipotent, omniscient God that shone through these women as they released the lies and experienced His love, was evidence of a powerful exercise that encouraged them to persevere in their faith.

Still, however, their bellies were empty. So before leaving, Dave announced that we were going to use the funds we brought for team expenses to buy food–ten pounds of beans and five pounds of rice–for each woman; in addition, we would give each one of them a Bible translated in their common languages of Swahili and French.

The women were truly thankful, as they were desperately in need of the food. But what touched us Americans most was how these women clamored for the Bibles–how they received them, held them, and hugged them. Indeed, they found the value in God's Word to them–personally.

Meanwhile, I continued to work with Dr. Gudeman, fitting people for glasses. The waiting line snaked out the door, and after about ten hours with no break at all, our taxi arrived to take us back to the guest house, so we had to ask people to come back the next day. Fitting people for glasses was just one of many needs we had a chance to fill.

The last full day we had in Congo we spent touring the ATC-supported facilities, including a church, a hospital, a feeding center and farm, a school at an orphanage, and a site where ATC is building a women's shelter for many of the women we had encountered just a few days before.

At the Panzi General hospital we met with the chief doctor, an incredible Christian man who also serves as a pastor at a local church, preaching the Word of God every Sunday. He has twelve doctors working for him, and he graciously took the time to meet with us in his office, giving us statistics and answering all our questions. I was especially impressed to hear him say he believes in treating the "whole woman." Most of his patients are women and children, primarily rape and torture victims. In addition to providing medical services, he feeds them, prays with them, and encourages them to find hope in Christ. He brings in women from outside to help teach skills his patients can use to earn an income once they're released from the hospital–so valuable when husbands and fathers often won't allow raped women to return home.

During our tour, this dedicated doctor pointed out one woman on whom he had already conducted six surgeries over a three-year period. He also gave us such statistics as the age range of his patients: from two years to eighty-five; the number of patients he expects the hospital will treat this year: 4,000; and how it is impossible to estimate the number of women who die out in the bush because they cannot get to the hospital. Though obviously an emotional strain for him to do so, he related the story of one woman who was so savagely raped with a bayonet that she begged for him not to perform any surgery on her, but rather to let her die. He then took us on a tour of the hospital, showing us first the post-op room, which looked a lot like a MASH unit, with all the cots lined up in rows and IV bags hanging at each bedside. Dr. Fuller asked if a particular patient was getting a blood transfusion. No, he was told; that was a urine bag, draining the blood. But the most amazing thing of our entire meeting with this doctor occurred when we entered the room full of patients. The impact he has on those he cares for is evident. When he explained who we were and why we were there, all those who were physically able began singing praise songs!

Our entire team was stunned, as we struggled to grasp the scene that was playing out in front of us. These women who had been through a living hell were greeting us from their post-op hospital beds—simple cots—not with complaints but with songs of praise to God. Dr. Fuller then led us in prayer for the women, and we all left that room a little different than when we entered.

Next on the tour was "pre-op," which was actually just an open area under a roof, with picnic tables and scores of women—probably 1,000 or so—sewing, knitting, doing whatever they could to keep busy until they could have their surgery. Again, our chief doctor announced us as visitors and told the reason for our visit, and then allowed us to pray with this group of women. And, as the group of patients before them, they sang for us a beautiful praise song, a song of hope and faith in the promises of Jesus.

Before we left we were introduced to a grandmother and her granddaughter, three-year-old Julie, the youngest patient at this hospital for rape and torture victims. Our team was so struck with the sickening feeling of the knowledge of what had been done to this precious little one that many of us broke down and cried. Even after we'd managed to regain our composure, we were silent and withdrawn for quite a while. But we were comforted to know that God would continue His work through little Julie. Little Julie was brought to the U.S. where she has undergone several surgeries to repair damage to her insides, after being raped and shot and left for dead. She has been adopted and now lives in the U.S. and has become the inspiration for The Julie Project, the ATC-sponsored shelter built in her homeland.

In awe of the work God has already done through this chief doctor and those who work for him, we left the hospital and headed for the ATC-funded school, which is built on the property of an orphanage. Hundreds of children at this orphanage have nothing more to eat than one cup of porridge each day.

After the children sang for us we were given the honor of handing their cup of porridge to them, an experience every American should have at least once. Then the eight of us were asked to pair up and go into one of the four classrooms, and then just do whatever the Spirit led us to do. I was paired up with Jamie, and we chose to pray for each of the 100-130 children individually, while placing our hands on their heads as we went down the rows of benches. As we did this, the kids stopped eating and sat quietly. This was a difficult experience, emotionally taxing and stressful, and yet I wouldn't have missed it for anything. But what I am about to tell you next had incredibly huge meaning for me personally.

Holy Moments with the Children

I had asked the Lord to show me what to pray for each child, believing I had been placed there for a reason, and I wanted to be faithful to that cause. As I placed my hands on the head of each child, words came to me, and I prayed them out loud. About halfway through the group, toward the end of one of the rows, I had my hands on a little boy's head when I was given these words to pray: "Father, protect this child—where he eats and where he learns, where he lies down and where he wakes up, where he plays and where he works. Lord, protect him with your army of angels. Let him be a child; let him laugh and run, and grow big and strong and jump real high." When I heard those words spill out of my mouth—"grow big and strong and jump real high"—it was as if God were saying to me, "In honor of your children, Linda, I am listening. Your prayers are not wasted; I am here." I could almost hear Austin and Jessie, praying as they did before meals: "God, please bless this food so we can grow big and strong and jump real high!" I was sure I sensed a holy presence, not only God's but that of my own children there with me. Whether that was the case or not, the moments were holy ones indeed.

Later, as I sat at my laptop in the dining room to type this part of the manuscript, I had to take several deep breaths, wipe tears from my face, and even get up from the computer and walk through the house, taking breaks in order to get through it. It took me hours to get to the point where I could actually type these words, and that was after the three weeks it took just to consider sitting at the computer to attempt it. I wasn't even able to share this meaningful prayer with my teammates while we were in Africa. This is something so sacred to my heart, something so important, so valuable: *the words and prayers of my children.* Their very words have now been used in prayer for other children. This is huge for me to see God use my family to pray for people on the other side of His world, and bring Him glory.

It was hard to leave that place, with hundreds of children swarming around us. They were so happy we had come to see them, and it was heart-wrenching to say goodbye.

Next we visited a feeding center supported by ATC. The center has grown from its initial capacity to serve twenty children to serving fifty, but there are so many more outside the gate who are hungry and alone. I saw children as young as four or five, many carrying smaller children on their backs, waiting and hoping for something to eat.

We were welcomed into the feeding center, where a screening process is used to determine the most vulnerable children—the youngest ones, the sickest ones, those who are crippled and least likely to be able to run from soldiers or other danger. Again we were blessed by the music of the children's voices, as they sang their beautiful praise songs. Then we were given the honor of handing out plates of beans and rice to these children, who sat on a tarp spread over the ground under a tin roof to protect them from the sun. I sat on the ground at one edge of the tarp just because I wanted to be right there with them. Our cameraman, Kirk Wray, who is also a young father, was so moved by this scene—very small children with no parents, waiting to be fed, with hundreds more for whom there was no room peering through the thatch from outside the center, looking longingly at the food—that he asked to be the one to deliver the blessing for the meal. He struggled to get the words out, as his voice faltered and cracked several times. And again, I sat there and wished every American could share in this experience.

The feeding center now has a farm where they grow their own food and sell any excess to support further expansion. My prayer is that someday those children hanging around outside the walls of the feeding center will be able to come in and be fed.

The Final Stop

Our final stop of the day was at the ATC-sponsored church. With three sides, half a tin roof, and a dirt floor, the church is alive with people praising and praying. While most of the money donated to ATC has gone toward building feeding centers, clinics, and schools, purchasing farms, and stocking clinics with medical supplies, there is so much more the organization would like to do. We looked at the property near the church, the site of ATC's Julie Project, the women's shelter for rape victims of that area—the very women we met who are at such high risk for further abuse and torture. In the shelter women will be fed, cared for, and taught marketable skills so they can eventually return to society and take care of themselves.

After a full day of touring these sites, we returned to the guest house. We would leave the next day for Rwanda, spend the night there, and then head on to Nairobi and eventually back to the States. At the Swedish guest house we had watchmen who kept guard at the gate to the compound, with two guards being on duty each night. On that last night, a young boy came running to the compound to get his father, who was one of our guards. He wanted his father to come home because soldiers had come and beaten the boy's mother into unconsciousness. The man understandably had to leave his post to get his wife to the hospital.

Now we were down to one guard, and soon someone else came to the remaining guard with the news that soldiers had come and taken away his father, who was a pastor. Because this night watchman was the only remaining guard the compound had until the morning shift came at 7 a.m., he stayed on duty. When I spoke with him about 6:30, as he anxiously awaited the time when he could leave to begin looking for his father, I was so affected by the grief and fear these people live with every day. This young man sobbed as he told me how his father had made him into the man he was; that he had learned everything he knew about God from his father; and that he did not know who took him, where they had taken him, or why. Since there is no justice and no real law in Congo, that information would be difficult to obtain. He would have to spend his day walking Bukavu, a city of about 420,000 people, looking for his father, and then return to duty that night. He would get no sleep until at least the next day.

This poor man was obviously scared, so I asked if we could sit and pray together. He agreed, and we did. I later learned he had located his father, but it was not good news. His father was to be "in court," which over there is not like it is here. There is no justice, no right of appeal or court-appointed lawyers or bail bondsmen. I asked this young man if he would continue to trust God or if he would allow this to silence him. He said he would continue to trust, and this would not silence him because his father had taught him everything that was right.

Leaving Congo after all we had seen and experienced, we knew that not a one of us was the same as when we first arrived. Congo and Rwanda have beautiful countryside rich in agriculture, forests, minerals (including diamonds), and other natural resources, yet also filled with hatred, atrocities, oppression, war, greed, and evil.

We also learned that the Muslims may again attempt to move into the area, offering to build schools and pay teachers a high salary. As Christians we are concerned about the hatred that will be spread by the Islamic system and the harm that could come to these people, who so desperately need our prayers and support.

By the time we left Africa to return home, I had recovered from the infection, and as a plus, I got to co-pilot during two of our chartered flights. All in all, it was a two-week trip I will never forget.

Isaiah 40:31

[b]ut those who hope in the LORD
will renew their strength.
They will soar on wings like eagles;
they will run and not grow weary,
they will walk and not be faint.
(NIV)

Chapter 22

Where Does It All Lead?

Just before leaving on that memorable trip, we received news of the diagnosis of an additional disease in my grandson Myles. In May his tummy aches were investigated and found to be caused by B-cell lymphoma. Two cancerous tumors were discovered in his abdominal cavity, doubling in size every forty-eight hours. The surgeon opened him up, took a look at the complexity of the tumors, and sewed him back up. Treatment would have to be quick, and as aggressive as his little body could endure. He began chemotherapy immediately, and seven months later was tumor-free. Today he continues to battle and often suffers from the complexities of having a compromised immune system, as well as the risk of further lymphomas and other cancers, arthritis, asthma, and other auto-immune diseases. But through it all, I am so very proud of Angie, as I see how she responds to the blows she's been dealt. She has grown into a fine young lady, a most admirable mother, and a stronger Christian than I think she realizes.

Then, in December, 2005, Missy gave birth to my third grandson and named him Caleb Mycol Austin Henderson. I am honored that this precious little chunk of joy will carry on such important names.

Pulling It All Together

A Christian family, a dream home, a fiery tragedy, a heartbroken wife and mother, a toy U-Haul, a wedding ring, a crayon drawing, prayers and fasting, people who love so deeply they will come and enter the pain, a very sick grandbaby, spiritual warfare and proclaiming the gospel of Jesus Christ in the 10/40 Window, people who spent time with my family and filled in gaps of time I missed, a police officer, a firefighter—hundreds of police officers and firefighters, actually... Where does it all lead?

This book is not written to be a dramatization or a fantastic story; I'm not reaching for any literary prize or acclaim—God's love is so much more than that—but to simply expose the Truth as I have experienced it. My prayer is that you will receive from this courier a message of hope, of God's love, of the Good News of Jesus Christ, and become a courier of that message to others.

I will not tell you I understand all that happened or why; I don't. Nor will I tell you I am "all better now." (You already know how I feel about that phrase!) I miss my family, and it hurts. But even though I don't understand, I serve a God who does. I was made by the God who made this universe, the same God who made you and who understands His own plan. I will never understand in this lifetime why I've been given this assignment, but I want to be called faithful—Hebrews 11 faithful—and so I am thankful for each and every person who continues to love and support me and pray for God to carry me through this.

In all that's happened since the fire on January 27, 2003, I have come to know, really know, that Jesus really did walk this earth and that He really did everything He said He would do up to this point. Consequently I don't have any reason to doubt that He will come through on His promise of heaven and eternal life.

I have come to believe more strongly in the existence of spiritual warfare and its desire to deceive, divide, destroy, lie, steal, and conquer. There is something significant about offering to share the gospel, the good news of Jesus Christ, in the 10/40 Window, and it is quite ironic how this has played out in my life in significant ways and on important days. Satan may have tried to sift me, and he may have been successful for a time, but I realize now what was going on, and I will continue to trust in God's promises. There is ample evidence, as author Josh McDowell so aptly put it, to demand a verdict.[vi]

Where was God at the time of the fire? Why didn't He save my family? Why didn't He wake Mycol up so they could escape? Why were we separated, preventing me from "moving to heaven" with them, instead being left behind to grieve?

All I can say is, God was here, where He always is—present—even during the fire. I have landed in a place of deepened faith. He is my Father; He has never left me nor forsaken me. He is not my enemy; He has grieved with me and has compassion on me. And He offers me the choice of eternal life in heaven, with Him and with my family.

Psalm 107 came to my sister Barbara during prayer and fasting, and it spoke to us of our own experience, of our desire to settle in a better place, to raise our family in a more desirable location. Mycol and I found incredible significance in that psalm. I even said it "became a stronghold of promise to us, of God answering prayer, confirming as we listened." That's where I was wrong. It's right to read scripture and seek guidance from God's Word, but if our "stronghold of promise" is based on a concept of our limited understanding, no wonder we can't understand the bigger picture when it unfolds in a way contrary to our expectations. I was trusting in a concept; I was trusting in my expectations. I was not putting my trust in the Person of Jesus Christ.

Job made a bold statement as he argued with his friends: "Though He slay me, yet will I trust Him." (Job 13:15) Now I can't say this is what God did to me and my family, since I can't possibly know the mind of God, but I have learned that even if He takes everything away from me, my hope and my faith remain firm in His promise of salvation through His Son.

The Bible speaks to me of a personal relationship between God and man. God wants me to seek Him; He wants me to persist. Doing so has allowed me to see that He was there before the fire, and that He has been with me ever since. Mycol, Austin, and Jessie went to sleep that night, breathed in some carbon monoxide, then smoke and soot, and were finally awakened and "moved to heaven," hand-in-hand with Jesus.

Mycol's favorite section of the Scriptures was from Romans 8:

Romans 8:18, 24, 26-27 [18]I consider that our present sufferings are not worth comparing with the glory that will be revealed in us... [24]But hope that is seen is no hope at all. Who hopes for what he already has? [26]In the same way, the Spirit helps us in our weakness. We do not know what we ought to pray for, but the Spirit himself intercedes for us with groans that words cannot express. [27]And he who searches our hearts knows the mind of the Spirit, because the Spirit intercedes for the saints in accordance with God's will. (NIV)

Christ prays for us! Isn't that awesome? And here is the rest of Mycol's favorite section of Scripture:

Romans 8:28, 34-35, 37 [28]And we know that in all things God works for the good of those who love him, who have been called according to his purpose... [34]Christ Jesus, who died—more than that, who was raised to life—is at the right hand of God and is also interceding for us. [35]Who shall separate us from the love of Christ? Shall trouble or hardship or persecution or famine or nakedness or danger or sword? ...[37]No, in all these things we are more than conquerors through him who loved us. (NIV)

There it is again: Jesus prays for us. In John 17, as Jesus was preparing to be taken away and crucified, He prayed for Himself, for His disciples, and then–for us; for you and for me!

John 17:20-26 [20]"My prayer is not for them alone. I pray also for those who will believe in me through their message, [21]that all of them may be one, Father, just as you are in me and I am in you. May they also be in us so that the world may believe that you have sent me. [22]I have given them the glory that you gave me, that they may be one as we are one: [23]I in them and you in me. May they be brought to complete unity to let the world know that you sent me and have loved them even as you have loved me. ²⁴Father, I want those you have given me to be with me where I am, and to see my glory, the glory you have given me because you loved me before the creation of the world. ²⁵Righteous Father, though the world does not know you, I know you, and they know that you have sent me. ²⁶I have made you known to them, and will continue to make you known in order that the love you have for me may be in them and that I myself may be in them." (NIV)

One in unity; God in us—that's what Jesus prayed for each of us.

The Scriptures tell us that God causes the sun to rise on both the evil and the good, and sends rain on the righteous and the unrighteous. Now that I've shared my experience of faith in the midst of tragedy, I pray that God uses this story somehow in your life. This is my experience, but the message is His. My family and I, and this book, are simply the couriers.

You're in a better place, I've heard a thousand times
And at least a thousand times I've rejoiced for you
But the reason why I'm broken the reason why I cry
Is how long must I wait to be with you
I close my eyes and I see your face
If home's where my heart is then I'm out of place
Lord won't you give me strength to make it through somehow
I've never been more homesick than now
Help me Lord because I don't understand Your ways
The reason why I wonder if I'll ever know
But even if You showed me the hurt would be the same
Because I'm still here so far away from home
In Christ there are no goodbyes
In Christ there is no end
So I'll hold on to Jesus with all that I have
To see you again

—From "Homesick" by Mercy Me[vii]

Epilogue

Walking with a Limp

As I worked on the manuscript for this book, I complained to Rusty on several occasions, "I don't know how the book ends."

"God will give you that," he reassured me. "Be patient." He was right.

Not all endings are happy ones. In fact, in real life we have pain. And so, this book is real.

By the grace of God I have moved from a woman paralyzed with grief, lying in a fetal position on Mycol's bed, to one who is doing my best to serve as a courier. The transition from my state of "being" on January 27, 2003 to returning to work, learning to fly, and writing a book, is the result of many gifts of grace, gifts of time, and a whole bunch of prayer. It is fed by the ongoing encouragement Mycol left to me as a loving husband. He gave me a gift that will last the rest of my life in the way he lived his. Because of his love for God and for our family, I can hear Mycol cheering me on, telling me to live and bring glory to God as long as I have breath.

A phenomenal change has taken place within me, but because I don't see myself ever "getting over" the fire, it's only natural and reasonable that I continue to view life through a lens of at least partial grief. My desire to be a courier of God's love and compassion and good news is based, to a large degree, on the sadness and pain that will always be a part of my life. It is the very reason I am willing and able to empathize with others. It is "walking with a limp" as Jacob did after he wrestled with the Angel of God; it became a painful but identifying mark of God's hand on his life. Mine too.

Though none of us knows what tomorrow will bring or how the next chapter of our lives will read, we can rest in the fact that we know the One who holds the future in His hands. And while it has taken years to write this book, what a gift that it was submitted to the publisher on the day we would honor the tenth birthday of the cover artist – our little Jessie.

I am committed to my desire for God to work through me, to use me for His glory, and to carry the good news of His great love and mercy to everyone who will listen to His promise.

May you make a commitment, as faithful couriers in His service, to know God's presence and be blessed, and may you…

"Have a hundred-forty-sixty-hundred-ninety-hundred nice days!"

A P.S. from Rusty

Linda,

You know I am not a writer, and this is another stretch for me, way out of my comfort zone. This stretching is a place that you and I seemed to frequent, and dwelt often in months past.

You have endured much since Mycol, Austin and Jessie's "move to heaven." I have witnessed your journey from total devastation, mental, physical exhaustion, and spiritual emptiness. I had never seen nor experienced a person so overwhelmingly hopeless at the onset of this tragedy, but one who chose to set out on a journey to find out who God is and what one's purpose is.

You have traveled a long road which has had many turns, steep mountains, narrow lanes, and a few dead ends. But God has walked with you every step of the way, just as His word says, "I will never leave you nor forsake you." God placed markers along that road, to give you hope and restore your faith; the toy U-Haul, the drawing, the ring are a few examples. And God has directed others to cross your path for His purpose.

Your physical and spiritual travel has led you to become a woman full of God's grace, which you had expressed to me as your desire, a few weeks after the tragedy.

While tragic, your journey has been a true inspiration to me and many others who have witnessed the transformation.

Sincerely yours,
Bro' Rusty

To my loving wife Lynna,

I love you with all my heart and want to thank you for allowing me the freedom to be a vessel used by God in this situation. Your unselfishness, and trusting God, allowed us both to play a small role in Linda's journey. Your unfailing love for God, me, and continual prayers for Linda and the family, I believe played a significant role in her and our healing.

Rusty

i Lee Strobel, *The Case for Faith* (Grand Rapids, MI: Zondervan, 2000), pp. 66-67.

ii Fincastle Herald, Letter to the Editor, March, 2003. Used by permission.

iii Cody Lowe, "Her family dead, woman seeks solace at Graham festival," *Roanoke Times*, May 5, 2003. Used by permission.

iv Sam Woolwine, "Hall of Fame Guests Hear Pumpyisms," *Chattanooga Times Free Press, Inc.*, November 21, 2001. Used by permission.

v Used by permission, Fire Chief Greg Sleboda.

vi Josh McDowell, *The New Evidence that Demands a Verdict Fully Updated to Answer the Questions Challenging Christians Today* (Nashville, TN: Thomas Nelson Publishers, 1999).

vii Mercy Me, "Homesick." Used by permission.

www.ingramcontent.com/pod-product-compliance
Lightning Source LLC
Chambersburg PA
CBHW030147100526
44592CB00009B/161